THE AGE OF
VELIKOVSKY

C. J. RANSOM

THE AGE OF
VELIKOVSKY

A Delta Book

To Linda

A DELTA BOOK
Published by
Dell Publishing Co., Inc.
1 Dag Hammarskjold Plaza
New York, New York 10017

Reprinted by arrangement with the author.

Delta ® TM 755118, Dell Publishing Co., Inc.

ISBN: 0-440-50323-X

Printed in the United States of America

First Delta printing—May 1978

VB

ACKNOWLEDGEMENTS

I would like to thank the following people for their interest and providing helpful discussions, correspondence and references.

Dr. John Lynde Anderson, Dr. Donald Anthony, Dr. Jerry Arnet, Dr. Ram Babu, Dr. Elizabeth Chesley Baity, Dr. Robert W. Bass, Prof. John M. Bell, Dr. Donna Boutelle, Dr. George Brigman, Dr. Geoffrey L. Broderick, Dr. Mary Buckalew, J. B. Bulloch, Dr. Albert W. Burgstahler, Dr. Leonard P. Caccamo, Dwardu Cardona, Dr. David C. Carlyle, Dr. Harris Carter, Prof. Richard W. Chadwick, Dr. Melvin Cook, Dr. A. Lucile Cox, Duncan B. Cox.

Dr. B. C. Deaton, Vine Deloria, Jr., Prof. Martin Dickson, Prof. Patrick Doran, Robert B. Driscoll, Dr. H. C. Dudley, Dr. James A. Durham, Dr. H. R. Dvorak, Dr. Stephen Epstein, Dr. Felix Fernando, Dr. Jorgen Fex, Dr. Reuben Fields, Leo Fox, Dr. Richard Freeman, Prof. Alexander H. Friedman, Dr. Dan Gibson, Dr. James Gilcrest, Prof. Cyrus Gordon, Dr. Alan Gowans, Dr. Alfred de Grazia, Prof. Lewis M. Greenberg, Dr. David Griffard, Dr. George Grinnell.

Dr. Richard F. Haines, Dr. Joyce Harden, D. C. Helton, Dr. G. C. Henderson, Dr. T. Walter Herbert, Dr. Robert H. Hewsen, Dr. Hilton Hinderliter, L. H. Hoffee, Dr. W. G. Holmes, Dr. David Huebner, Edward Imparato, Frederic B. Jueneman, Ralph Juergens, Dr. Michael Kamrin, Prof. Emeritus Norman M. Kastler, Dr. J. C. Keister, Dr. Dorothea Kenny, Dr. K. G. Kibler, Dr. J. B. Kloosterman, Dr. Leroy Lewis, Marvin A. Luckerman.

Dr. Euan MacKie, Dr. A. J. Mantura, Dr. Joseph May, Dr. Pat McDade, Dr. Daniel McLallen, Dr. Earl Milton, Dr. William Mullen, Baxter Mullins, Dr. Robert Oliphant,

Dr. G. W. van Oosterhout, Dr. James Outenreath, Prof. A. M. Paterson, Roy Patience, Dr. Robert C. Pollock, Dr. J. C. Redman, Dr. John Regalbuto, Dr. William Regelson, Dr. Ellis Rivkin, Dr. Zvi Rix, Dr. Robert Rock, Dr. John Romanko, Prof. Lynn E. Rose, Prof. Emeritus Alexandre Rothen, Dr. Lionel Rubinov.

Dr. Ron Sanders, Prof. Claude Schaeffer, Prof. Albert Schatz, Dr. Hans Schluter, Eddie Schorr, Dr. Charles Scott, Prof. A. J. Sharp, C. S. Sherrerd, Dr. Steve Sims, Prof. Warner B. Sizemore, Dr. C. Ray Skipping, D. O. Smith, J.D., Dr. Joseph A. Soldati, Dr. Jon Sollid, Dr. H. C. Sorensen, Dr. George W. Spangler, Dr. Leonard Spialter, R. Standfield, Dr. Livio Stecchini, Dr. Harold Stern, Prof. David Stove, Prof. Carter Sutherland, Dr. Jerry Swint.

Prof. J. Terasmae, Dr. Charles B. Thaxton, Dr. C. W. Tow, Prof. Lynn Trainor, Robert Treash, Harold Tresman, Raymond Vaughan, Dr. Immanuel Velikovsky, Prof. S. K. Vseksvyatskii, Dr. Robert L. Wadlinger, Dr. Irving Wolfe, Dr. James Wilson, Dr. B. G. W. Yee, Henry Zemel.

(Over 30% of these people have degrees in physics. Other disciplines include astronomy, archaeology, chemistry, geophysics, history, philosophy, and psychiatry.)

I would also like to thank the following organizations for their efforts in behalf of this work: The General Dynamics Management Association, Universal Map and Drafting Co., Electronic Monitors, Inc., The Fort Worth Museum of Science and History, The Fort Worth Astronomical Society, Cosmos and Chronos, Inc., all of Fort Worth, and KRONOS of Glassboro, New Jersey, and Innovative Concepts Associates of San Jose, California.

In addition, I would like to thank the following for their help with typing the manuscript: Betsy Caraway, Wanda Marstrand, Susan Weber and my wife, Linda. Linda also provided a number of references relating to Native American and Mesoamerican cultures. Pertinent references were also made available by Helen Davis and Mildred Onken.

Also I would like to thank the following for their many helpful suggestions with regard to the presentation of the material: Dr. James A. Durham, Darrell H. Hanson, Ralph Juergens, Dr. Dan McLallen, Dan Ray Moore, and Dr. and Mrs. C. W. Tow.

My sincere gratitude is extended to Professor Lewis M. Greenberg, Ralph Juergens and Professor Lynn E. Rose for reviewing the material and making valuable editorial suggestions.

I would also like to thank Professor Lynn E. Rose for the title and Jay M. Wilson and my daughter, Michelle Ransom, for assistance in designing the cover.

Finally I would like to extend special thanks to Dr. Immanuel Velikovsky for his encouragement during the preparation of this book.

PREFACE

In the 1940's, Dr. Immanuel Velikovsky developed a unique model for the recent history of the solar system. His ideas were eventually presented in the form of a cosmological reconstruction titled *Worlds in Collision*. The most familiar aspect of this work dealt with close encounters of some of the planets (i.e., Venus, the Earth, and Mars) in historical times.

Velikovsky also challenged the chronology used for certain historical periods (i.e., the period from the fall of the Egyptian Middle Kingdom to the time of Alexander the Great's successor in Egypt, Ptolemy I) which he viewed as being Ages in Chaos.

Since these ideas were first presented, considerable evidence has accumulated which supports both the historical reconstruction and the possibility that the proposed physical interactions did occur. Many discoveries of the Space Age were anticipated by Velikovsky's theory. But more important, whether or not these discoveries were anticipated, these and other space probe data fit exceedingly well with the model he proposed. Also important is the fact that many of these discoveries were not anticipated by conventional thinking of the late forties and early fifties. In fact, in some cases, the opposite of what was expected was found.

In addition to not having been expected, some of these data require strained *ad hoc* hypotheses for explanations under accepted theory. In light of the historical and physical evidence, it seems that it would be in the best interest of the scholarly community to consider Velikovsky's suggestions as a reasonable alternative to the opinions presently taught about the history of the Earth.

Unfortunately, many scholars have not investigated Velikovsky's theory properly because they have been told the ideas are unreasonable. Obviously, everyone cannot take the time to study in detail every new idea that is postulated, so even scientists often must rely on the word of others.

At first it was relatively easy for some scientists to persuade other scientists not to take Velikovsky's work seriously because his ideas were not the opinions that had been held sacred by the scientific community. Distorted sensationalized reviews and misrepresentations about what Velikovsky said made it even easier to convince some scientists that they need not investigate the theory.

As more was learned about our solar system, a number of scientists began to realize that Velikovsky's theory conflicted only with accepted *opinions* and did not actually conflict with known facts. Some scientists, who originally committed themselves to irrational attacks on Velikovsky and his work, then felt constrained to defend their actions.

One of their methods was to try to convince the public, and as many other scientists as possible, that no qualified scientist or historian would ever investigate anything Velikovsky said. This is completely unfounded, as will be demonstrated throughout this book. Another method was to repeat previously accepted dogma, as if it were unalterable fact, and have defenders of this dogma publish supposedly scientific treatises which were irrational or irrelevant, and sometimes unethical. This book contains replies to the most common misrepresentations. In addition, this book was written to provide a complete overview of the theory and to demonstrate that this well thought out theory has considerable support from many fields.

For a more complete understanding of Velikovsky's ideas, the reader should refer to Velikovsky's books and the continuing analysis of his ideas which is available in the journal KRONOS, from Glassboro State College, Glassboro, New Jersey.

Although Velikovsky has encouraged me during the preparation of this work, *he did not see the manuscript before publication.* All of the mistakes are mine, and his work should not be judged harshly on the basis of any errors that are my own.

C. J. Ransom
Fort Worth, Texas
1976

EARLY LIFE OF DR. VELIKOVSKY

Immanuel Velikovsky was born in Vitebsk, Russia, on June 10, 1895. He learned several languages as a child, and graduated with full honors from Medvednikov Gymnasium in Moscow. He then studied at Montpellier, France, traveled in Palestine and in 1914 began pre-medical studies at Edinburgh, Scotland. His studies were interrupted by World War I, and he returned to Moscow. There he studied law and ancient history at the Free University. He continued his work toward a medical degree and in 1921 received his medical degree from the University of Moscow.

Dr. Velikovsky then traveled to Berlin where he and Professor Heinrich Loewe founded and published *Scripta Universitatis*, conceived as a cornerstone for what would become Hebrew University at Jerusalem. The journal contained contributions from outstanding Jewish scholars in many countries. The articles were published in the authors' native languages and in Hebrew. Albert Einstein edited the mathematical-physical volume of *Scripta Universitatis*.

In 1923, Dr. Velikovsky married Elisheva Kramer, an accomplished violinist from Hamburg. That year they moved to Palestine, and he began medical practice. He was a general practitioner and after studying in Vienna under a student of Freud's, Dr. Velikovsky began practicing psychoanalysis. In 1930, Velikovsky was the first to suggest that pathological encephalograms would be found characteristic of epilepsy. Distorted and accentuated brain waves were later found to be important clinical diagnostic symptoms of this problem. Velikovsky edited *Scripta Academica Universitatis* and published some articles in Freud's *Imago*.

In the summer of 1939, Dr. Velikovsky came to the United States to complete research for a book. The intended book was to be about Freud's dreams and three characters of interest to Freud: Moses, Oedipus and Akhnaton. The book was nearly completed when other research led to discoveries that would change the course of his life.

CONTENTS

Chapter I

THE REVIEW

In 1950, the Macmillan company published Dr. Immanuel Velikovsky's *Worlds in Collision*, but before it was in the book stores, opposition to the ideas expressed in the book had grown so strong that Macmillan had considered not publishing it. Nonetheless, after receiving approval from two of three referees, the book was published. The day before publication, Gordon Atwater, head of the world famous Hayden Planetarium in New York City, was to publish an article suggesting an unbiased investigation of Velikovsky's work. *This Week Magazine* carried the article even though a number of noted scientists had told Atwater not to publish it. By the time the article was printed, Gordon Atwater was no longer head of the Hayden Planetarium nor employed with any other position related to astronomy. It remained this way for twenty-three years.

Two months after publication, opposition to the book had grown even stronger, and Macmillan was forced to cease publication of *Worlds in Collision*. The editor who had accepted it for publication was fired, even though he had been with the company for twenty-five years. Unlike Macmillan, the Doubleday book company was not financially vulnerable to those who wished to protect the public from new ideas. Doubleday, therefore, purchased the rights to *Worlds in Collision* and continued printing this book as well as Velikovsky's later books. Yet, opposition continued to be extreme, and for a while the book was even banned in Germany. A professor at Southern Methodist University declared that the theory would subvert our traditional way of life more radically than would communism and prostitution combined. The book and its author were recipients of an irrational reaction which was unprecedented in the scholarly world.

The following will contain a discussion of the initial reaction to the book as well as a review of the ideas presented by Velikovsky. The theory is generally divided into the categories of history and physical science, although the historical observations are the basis for the suggestions related to the physical sciences. Descriptions of the physical events associated with the catastrophes will be given in Chapter II. Some of the physical events will be correlated to familiar historical events.

After medicine and psychoanalysis, Velikovsky's initial investigation was in the field of ancient history. There appears to be very little correlation between certain time periods of the history of Egypt and Hebrew history, though these nations resided side by side and supposedly interacted extensively. It was an investigation of the historical problem that eventually led to Velikovsky's discovery that the ancient world's literature contained descriptions of global catastrophes. His historical reconstruction of the ancient Middle East is basically independent of these catastrophic events. Some of the salient points of this reconstruction will be reviewed in Chapter III. Reference will also be made to Velikovsky's book *Oedipus and Akhnaton* in which he identifies Oedipus, thought to be purely legendary, with the known historical character Akhnaton.

After a review of the major and some minor points of Velikovsky's work, supporting evidence will be given for the view that the described events are physically possible. Also, evidence will be cited indicating that something did happen in the periods discussed and that the historical reconstruction solves many major problems created by the conventional chronology. Most of the references used are generally known, but two less familiar sources are the journal KRONOS and a ten issue series of the magazine, *Pensee.* Information about these sources is easily obtainable.[1]

The discussion of the controversy in this section draws information mainly from *The Velikovsky Affair*, a book published in 1966, and is related to the initial reaction to the theory. Unfortunately, there are some more recent events in this affair and a number of these will be discussed in Chapter 8. This includes a discussion of the session about Velikovsky held by the American Association for the Advancement of Science in 1974.

The AAAS meeting was advertised as a scientific appraisal of Velikovsky's theory. But, at the very opening of the meeting, the attendees were informed that the subject was not worthy of scientific discussion and the meeting was being held to point this out to any minds which had strayed from the uniformitarian faith. Several of the participants certainly lived up to the claim that they would not discuss the subject scientifically. References to some of the participants will be made throughout the book, but a general review of the meeting will also be given in Chapter 8.

THE REACTION

The reaction to *Worlds in Collision* by many members of the scientific community can provide research material to interested psychoanalysts for decades. As Ralph Juergens pointed out in *The Velikovsky Affair*, "the violence of the reaction against it seemed all out of proportion to the book's importance if, as most critics insisted, the work was spurious and entirely devoid of merit."[2]

Recent discussions by scientists, about this reaction, have two basic points. First, scientists claim they really did not react violently and no acts were committed which could be construed as unwarranted. Second, when confronted with evidence of unethical actions, they claim that these actions were justified to protect the public. From the data compiled by Juergens and others, it is apparent that the unscientific and unethical actions did take place, and that no amount of rationalization can justify these actions. Only a portion of the evidence will be repeated here, but it should be sufficient to demonstrate that much of the scientific treatment of Velikovsky and his work was *not* scientific.

Many of the actions were personal assaults on Velikovsky, or others who happened to be in the line of fire. These actions were inexcusable even if Velikovsky were wrong. However, the fact that his name was slandered and prevarications about his work and intentions were common does not make his theory correct. The review of the inane actions of some scientists is not presented as an attempt to support Velikovsky's work. His work must be judged on the merits of the evidence alone. A knowledge of these events, however, reveals that many of the opinions about his work originated from other than analysis of the evidence. On the rare occasions that the opposition did consult the evidence, often no distinction was made between assumptions and facts.

We acknowledge, then, that the way Velikovsky was libeled and his work intentionally misrepresented does not make his theory correct. However, the important point is that scientists who have an unfavorable opinion of Velikovsky's work often obtained this opinion by reading the unscientific reports of other scientists who were, at best, misguided in their attempt to protect the world from new ideas. After 25 years, the opinions of science have changed to the extent that Velikovsky's ideas about what *could have happened* in the past are no longer unusual. The only major difference between what in 1950 Velikovsky suggested for the earth's history and what many scientists have recently hypothesized is *when* the events may have occurred. Unfortunately, many scientists still think that Velikovsky was proven wrong in 1950 and that he, therefore, must still be wrong. By discussing the controversy we see that his ideas were not properly considered when they were first presented, and have been treated just as irrationally in many circles recently.

Also, a review of the reactions of some scientists reveals that they are human and not all of their actions are based on logic or on a full analysis of the available information. Sometimes, their "scientific" opinion is influenced by factors such as vested interest in an opposing theory. Another influence can possibly be connected to Velikovsky's suggestion of "collective amnesia", which will be discussed briefly in Chapter 8.

Some people have mentioned in conversations with me, and some, such as Harrison Brown, have said in print, that the reaction given Velikovsky's work was justified since he violated the "proper" procedural code by publishing his work in book form for public sale instead of seeking the opinion of accepted scholars and publishing articles in accepted journals before publishing the book. At least four things should be considered by anyone who might take this rationalization seriously. First, Velikovsky did have the material reviewed by known scholars, and he did ask to have experiments performed. Second, just as a person's being unjustly and unethically abused does not make a theory correct, not following artificial procedural customs does not make a theory wrong. Third, no one really thinks that Velikovsky would have been allowed to publish in standard journals. Fourth, many scholars have chosen to publish their ideas in book form without first having published those ideas in the form of articles.

The late Dr. Horace M. Kallen, a noted scholar and educator, was familiar with Velikovsky's work. Before the publication of *Worlds in Collision*, Kallen asked Harlow Shapley, who was then director of the Harvard College Observatory, to consider performing some experiments suggested by Velikovsky. This followed the procedure set down by Shapley himself when he earlier (1946) told Velikovsky that consideration would be given to the experiments if Velikovsky had a noted scholar review and recommend the work. However, after Velikovsky followed Shapley's instructions, Shapley still refused to read the manuscript or consider the experiments. Shapley later expended a liberal amount of energy trying to insure that others would also not read the book.

Other noted people also read the manuscript before it was published. Among these were Atwater, John J. O'Neill, the science editor of the New York *Herald Tribune*, and Dr. C. W. van der Merwe, Chairman of the Physics Department at New York University. So, as if it would have made any difference, the claim that scholars were not contacted is unfounded and the scholarly world was not totally taken by surprise with the public disclosure of a new work.

It might have been better if some of the ones who read about the work in review articles had been surprised by the book instead. *Before the book was published*, review articles, which appeared in magazines and newspapers, emphasized the sensational aspects of the book, but did not accurately portray the conclusions or the scholarship which led to these conclusions. Unfortunately, the information in the review articles was the basis of the first attacks by the scientists, since the book had not yet been published when the refutations started appearing. Some writers never came closer to the original than a review article, and they wrote articles refuting what *others* thought Velikovsky might have said. Oddly enough, some of these same people claimed that Velikovsky did not use proper sources.

Even after the publication of *Worlds in Collision*, people who claimed it was totally wrong also bragged about having never read it. For example, Dean B. McLaughlin, an astronomer at Michigan, wrote to Macmillan that the book was nothing but lies and that he had not read it and would never read it.[3]

The common action of scientists claiming they could refute in detail a book which they had not read is perhaps what prompted astronomer J. Derral Mulholland to say at the AAAS meeting: "Before I am asked the question, I would like to point out that I first read Dr. Velikovsky's work in 1950 in *Colliers Magazine*, and I have read [it] three times since, most recently yet this year." It is not clear if the "it" should refer to his tattered copy of *Colliers*, to *Worlds in Collision* or a combination thereof.

From the misunderstandings repeated by Mulholland, there easily can be some doubt that he obtained his information from the book. If he obtained the information from *Colliers*, even Velikovsky would agree that the presentation there was not substantial. The editors of *Colliers* published two parts of a planned three part series about *Worlds in Collision*, but Velikovsky so objected to the exceedingly improper treatment given the work that the third part was never published. [4]

People can probably successfully attack *Colliers*, but then that has very little to do with Velikovsky's theory. Unfortunately, many scientists formed opinions of the theory from reading sensationalized reviews such as that presented in *Colliers*.

SUPPRESSION

In addition to having no desire to read the book, some members of the scientific community desired that no one else be allowed to read the book. Shapley wrote that he was astonished that Macmillan had ventured into the "Black Arts". Later, he wrote that, if Macmillan published *Worlds in Collision*, this act would "cut off" all relations between Shapley and the book company. He also said that he hoped Macmillan had investigated Velikovsky's background, but "it is quite possible that only this *Worlds in Collision* episode is intellectually fraudulent". [5]

Having been shaken by Shapley, the president of Macmillan gave the book to three impartial censors and decided to go with the majority opinion. The majority favored publication and the book was published on schedule on April 3, 1950.

Professors in some large universities refused to see Macmillan salespersons, and Macmillan received letters from scientists demanding that the sale of *Worlds in Collision* be stopped. By May 25, 1950, although the

book topped *New York Times* best-seller list, Macmillan
gave in to the pressure and asked Velikovsky to transfer
the rights of publication to Doubleday, which did not have
a vulnerable textbook department. The remaining Macmillan editions were burned. To insure that there was no
further contamination, and as partial penitence, James
Putnam - the editor who accepted the book for publication - was fired.

The newspapers reported that Shapley had engineered
the suppression of *Worlds in Collision*, but he claimed that
he did not "make any threats and I don't known anyone
who did." [6] While Shapley was playing "Mr. Clean", other
people were jealous because Shapley was getting all the
credit for something they bragged about helping to do.

Suppression attempts did not stop with the transfer of
the book to another company. Doubleday owned Blak-
iston company which published *Earth, Moon and Planets*,
written by Fred Whipple. He was the successor to Shapley
at Harvard. Whipple wrote Doubleday that he would not
do any updating of his book as long as it was owned by
Doubleday and they published the works of Velikovsky.
Doubleday, not bowing to irrational pressure, told Whipple
what he could do with the *Earth, Moon and Planets*.

RATIONALIZATION

One might think that people would have good reasons
for having articles and books suppressed and burned, and
competent employees fired. After exuding a myriad of words
to convince the public that the scientists were right, Shapley
and other scientists noticed that the public and other scientists were not accepting the word of scientific authority,
and people were asking for reasons. Shapley instructed
Cecilia Payne-Gaposchkin to make a definitive analysis
showing that the book was wrong, before it was published.
Forming the conclusions before the analysis is not the re-

commended scientific procedure, but performing the analysis before the book was published was even less scholarly. However, Payne-Gaposchkin managed to finish her "analysis" before publication of *Worlds in Collision.*

Payne-Gaposchkin mailed mimeographed copies of her report to several scientists. After people pointed out a number of gross errors in her thinking and calculations, she published a revised edition in *The Reporter.* This, plus five articles, by five "authorities", which were published in *Science News Letter*, headed by Shapley, comprised the major first round rebuttals to Velikovsky. All were published before *Worlds in Collision.* The easy thing about doing it this way was that you could make up things and claim Velikovsky left out certain items he really included, but no one could check the statements until after the damage was done. Since corrections are old news, no one felt obliged to print them.

At least one of Payne-Gaposchkin's major fallacies was repeated by others, such as Frank Edmondson and, more recently, by Isaac Asimov, who repeated the idea although not the numbers. Apparently, they did not notice that this argument was prepared during a mental short. Edmondson, then director of the Goethe Link Observatory, said that "Velikovsky is not bothered by the fact that if the earth stopped, inertia would cause Joshua and his companions to fly off into space with a speed of nine hundred miles an hour."[7]

It seems that Edmondson was not bothered by the fact that neither he nor Payne-Gaposchkin, in her original report, mentioned any length of time. Some people used to think. cars could never go thirty miles an hour because, if they stopped, the people would fly out or hit the front so hard that an automatic putty knife would have to come out and wipe them off the windshield. They evidently thought that hitting a brick wall was the only way to stop a car. Although some drivers seem to use this technique, there are other methods open to the driver, most of which involve *a reasonable length of time* for stopping, and hence no one goes sailing anywhere.

Velikovsky did not claim that the Earth stopped instantaneously. In fact, he did not claim that the Earth must have stopped at all during the time of Joshua. Velikovsky pointed out that a change in the tilt of the earth's axis could also give the appearance of an extended day. But assuming for a moment that the earth did change its rotation rate, one must consider a span of time for determining the acceleration rate which is then used to determine the force on a person.

If we assume that the earth totally stopped in six hours, then the velocity of an object at the equator would change, under present conditions, from about 1050 mi/hr. to zero in six hours. This is about the same deceleration as a car going 60 mi/hr. and stopping in 20 minutes. Putty knives are not needed for this operation, and no one would fly off the earth at 900 mi/hr. A more normal situation of a car going from 60 to 0 in thirty seconds would give a deceleration rate approximately equivalent to the earth stopping in 8.7 minutes. This would not have led to an early invention of seat belts.

Although one may well question the justification of writing a detailed critique of an unread book, it is understandable that Payne-Gaposchkin would misquote *Worlds in Collision* since she had not read it. Even a few casual mistakes in analysing a book that has been read are also understandable, but Payne-Gaposchkin's continued misrepresentation of the book later, after she claimed to have read it, can be understood only in terms not associated with ethical scholarly behavior. She accused Velikovsky of misquoting and adding new portions to ancient texts he described. To support her statements she not only misquoted Velikovsky, she misquoted and deleted important sections of the original texts she supposedly consulted.

These are just a few of the initial injustices and illogical reactions related to the Velikovsky controversy. This procedure has continued since the publication of *Worlds in Collision*. However, as more and more scientists began to investigate the theory, some of the scientists who originally committed themselves to irrational defamation of

Velikovsky's work tried to cover up the fact that some scientists were willing to investigate portions of Velikovsky's theory. Propaganda is prevalent that no scientists or historians would take seriously anything Velikovsky said; whereas, the fact is that a number of noted scientists and historians are actively engaged in research to determine the correct portions of the theory. Some scientists, however, still try to make it appear as if the originator of the theory is the only person·interested. This way their arguments against the individual still sound impressive to the uninformed. As long as they can perpetrate the myth that "no scientists" would consider discussing the theory, they do not feel obliged to print other than defamatory remarks about Velikovsky and they do not feel that it is necessary to use logic for the public since "science" has spoken.

ACCEPTED ASSUMPTIONS OF 1950

Since many opinions about Velikovsky's work were formed as a result of the initial reaction, it is informative to mention certain attitudes which were widely held in 1950. With present scientific journals containing numerous articles relating to changes in the Solar System, and catastrophic events on Earth caused by external bodies, it is difficult to fully understand why such an irrational reaction occurred. As we shall see, what were thought in 1950 to be facts were merely opinions, and Velikovsky challenged nearly every major opinion about the recent history of the Earth and Solar System.

PLANETARY ARRANGEMENT

Earth is now the third planet from the Sun. Mercury is the first planet and then come Venus, Earth, Mars,

Jupiter, Saturn and the remaining planets. Modern astronomers have recently postulated that this may not be the original order of the Solar System. Theoretical discussions have been made about our Moon having been formed as a planet inside the orbit of Mercury and about Mercury having been a moon of Venus. Suggestions about the original system have the Earth being anywhere from planet number two to planet number four or even not existing in the original system. However, in 1950, it was *assumed* and widely believed that all of the planets were formed in their present orbits several billion years ago. Orbital changes of planets were suggested by Velikovsky at a time when such suggestions were considered heresy. Much of the opposition to Velikovsky's work was based on the *assumption* that no changes had or could have occurred in the Solar System. Velikovsky has called it "a system without a history" according to orthodox cosmological theories of the pre-1950's.

UNIFORMITY

The idea of uniformity, or the theory of uniformitarianism, states that it is possible to explain all geological features on the earth today by processes now acting on the earth. It was thought that, given enough time, gradual processes could shape the earth the way it is today. No agents external to the earth were required. A number of modern geologists realize that some features of the earth are more easily explained by random, rare, sudden events, and even natural agents external to the earth are suggested as the cause of some of these events. However, in 1950, the reasonable first approximation "possible to explain" had actively (whether or not officially) been replaced by the dogma "must be explained".

Velikovsky did not adhere to this dogma and even presented evidence that sudden or discontinuous changes might reasonably explain some features of the earth which strained the hypothesis of uniformity. Some of the opposition to Velikovsky's work was based on the assumption of uniformity. The apparent logic was that, since it was assumed that nothing happened, this proved that Velikovsky was wrong when he said something did happen.

EGYPTIAN CHRONOLOGY

Ancient Egyptian history has been used for years as the standard by which to determine the chronological order of other countries. This has caused a number of problems in the historiography of the Ancient Middle East and Greece. By force-fitting the histories of these regions to the assumed history of Egypt, "dark ages" have been created and one country will appear to copy the customs and fads of a neighboring country five hundred years after the first nation is buried in the dust. Recently, more historians are beginning to realize that there are many problems with the accepted chronology of Egypt. However, in 1952, it was assumed that basic Egyptian history was accurately known from then to over 4000 years ago and only a few details needed to be added. Velikovsky did not adhere to this assumption.

Velikovsky pointed out that the assumptions of astronomy, geology and history *were* merely assumptions, and he presented, among other things, a new model for the recent history of the Solar System which did not accept these assumptions. This model also explained more data and contained less inconsistencies than previous models. The circumstances leading to the development of this model and the basic catastrophic and historical events associated with it will be reviewed in more detail in Chapter II.

ORIGIN OF DOUBT

Dr. Velikovsky studied under Dr. Wilhelm Stekel, a student of Freud's, and then practiced as a psychoanalyst in Haifa and Tel Aviv. Velikovsky published a number of papers in psychology and some appeared in Freud's *Imago*. In 1939, Velikovsky came to the United States to do research about Moses, Oedipus and Akhnaton, three characters of interest to Freud. A review of this work will be deferred until   page 245   since there is only a slight tie-in to his later discoveries. When most of the research was completed, Velikovsky began preparing for the publication of the book and his return to Europe. Meanwhile, he got into a discussion with a friend which would eventually cause the cancellation of his family's return to Europe and change the course of his life.

During the discussion, a question arose about the Exodus. If it had actually occurred, why does there seem to be no record in Egyptian history? In Hebrew history, the Exodus from Egypt is a very important event. If the event took place with only half the fanfare described in traditional accounts, Egyptian history should contain a record of this event. Using the conventional chronology of Egypt, historians are divided over the question of when the Exodus occurred. During the time periods that some historians are willing to consider for the Exodus, there are problems which make certain correlations questionable. For example, some pharaohs who were considered as the possible ruler at the time of the Exodus were too powerful to let any slaves go, and there are no indications that the Hebrews had even been in Egypt in the time of these pharaohs. Under some of the weaker pharaohs, the land entered by the Hebrews was still ruled by Egypt, so there would have been no real exodus from Egypt.

Problems occur not only with the Exodus, but with other major historical events in Hebrew history. There appears, under conventional chronology, to be no counterpart in Egyptian history for many of the events in Hebrew history. The histories of the two nations should have many noticeable correlations if the two nations actually intertwined as closely as suggested by their proximity and Hebrew history. The lack of correlation is so striking that some historians have postulated that Hebrew history is largely fictional. However, there is abundant archaeological support for great portions of Hebrew history, so it is reasonable to investigate the possibility that the chronology of either Hebrew or Egyptian history is not exact. Velikovsky was led into this investigation from a consideration of the Exodus question. If it occurred, and if the Egyptians mentioned it in extant literature, where should it be placed in Egyptian chronology?

Velikovsky soon discovered a translation, by A. H. Gardiner, of an ancient Egyptian papyrus called the Papyrus Ipuwer. The description of events by Ipuwer was strikingly similar to the narrative of the Exodus. When he made the translation, Gardiner did not think that the papyrus discussed the Exodus, so the similarities of the descriptions of events could not be attributed to biased translation. Still, the descriptions are so similar in some cases that, even for one only vaguely familiar with the Hebrew version, it is difficult to distinguish between portions of the Hebrew and Egyptian records. However, the Papyrus Ipuwer was composed at the end of the Middle Kingdom of Egypt.

Under conventional chronology, the Middle Kingdom is thought to have ended some five hundred years before the Exodus could have occurred. Subsequent investigation by Velikovsky reveals that a number of major historical events described in the Hebrew records had a corresponding event about five hundred years earlier in the Egyptian records. It appeared that this offset was caused either because Hebrew history was too short or Egyptian history too long. Either solution would have been controversial.

Further examination of the historical evidence led Velikovsky to conclude that Egyptian history was padded with an excess of five to eight hundred years. Portions of this excess period contained real history, but it was about people found elsewhere in Egyptian history. Part of the problem originated because a number of names were used by the same person, so sometimes the acts of one pharaoh were attributed to more than one person. When these details were corrected, Velikovsky's revised chronology contained an exact one-to-one correlation between the Hebrew and Egyptian chronologies.

In 1945, Velikovsky published a booklet titled *Theses for the Reconstruction of Ancient History*. This was an outline of the major changes that he felt would provide a more accurate chronology of the ancient world. One-half of this work was expanded to provide detailed support of the reconstruction for the time of the Exodus to the period of Akhnaton. This was published as *Ages in Chaos* in 1952 by Doubleday & Co. Additional information about the reconstruction has been published in KRONOS and *Pensee*, and will later be available in additional historical volumes by Velikovsky. These include *Ramses II and His Time, Peoples of the Sea* and others.

BASIC EVENTS

In *Ages in Chaos*, Velikovsky synchronizes the Exodus with the sudden and dramatic end of the Middle Kingdom. These simultaneous events were determined to have occurred around 1450 B.C. Some of the details leading to this synchronization are discussed in Chapter III. After having made this correlation and others in the histories of these two nations, it became obvious that the description of the plagues of the Exodus and the disruptions at the end of the Middle Kingdom were actual natural events. Two questions then arose. How widespread were these events and what caused the events?

To answer these questions, Velikovsky examined a plethora of pages of text from the histories and so-called mythologies of many of the ancient cultures. He started with the regions adjacent to Egypt and Israel and quickly discovered that the events were seen throughout the Middle East. Investigation of other areas revealed that many locations in the world seemed to have created the same "mythology" about these events at about the same time in history. It was eventually clear that a global catastrophe had occurred around 1450 B.C., but it was not the first nor the last.

From the ancient writings, Velikovsky tried to remove extraneous material which appeared to be local ornamentation. If, for example, the people on one side of a volcano said their king made it erupt and the people on the other side said their olympic champion made it erupt, Velikovsky used the basic information that the volcano erupted.

A culture that attributed this kind of capability to mortals would not always use the straightforward phrase "the volcano erupted", so interpretation of the writings is sometimes required. This is true whether one is interpreting in support of catastrophes or uniformity. The people with the king may have said that the king wanted protection from an enemy, so he made the mountain throw smoke and rocks on them. The group on the other side may have thought the olympic champ hacked off the mountain by sticking a spear in it, so it bled molten rock all over them. So, without force-fitting the data in the manner of the accepted scholars, Velikovsky ascertained that the ancients actually observed the events which he described in *Worlds in Collision* and other writings. These major events will be reviewed below, and a more detailed discussion of these events can be found in later chapters.

Worlds in Collision contains information about the time period from 1450 B.C. to 687 B.C. Velikovsky has written a book about events before 1450 B.C., but this has not yet been published. This is partly because events of that time are more difficult to determine and require even more demanding analysis.

As of this writing, others, in addition to Velikovsky, are also now attempting to reconstruct the events of the pre-1450 B.C. era. Because of the unpublished nature of most of this work, I will refer to only one pre-1450 B.C. event, the Deluge, to give a tie-in to the triggering mechanism which may have caused the series of events described in *Worlds in Collision.*

Velikovsky noted that abundant ancient literature indicates that Saturn was once disrupted and became a nova. Saturn is now about ninety-five times more massive than the Earth, but Saturn was apparently larger at one time. The planet expelled debris, some of which was absorbed by Jupiter, and some of which eventually encountered the Earth and other planets.

It is striking that there are universal accounts about a great flood. This occurs also in arid regions that do not have even seasonal floods. That this is true has been recently reiterated by Bratton in his book *Myths and Legends of the Ancient Near East.* [8] It is not always observed, however, that these accounts strongly suggest that the water causing the Deluge was not a result of statistically expectable extra-heavy rainfall. The implication from the ancient writings is that some of the water was debris from Saturn's disruption. The exact time of this event has not been determined.

Jupiter later ejected a massive body into an orbit which, after an unknown number of years, allowed it to have a near encounter with the Earth. The instability of Jupiter may have been created in part by the debris from Saturn and the close approach of Saturn. Possible physical mechanisms will be discussed in Chapter V. Whatever the theoretical explanation, the observation by the ancients was that the body appeared to be expelled from Jupiter and interacted with other bodies in the Solar System until it acquired a stable orbit and became known as the planet Venus. Hence, the Greek "mythological" claim that a planetary deity representing Venus sprang forth from the head of Jupiter or was spewed out from Jupiter.

The body that was to become Venus orbited the sun for hundreds or perhaps thousands of years before it was in a position to encounter the earth. The first encounter occurred around 1450 B.C. and created the natural catastrophes associated historically with the Exodus. Similar descriptions are found in the writings of other ancient cultures. Great earthquakes and tidal waves occurred. Volcanoes erupted and meteorites fell. The atmosphere was polluted not only with volcanic ash, but with material created by the interaction of the earth's atmosphere and the elongated comet-like tail of Venus. This pollution caused partial darkness for an extended period. Cities and nations were destroyed. Mass migrations took place as people searched for locations that had not been devastated.

About fifty years after the first encounter, Venus had another close approach to the Earth. This second encounter appears to have been not quite as destructive as the first, although there were major events described by people throughout the world.

Venus continued to appear to be threatening the Earth about every fifty-two years, but there were no more exceptionally close approaches to Earth. However, about the ninth or eighth century B.C., Venus encountered the planet Mars, knocking Mars into an orbit which then caused Mars to endanger the Earth. Mars had encounters with the Earth around 776, 747, 717, or 702 and 687 B.C. These dynamical encounters were also adjusting the orbits of these bodies so that after 687 B.C. Mars and Earth were closer to their present stable orbits and the body which appeared originally to be ejected from Jupiter acquired its present position in the solar system and became known as Venus.

This series of events was not the first. It is not as if the Earth orbited the sun peacefully for billions of years and then-wham! The earth, however old it is, appears to have undergone catastrophes throughout its geological history. One need not calculate the probability that the Earth was a perfect ball of uniformity until the time of man, when it was suddenly introduced to the game of planet billiards.

Chapter II

THE EVENTS

Velikovsky postulated a model for the recent history of the Solar System designed to fit observations made by the ancients. Therefore, a better understanding of this model can be acquired by studying the historical testimony of past civilizations.

There are historical records from almost every culture imaginable, and information from these many cultures will be included where applicable. However, since it is reasonable to assume that the majority of the readers of this book will be more familiar with Hebrew history than Hindu or Mesoamerican histories, many of the historical associations relative to cosmological events will be from the Hebrew history. Use of many Hebrew sources should not be misconstrued as representative of the ratio of abundances of sources from other histories. Also, the sources are considered as historical only, and no theological significance is attached to them.

VENUS-EARTH ENCOUNTER ONE

After an unknown number of orbits which were uneventful, but probably impressive from the stargazers' standpoint, Venus had its first major encounter with the earth about 1450 B.C. The results of this encounter were recorded by many ancient cultures, but these events are most noted for being the plagues associated with the Exodus of the Hebrews from Egypt. The first physical evidence was a reddish material falling through the atmosphere.

RED

Rayleigh showed that practically all the light seen in a clear blue sky is a result of scattering by the molecules of air. If it were not for the atmosphere, the sky would look black. However, as the amount of the atmosphere increases, the scattering removes the blue rays from the direct beam more effectively than the red. At sunset, the light travels further through the atmosphere to the observer, so the transmitted light has an intense red hue. This is even more impressive when you add sand or dust particles to the atmosphere.

Dust particles added to the atmosphere were the first visible sign of the encounter with Venus. The atmosphere turned a deep red, but even those ancients without scientific training quickly determined that the red was not due entirely to "Rayleigh scattering". The dust had a reddish hue of its own, and was perhaps a ferruginous material, such as "limonite" (ferric oxide). This settling material turned the world red.

The red-pigmented dust not only covered the land; it ruined the water. In the Ipuwer papyrus, it says: "The river is blood", and "Plague is throughout the land. Blood is everywhere."[1] The Hebrews recorded that: "All the waters that were in the river were turned to blood. There was blood throughout all the land of Egypt."[2] The Mayas tell of days of great cataclysm involving earthquakes, apparent disruption of the regular motion of the solar system, and rivers turned to blood. The Finns say the world was sprinkled with red milk, and the Altai Tartars tell of a catastrophe when "blood turns the whole world red."[3]

Why is the Red Sea called "Red"? Red River, at least in many places, looks red. It is not so obvious for the Red Sea. However, it was renamed and probably received its new name at a time when it did have a red tint. Other places were, at the time of these events, renamed "Red" also, such as Edom (red), Erythrea (erythraios-red in Greek), and Haemus.

The fish did not fare any better in this pre-industrial pollution. The fish died, decomposed and smelled just as today. "And the river stank", said the Israelites.[4] "And all the Egyptians digged round about the river for water to drink; for they could not drink of the water of the river."[5] The Egyptians agreed with the Israelites when they wrote: "Men shrink from tasting; human beings thirst after water," and "That is our water! That is our happiness! What shall we do in respect thereof? All is ruin."[6]

Other problems one would expect from not having clean water for man and beast were also reported. Skin sores were prevalent because there was no way to cleanse the body.

METEORITES

As the earth entered further into the extended atmosphere of Venus, the particles became larger. Soon meteorites were abundant. Contemporary concepts of Hebrew history leave the impression that the "hail" which fell on Egypt was the type of hail now associated with spring rains. However, the original word "barad" means hot rocks. Since the translators can not imagine hot rocks falling from the sky, they substitute the most reasonable alternative under acceptable experience.

PETROLEUM

Along with the "hail" of rocks falling, a blazing sticky substance fell from the sky and ran along the ground. Velikovsky cited numerous instances of ancient references to a time when the "water of fire", "fire rain", or a fiery,

sticky liquid fell from the sky and caused great destruc-
tion. Evidence is given from the Popol-Vuh of the Quiche
Maya, Annals of Cuauhtitlan, Book of Exodus, and the
Midrashim, as well as from stories of the mythologies of
Siberia and of the East Indies. The descriptions all indi-
cate a petroleum product was precipitating.

The people were obviously unfamiliar with petroleum.
When unburned portions accumulated, they experimented
with it, and used it in offerings to the gods. When some
people were unexpectedly engulfed in flames, this was attributed to the anger of the gods. For years after the "fire
rain", the liquid was used in religious ceremonies even unto
the present in the "anointing" of royalty.

DARKNESS

Sources in the Middle East refer to a time when there
was an extended darkness. People were unable to keep a
fire going because of gale-velocity winds, and it was so
dark they could not see anyone next to them; and for many,
the lights went out for the last time. According to the rabbinical sources, forty-nine out of fifty Israelites are said to
have perished in this plague of darkness.

This was not just an unusually dark night. The records
do not indicate that people on the street casually asked,
"Did you notice how dark it was last night?" The Egyptians
recorded that no one left the palace "during nine days, and
during these nine days of upheaval there was such a tem-
pest that neither men nor gods [the royal family] could
see the faces of those beside them."[7] The Hebrews claimed
that "there was a thick darkness in all the land of Egypt
three days. They saw not one another, neither rose any
from his place for three days."[8] Other rabbinical sources
indicate that wind and darkness endured for seven days
and "on the fourth, fifth and sixth days, the darkness was
so dense that they could not stir from their place."[9]

The rabbinical source says seven days, and the Bible three, but the rabbinical source does say three days of *intense* darkness, so the records may not be all that dissimilar. Also, there could be some confusion as to whether a dark day and a dark night might be called two dark days. The Egyptian source said nine days, but it is difficult to measure exactly if one of your best time pieces is a sundial, and if it is too dark to read the water clock which may be clogged up by that time anyway.

There could also be a magnification differential because of the "second story-teller syndrome". If one person said it was dark for four days in his country, a visitor from the next country might say that there was at least five days of darkness where he was. It has been fairly well established that different observers do not always report identical details about an event; however, the overall picture, such as "the big truck knocked the Honda off the bridge", is usually consistent. In this case, the difference in the number of days does not mean that there was no darkness.

Modern atmospheric pollution can make a city sometimes look very gloomy when there are also clouds, but even adding a few clouds would not make one think that the sun had foregone its morning ritual. The darkness was described as if the sun did not rise on time; and the stories do present the logical characteristics one would expect if a long night occurred in part of the world.

If the earth's spin rate had been reduced (see Appendix I), perhaps in addition to the axis being tilted, stories should indicate that there was an extended day somewhere. While, from the New World to Egypt, people were making it slowly through the night, the people in Iran, just to the east of Egypt, were experiencing a "threefold day" and then a "threefold night". [10] Further to the east, China had an even longer "day". A story might travel around the world and have details changed to fit the location, but having a story acquire the proper day-night sequence, as it traveled, is probably too much to ask of the theory that says myths originated in one location and "diffused" throughout the world.

EARTHQUAKES

As Venus and Earth had a close encounter, gigantic earthquakes occurred. According to Ipuwer, "The towns are destroyed. Upper Egypt has become waste... All is ruin" and "The residence is overturned in a minute." Even Gardiner, in his commentary about the Papyrus Ipuwer, commented that "overturned" was used in the sense of overthrowing a wall.

The Hebrews also talked of a tenth plague wherein the Egyptians and their houses were destroyed, but according to some sources, many of the houses of the Hebrews were not ruined. This can be understood by the ruler-slave relationship of the Egyptians and Hebrews. The Egyptian overlords lived in more massive, larger homes made of rock and brick; whereas the Hebrews lived in smaller dwellings made of clay and reeds. When the earthquake struck, the Egyptian abodes were the most likely to be destroyed in a manner which would do bodily harm to the occupants.

Velikovsky also cited a description in the Mexican annals which mentions a catastrophe accompanied by a hurricane and earthquake. Again, people living in small log cabins survived while the tenants of larger dwellings were annihilated.

In Exodus it says that "the Lord smote all the firstborn of the land of Egypt,..."[11] Critics have said that Velikovsky cannot explain how a natural catastrophe could kill the firstborn of a particular group. Velikovsky, however, is not a fundamentalist whose purpose is the verification of every detail of the Bible. Contrary to scientific propaganda, his work was initiated to determine, as accurately as possible, the actual events which transpired during the time period under question, and not to make up anything necessary in order to "prove the Bible".

As a matter of fact, it turns out that, in this case, just the opposite occurred. Velikovsky said that this version has a distinctly supernatural quality and "an earthquake which destroys only the firstborn is inconceivable". Further-more, he said that "no credit should be given to such a record." [12] Either the story is fiction or it contains a corruption of the original text.

Additionally, he said that before proclaiming the entire section to be one which was inserted after the original, "it would be wise to inquire whether or not the incredible part alone is corrupted." Analysis of other locations in the scriptures where this phraseology is employed revealed that the translation resulted in "chosen" instead of "firstborn". The words in the original language are almost identical.

If the "chosen" or elite or select of Egypt were killed, this would then seem reasonable in relation to the earthquake which destroyed the homes of the elite.

MIGRATIONS

Since many Egyptian soldiers were killed, the Hebrews seized upon the opportunity as a reasonable chance for escape, and thus left Egypt. The surviving Egyptians may have pursued the Hebrews in order to retrieve escaping slaves, or the Egyptians may have set out to defend their country against the invading Hyksos, and, therefore, only appeared to be pursuing the Hebrews.

The Exodus was then a result of these events instead of the events happening just as the Exodus occurred. Ben Bova, editor of *Analog*, naively asked why the plagues happened along when the Hebrews were exiting. [13] Dr. James A. Durham pointed out that this would be like asking why Vesuvius erupted just as the people of Pompeii were suffocating. [14]

An interesting by-product of Velikovsky's basic work is a speculation about origin of the fear of the number thir-teen. Many cultures have had this superstition for thousands of years. There does not seem to be a record of this superstition dating from before the Exodus. However, the Israelites did not share the fear of the number thirteen.

The Egyptians claimed that the thirteenth day of the first month was a very bad day. "Thou shalt not do anything on this day." [15] Similarly in the New World, a new *world age* was said to have originated on the thirteenth day of a month called "earthquake". The peoples involved started the new day at sunrise. The Hebrews then and now count the new day at sunset. Their month Aviv is called the first month.

The Passover, or close approach of Venus to Earth, which created extensive damage, occurred at midnight on the fourteenth day of the month of Aviv. For much of the world it was a terrible and destructive thirteenth day; whereas, the Hebrews considered it not only a day of liberation, but the fourteenth day of the month.

It sounds repetitive to say that many ancient cultures had stories of a time when great tides existed, but this is the case. The order of events in these stories is also the same. After the darkness and earthquakes came the tidal waves. From the Choctaw Indians to the Chinese and from Peru to Northern Europe, the stories are similar. A Laplandic epic says that the sea gathered "together itself up into a huge towering wall...". [16] The Indians of Yucatan had an ancient tradition about a time when their ancestors had escaped the pursuit of the opposition when a passageway was opened for them in the sea. This was strikingly similar to the Jewish tradition; however, the story did not necessarily reach the Yucatan Peninsual by diffusion. (See Mullen, *Pensee IX*). A migrating story often retains details uncharacteristic of the region to which it migrated. (For example, see the section on *Oedipus and Akhnaton*.)

The Hebrew history indicates that going beyond the Sea of Passage would not have been possible except that physical interactions had rent the waters. Many Hebrews made it through the gap to the other side, but many did not. These were alluded to later as "My people who were left in the sea." [17]

According to the Hebrews, the Egyptians did not do as well. The Egyptians, seeing the escaping slaves, in one last desperate plunge tried to overtake them. The Egyptians' timing was off, and the Pharaoh and a large portion of his already decimated army were drowned.

In present day el-Arish, a black granite shrine was found inscribed with hieroglyphics and performing the un-shrinely task of being a cattle trough. The name King Thom was written in a royal cartouche, which indicates an historical instead of mythological characteristic of the writing. Two cities were built by the Israelite slaves for the Pharaoh of the Oppression. One was Pithom. Pi-Thom means "the abode of Thom".[18] So it is possible that the inscription concerns the time of the Exodus, although this is not where it is placed under conventional chronology.

In the mutilated description, there is mention of a time of great upheaval in the residences and a time of nine days during which people could not see adjacent people. After a series of events similar to those described by the Hebrews, the writing on the shrine says, "His Majesty leapt into the so-called Place of the Whirlpool." The location of this action was Pi-Khiroti.

The translator noted that this was the only known reference to this location. However, Velikovsky pointed out that Exodus says, "But the Egyptians pursued after them, all the horses and chariots of Pharaoh, and his horseman, and his army, and overtook them encamping by the sea, beside Pi-ha-Kiroth (Khiroth), before Baalzephon."[19] The "ha" is the Hebrew definite article and belongs between Pi and Khiroth. Velikovsky also mentioned that the vowels of the Egyptian translation are assumed by the translator, and the name can also be read Pi-Kharoti.

The Egyptians and Hebrew locations are identical. Therefore, Velikovsky believed that "the question, centuries or even millennia old, as to where the Sea of Passage was, can be solved with the help of the inscription on the shrine. On the basis of certain indications in the text, Pi-ha-Khiroth, where the events took place, was on the way from Memphis to Pisoped."[20]

The name Jam Suf is commonly thought to be the Red Sea. Some argue that Suf means *reed*, and since papyrus reed does not grow in salt water, Jam Suf must have been an inner lake on the route from Suez to the Mediterranean Sea. However, Velikovsky suggested that the name "Jam Suf is derived not from *reed*, but from *hurricane*, suf, sufa, in Hebrew."[21]   He says that the Red Sea in Egyptian is *shari* which signifies the sea of percussion (mare percussions) or the sea of the stroke or of the disaster." Disaster would probably fit with Thom's impression.

All over the world people were forced to migrate as a result of the natural disturbances which uprooted them *en masse.*

As the Hebrews were exiting Egypt, they met a group which had been forced to leave its desert home. The Hebrews called the group the Amalekites. The Egyptians called them the Amu, or later the Hyksos. After a few skirmishes with the Hebrews, the Hyksos (Amalekites) entered Egypt. They conquered Egypt and ruled there for about five hundred years. These identifications were made by Velikovsky in *Ages in Chaos*, and will be discussed in Chapter III.

AERIAL DISPLAY

During the time of activity on both sides of the Red Sea, and while a good part of the world observed the freakish action of the water, the world also observed an impressive display in the sky which would be a source of discussion for centuries to follow. An enormous electrical discharge occurred between Venus and Earth, and the gigantic tides collapsed. The extended atmosphere of Venus became distorted and discharges passed between the tail and main body. At times it appeared as though a great battle were taking place between a serpent and the sphere. Sometimes the tail assumed shapes like an animal with legs and many heads. As the tail disintegrated and meteorites fell to earth, it appeared that the sphere had defeated the monster and dumped the body on the earth.

WHISPERING STRATA

For years, noise of the settling strata was thought to be voices or the groaning of the dragon that had fallen to the earth. Ipuwer describes this as the "years of noise". "There is no end to noise. Oh, that the earth would cease from noise, and tumult (uproar) be no more."

Many cultures interpreted the noise as voices of gods or devils. This interpretation of the noise may possibly depend on how well an individual felt about his recent actions. A name similar to Yahoo, Yao or Yahu for a god-ruler, spiritual god, or devil arose throughout the world, perhaps because most of the world heard a similar sound from the ground.

Some people in North America said that when the sky was low, they lifted it back up by shouting "Yahu" which was heard all over the world. At Mt. Sinai, the people heard "I am Yahweh". Velikovsky relates instances of people hearing this sound throughout the world.

When Cotlow published *Twilight of the Primitive*, he quoted from the notes of one of the first people to become closely associated with the aborigines of Australia. This person said that the group did not have a god, but they did have a devil named Yakoo. If anyone died, it was said that Yakoo took him.

FOOD FROM THE SKY

Many cultures have a tradition about a time of great catastrophes followed by a time period when the survivors of these catastrophes were fed by an edible substance which fell from the clouds. The different cultures used various names, but all essentially described the food similarly. Depending on the location, one ate manna, ambrosia, heavenly bread, food of the morning dew, honey from the clouds, amrite or great dew. The people on the border of Asia and Africa, the Hindus, the Maoris of the Pacific, the Icelandics and the Finns all describe a honey-tasting, breadlike substance which precipitated from the clouds. All agree that the original cause was an object external to the earth which was also the source of the great upheavals that had taken place.

All over the world phrases originated which basically claim that lands flowed with milk and honey. These phrases were not the result of a person with a degree in creative writing suddenly being inspired by natural beauty which had been present throughout his lifetime; they were created by people describing, in the vernacular, events that were unusual. When a yellowish-white material, which tastes like honey, is flowing in a stream of water or has melted and formed its own stream, poetical phrases are easily acquired.

THE COW

While in the desert. the Hebrews started the worship of bulls and calves. Although this seems strange, it turns out that the Hebrews were not the only ones instigating bovine worship at this time. This form of devotion became a favorite pasttime throughout the world. The Apis bull cult was revived in Egypt, and bovine worship became extensive in Minoan Crete and Mycenaean Greece. Elaborate ceremonies were conducted in many lands to commemorate the "great cow", the "celestial cow" or the "heavenly cow".

There is evidence that cows were, at sometime in the past, eaten in India. Later, they became very sacred, and were regarded as daughters of the *heavenly cow*. [22] Today in India, cows are still considered sacrosanct.

Velikovsky observed that "Isis, the planet Venus, was represented as a human figure with two horns, like Astarte (Ishtar) of the horns; and sometimes it was fashioned in the likeness of a cow." [23] Also, Velikovsky used a quote about primitive tribes on Samoa who did not develop writing but repeat even today that "the planet Venus became wild and grew horns out of her head". [24] Numerous other examples exist. Since the horns of Venus are described so often by the ancients, an explanation has been sought which fits with the uniformitarian concept.

Venus has phases like the moon. It has been suggested that the normal phases of Venus caused the ancients to refer to it as having grown horns. This suggestion does not seem entirely adequate, since the ancients did not seem to have the same fascination with saying the Moon grew horns. It seems even less reasonable because the phases of Venus cannot now be resolved with the naked eye. [25]

If Venus were closer to the earth, the phases could be seen. If the atmosphere of Venus were elongated (comet-like), the phases may have resembled horns more closely, but the appearance of horns may have had nothing to do with the phases of Venus.

Comets generally have extended atmospheres which take on various shapes. NASA publication SP198 contains numerous photographs of comets taking on various shapes. Drawings of some of the comets are included with the photographs.

One of the drawings is of Comet Daniel 1905. [26] This drawing without a caption has been exhibited in a number of classes and the students were asked what they thought was in the picture. All agreed that it closely resembled a bull's head. If people saw something in the sky that looked like the object in the drawing, thought it had just gored the world, knew it had created massive destruction, and heard sounds that were caused by shifting strata and were similar to the sounds of a mad bull, it is not surprising that they would be inclined toward bull worship.

There seems to have been some trouble in distinguishing whether this agent of destruction was male or female.

At first it was thought to be a bull, but then, when the milk-like substance started to fall, it was decided that the initial guess was wrong. As Velikovsky noted: "A horned planet that produced milk most closely resembled a cow."[27]

YEARS OF CLOUDS

Another set of poetical phrases originated; again not necessarily because of an agile mind, but as a result of casual observation. Owing to the violence undergone by the earth, the atmosphere probably contained enough volcanic ash and other debris to put the entire Environmental Protection Agency into a frenzy. This created an exceptionally gloomy period which was called the time of wandering "in the valley of the shadow of death". Nordic peoples called this time the "twilight of the gods". The Egyptians, not attempting to be aesthetic, merely said, "... the sun is veiled by clouds."[28]

This condition lasted for a number of years according to the transcriptions from the eastern hemisphere. Mesoamerican cultures, also with straightforward prose, said that the "faces of the sun and of the moon were covered with clouds." They claimed that this lasted about twenty-five years.

The people of the Pacific also have similar stories. One chief in the Central Polynesian area is said to have traveled to a new island, during the time of gloom, in a canoe named "Weary of Darkness".[29]

Other problems one would expect as a result of this condition also occurred. Plants would not grow and "noxious creatures" which were best suited for this environment were prevalent.

THE SECOND ENCOUNTER

As the dust settled and the smoke cleared, people saw that the agent of destruction was still a threat. During the time of darkness, Venus had been continuing on its orbit, and would soon cross the earth's orbit again. This approach could have been perfectly harmless, but the earth happened to be near the same point at the time.

MINOR QUAKES

The second near encounter was not as close or as destructive as the first. The Earth was not engulfed in the extended atmosphere of Venus although numerous meteorites hit the Earth. Earthquakes were also common.

About this time, the Israelites crossed the Jordan river and entered the "Promised Land" where they encountered the walled city of Jericho. This provides another example of how Velikovsky does not approach the subject mystically. He said: "The fall of the walls of Jericho at the blast of the trumpets is a well-known episode, but it is not well interpreted. The horns blown by the priests for seven days played no greater natural role than Moses' rod with which, in the legend, he opened a passage in the sea." [30]

The walls of Jericho have been excavated. [31] They were about twelve feet wide and were probably destroyed by an unusually large earthquake. Whether this earthquake was a residual quake from the previous encounter or among the first indicators of the impending disaster may not be known, but the second approach of Venus was soon to produce another event that would be noticeable worldwide.

APPARENT CHANGE OF MOTION

The second encounter is probably best known for being the time Joshua "made" the sun stand still. In the Middle East, the event happened in the forenoon according to indications in the stories. Supposedly Joshua could see that more time was needed than was available to complete the battle of Beth-horon, so he sought a longer day, and the sun stood still.

Velikovsky pointed out that the most informative part of this story is usually ignored. Meteorites played a major role in the battle. Great stones fell from the sky and killed more of the opposition than were killed by Joshua's soldiers. Great winds, earthquakes and tidal waves also occurred.

If no one else in the world happened to notice the sun standing still and the other events, then as Velikovsky said, this story would be "beyond the belief of even the most imaginative or the most pious person." [32] However, the rest of the world did seem to notice.

The same series is found throughout ancient mythology. Rocks falling from the sky, apparent changes in the motion of the heavenly bodies, earthquakes, whirlwinds, great fires and tidal waves were recorded by many nations. The basic theme is that the sun and moon or the stars stopped or went off course, and the details describe the local effects. These cultures would not be expected to associate these events with a change in motion of the earth unless the events had been observed.

MARS ENCOUNTERS

Mars was not an important deity before the ninth century B.C. People knew of Mars and observed its motions, but it was not considered to be all that significant. Suddenly, around the ninth century, Mars began to make people realize that it was not the innocent little celestial body that people had thought. Mars became the war god, the dreaded planet and the planet everyone feared. Before this time, Velikovsky notes, "Mars did not arouse any fears in the hearts of the ancient astrologers, and its name was seldom mentioned in the second millennium." (B.C.) [33] Why the sudden change?

VENUS DISTURBS MARS

A short time before Mars began terrorizing the earth, it had had its own problems with Venus. This did not occur as far in the past as the Venus-Earth encounter, and the records of this event are more extensive. Mythologies abound with descriptions of the battles between Venus and Mars. These encounters left Mars with orbital characteristics which later brought it into several close approaches with the Earth.

Mars has a mass of about 0.108 times that of the Earth and a radius of about 0.53 that of Earth. Venus, however, is only slightly smaller than Earth. So, in its encouters both with Venus and with Earth, Mars came out second. Velikovsky concluded, at a time when the supposed canals of Mars were still being debated, that "the contacts of Mars with planets larger than itself and more powerful make it highly improbable that any higher forms of life, if they previously existed there, survived on Mars." Also any canals "appear to be a result of the play of geological forces that answered with rifts and cracks the outer forces acting in collision." [34]

MARS ENCOUNTERS EARTH

Although Mars encountered the Earth more times than Venus and at a time when writing was better developed, Mars was much less destructive. Consequently, most records of the events are not as impressive as those of the Venus encounter. Damage could have been extensive but still appeared to be local in nature. Most of the destruction was caused by earthquakes and electrical discharges. Velikovsky has extensively discussed the "mythological" descriptions of these occurrences, and *Worlds in Collision* should be consulted for this detailed analysis. However, a few historical associations will provide a general understanding so that some miscellaneous items can be better understood. Although writing was more common in the days of the Mars events, the mythologies encompass the entire span; hence, the events are not always divided into time sections.

Most of the Mars events took place within less than ninety years. The regularity of these events was such that an astute observer could become quite a prophet. Amos started prophesying about an event which would occur around 747 B.C. Part of his reasoning may have been based on a similar event in -776. It is not clear from the literature if this event was merely activity in the sky or had done some damage to the Earth. The olympics were started in -776, possibly to honor this event. Velikovsky also mentions a damaging non-seasonal flood in Egypt during the time of Osorkon II of the Libyan Dynasty; Amos may have been referring to this event.

Whether because of previous damage to the Earth or only observations of the sky, Amos was predicting doom. Amos attempted to link morality with disaster and had the audacity to tell people that they were not acting properly, so they killed him. His death, however, did not deter Mars, and the catastrophe struck as predicted.

The catastrophe was known as the "raash" or commotion in the days of Uzziah, king of Judah. The Earth quaked, and part of a mountain was removed.

The unusual thing about the incident was that the people apparently left town before the earthquake. This was pretty remarkable without modern scientific techniques for "predicting" earthquakes. It would be remarkable even with some of the modern methods. However, if people saw Mars looming in the distance and remembered what had happened the last time something other than the sun or moon looked that size, they might reasonably try to find a place they would not fall into or where nothing would fall on them.

People in this region talked of "a day of thick darkness" and "the day dark with night". Velikovsky noted that astronomers, who assumed no changes in the order of the solar system, calculated that no eclipse was visible from Palestine between -763 and -586. They of course found it perplexing that these people spoke of an eclipse (it *must* be an eclipse), when there was none. More will be said about "eclipses" later. These dark days, however, were accompanied by events not commonly associated with eclipses. Also, many people seemed to expect doom, since the prevalent attitude, expressed coincidently in Isaiah 22:13, was "Let us eat and drink; for tomorrow we shall die".

Isaiah, Joel and Micah each predicted additional catastrophes. Another encounter did occur. Ahaz was king of Judah, but he died before the event. The Mars catastrophe occurred on the day Ahaz was buried. Supposedly, on that day, the sundial changed about 10° (about forty minutes). Velikovsky demonstrated that the evidence indicates that the terrestrial axis shifted or was tilted so that the sunset was hastened. This story, he said, "is related also in the records and told in the traditions of many peoples. It appears that a heavenly body passed very close to the Earth, moving, as it seems, in the same direction as the Earth on its nocturnal side." [35]

The last Mars event was in the time of Hezekiah who became the king after Ahaz. The Assyrians were interacting with Judah at this time. The narrative of eight campaigns of the Assyrian Sennacherib is found on what is called the "Taylor Prism". This is made of baked clay and has cuneiform signs on it. Part of this narrative corresponds to the Hebrew record. At the time, Sennacherib was running around the Middle East creating havoc, and said he would do the same for Hezekiah if Judah did not pay "protection" money to Sennacherib. Hezekiah paid, and Judah was left alone for awhile. Hezekiah put this time to good use and fortified the walls of Jerusalem. He also built up the army, and fixed the water supply so that the city would have water but could cut off that water to the enemy.

Sennacherib heard of this activity and the Hebrew threat to peace which consisted of building dangerous offensive weapons such as stone walls around Jerusalem. Hezekiah had also made treaties with Tirhakah, king of Ethiopia and Egypt. Sennacherib gathered his troops and marched toward Jerusalem. For the second time, he made his headquarters near Lachish, and sent someone to shout over the wall at the Hebrews and tell them to surrender. This was done by one of Sennacherib's generals, Rab-sha-keh, who was an ancient practitioner of the warfare propaganda game. He told the Hebrews that the Samarians also thought their gods would help just before the Assyrians crashed in, and everyone knew what had happened to the Samarians.

However, Sennacherib's army was destroyed by a "blast" from heaven. One hundred and eighty-five thousand men were killed in one day. (Sennacherib's sons were obviously not pleased with these results, for they slew him upon his return home.) Sennacherib's demise was recorded identically in the scriptures and in a cuneiform inscription of Esarhaddon, son of Sennacherib.

The "blast" was probably the result of the Mars encounter. One possibility is that it was interplanetary discharge. A phenomenon such as this could come closer to taking out the whole group in one day than the accepted explanation of a plague. A plague would have a distribution of deaths extending for days or weeks instead of the deaths all occurring in a single day.

This event occurred in -687 and was accompanied by a reversal of the tilt of the Earth's axis which occurred on the day Ahaz was buried. A celestial encounter which caused a perturbation that was later reversed has been observed in modern times. Wolf's comet had an approach to Jupiter which changed the orbit of the comet. Later another approach to Jupiter made the comet revert to almost its original course. [36]

The -687 event was the last Earth-Mars encounter. Many of the ancient records associated with planetary changes are not easily related to a specific date. From the writings, though, it is often clear that the ancients were describing changes which occurred in the solar system, and if any "interpretation" of these writings is necessary, it is only to force fit them into the uniformitarian concept.

There is an ancient Hindu astronomical text written in a logical, scientific manner, and it contains evidence that the writers were well versed in mathematics. [37] They knew that the earth is a globe and that directions in space are only relative. One chapter, however, is considered to be strange because it describes encounters between planets and claims that Venus is generally a winner in these encounters. Anything from saying the writers had a temporary mental lapse to saying that the section was inserted later is offered as an explanation of this "unscientific" section.

Some other writings may not be as clearly scientific in nature, but they also state that the appearance of the sky has made some drastic changes. The constellation of the Great Bear was said to have once contained the polestar. It was said that this constellation started setting toward the ocean, which it had not done before the planetary encounters. Later interpreters said that there was no reason for the ancients to say this, since the Great Bear must have always set toward the ocean. [38]

The *Iliad* also may contain descriptions of changes in the solar system. Velikovsky noted that there is a debate as to when Homer composed the stories about these changes. Velikovsky pointed out that the participants of the planetary encounters could give a clue as to the earliest time Homer could have lived. Some authorities place Homer as early as -1159 and as late as -685. [39]

Velikovsky suggested that, since the Venus-Mars encounter is implied, Homer must have written his works sometime after the ninth century B.C. Also, since the Earth and Moon have problems with Mars, the *Iliad* was probably composed after 747 B.C. Homer then would be contemporary with Amos and Isaiah or existed soon after them. Since the Trojan War was also during the time of the Mars encounters, Homer lived at the time of, or soon after, the Trojan War. [40] The conventional view is that Homer may have lived some *centuries* after the Trojan War.

The last planetary encounter was in -687, after which the solar system stabilized. The most pronounced catastrophic event after that was the modern-day arrangement of Egyptian history. These problems and how they occurred are discussed in the next chapter.

Chapter III

THE HISTORICAL CONSTRUCTION

Egyptian history is the standard for determining the absolute dates for the ancient histories of the world. If the standard is incorrect, archaeological problems will be created in the countries which use this standard as a reference. In *Ages in Chaos*, Velikovsky describes a number of these problems and demonstrates how these problems are resolved by use of a revised chronology. Some of these points will be reviewed here, but first it is interesting to see how flaws entered this standard for world history. This was discussed by Velikovsky in an article titled *Astronomy and Chronology*. [1]

ORIGIN OF THE STANDARD

For background, it is necessary to define relative and absolute dating. If it is known only that a certain king died three years after a major battle, then the time of the demise of the king is known only relative to the battle. Several other events may also be known to have occurred a given number of years before or after the battle. A relative chronology for the king's life can then be determined.

If it is established from the chronology of another country that the battle was fought in 1066 A.D., then the absolute chronology of the king's life can be determined. It would then be known that he died in 1069 A.D.

The relative internal chronology of a nation can be established basically by excavation. As with geology, the top layers are theoretically considered to be the youngest and, therefore, the layers are assumed to get progressively older the deeper they are. Correlations of pottery, literature and other art forms are made between differing locations in order to provide a time scale relative to another country. In the case of much of antiquity, the absolute dating of a culture is obtained by linking it to Egyptian history. The real key to absolute time, then, is the association of a given culture with Egyptian chronology.

This leaves the impression that Egyptian chronology is either exceedingly well-known or had an exceptionally proficient press agent. Unfortunately, as we shall see, the latter seems to be the case.

THE TIME SCALE

The ancient Egyptians did not use an absolute time scale the way we do today. They did not select a year and then relate the events of various dynasties to this date. Instead, they referenced events to the beginning of the rule of a particular ruler.

In creating an absolute chronology for Egypt, this practice caused ambiguity in at least two ways. First, in the case of a co-regency between father and son, it is not always clear if the time of reign of each includes the overlap. If a king is said to have ruled for twelve years and his son ten years and the co-regency is known to be three years, it is not clear if the two ruled for a total of nineteen years or twenty-two years or twenty-five years. Additionally, the highest regnal date known for a given Pharaoh may not be the actual full-length period of rule for that individual.

Second, the last *known* document of a given reign may have been written years before the end of the reign. If it described an event which occurred in the sixth year of a particular Pharaoh, it is often accepted that he ruled for six years; whereas, he may have actually ruled for twenty years. Compounding these chronological problems is the fact that the sequence of dynasties is not definitely determined. "Only in a few individual cases is there historical evidence to indicate the order of two dynasties that ruled consecutively."[2]

In addition to all of these sources of error, Velikovsky noted that the list of dynasties provided by the Egyptian historian-priest Manetho contained extraneous years in dynasties as well as extraneous dynasties. This tendency to exaggerate appears to have originated as an effort to demonstrate that the Egyptian civilization was considerably older than the Greek or Assyro-Babylonian cultures.

Two major problems arise with Manetho's list of dynasties. First, there are two versions (Eusebius and Africanus) which do not agree with each other. Second, it is not easy to determine which kings in Manetho's list correspond to kings mentioned in the monuments.

There are two dynasties (Eighteenth and Nineteenth) about which there is abundant documentary evidence. This evidence discredits Manetho's lists.[3]

Where there was no additional evidence to confirm or refute Manetho, his scheme was accepted almost without question. Velikovsky quotes Breasted as saying, regarding the chronology of Manetho, that it is "a late, careless and uncritical compilation, which can be proven wrong from the contemporary monuments in the vast majority of cases where such monuments have survived."[4]

Surprisingly, Hall, the same person who said that it "would be most unsafe to trust" the information attributed to Manetho, also claimed that the basic chronology of ancient Egypt is not speculative but is a certainty because of the "continuous literary tradition preserved by the Egyptian priest Manetho."[5] Hall then said that this basic scheme has been filled in and supported by archaeology. However, the archaeologists did *not* solidify this scheme by analyzing monumental inscriptions and correlating them with Manetho's list. As Velikovsky noted, "The strange fact is that long before the hieroglyphics were read for the first time, the kings of Egypt were placed in the centuries in which conventional chronology still keeps them prisoner." The few changes have been relatively minor compared to the chance for error provided by Manetho.

Perhaps this is part of the basis for Gardiner's 1961 statement that "what is proudly advertised as Egyptian history is merely a collection of rags and tatters."[6]

Actually, all of Manetho's work was not accepted exactly as he wrote it. His time values were considered "absurdly high", so astronomical evidence was used in attempt to fix some parts of Manetho's king lists to an absolute time scale. This is where sleight of hand enters the picture. The basis for conventional chronology changes hands faster than the eye can see. Historians and astronomers each say that the other has accurate data to support conventional chronology; hence, their *own speculations* must be true.

There are contradictions in the archaeological evidence which strongly indicate the possibility of a mistake in Egyptian chronology. Several examples will be discussed later. When historians are questioned about problems of this nature, it is quickly stated that conventional chronology has been substantiated by astronomers. When astronomers are asked about the reliability of their correlations, we are told that it must be correct because the historians have substantial correlative data. This circular support sounds impressive, but just *how substantial* is this mutual support?

ASTRONOMICAL SUPPORT

The star Sirius is thought to be Sothis, or Spdt in Egyptian, and the rising of Sirius is thought to be the basis for an absolute time scale of Egyptian history. However, Velikovsky gives support for the suggestion that what is known as the Sothic period actually pertained to *Venus* instead of Sirius. Knapp, who was with the astronomy department at University of Basel, also expressed this opinion as early as 1934.[7]

Some historians *assume* that the Sothic period was used for absolute time measurement, so an analysis of this "astronomical support" is of interest.

The Egyptian civil year of 365 days would concide with their astronomical year of 365 1/4 days only every 1460 years. Censorinus, a Roman author, said that this time period was called a "great year", "heliacal year" or "the year of the God". (Censorinus also described a "cataclysmic" year which was the time between two world catastrophes.) He also said that Sothis was the Egyptian name for Sirius, and that the "great years" begin with the heliacal rising of Sirius on the first morning of the month called Thot.

Heliacal rising designates the rising of a star just prior to sunrise when it is first seen again to the naked eye after its rising has been obscured by the brilliance of sunlight. If a calendar has only 365 days a year instead of 365.25, every four years the calendar is short one day. Therefore, with this calendar, the heliacal rising of a star would occur one day later every four years. Losing one day every four years would make a star rise heliacally on the same day only every 1460 actual years. Sirius would then rise heliacally on the first of Thot only every 1460 years. This is known as a Sothic Period. "There is no known instance of an ancient Egyptian event being recorded by the serial year of a Sothis period."[8] Although Sirius would rise heliacally on the first of Thot every 1460 years, modern scholars have assumed that this date was celebrated symbolically each year.

The historian Censorinus wrote during the time of about 238 A.D. Theon of Alexandria in Egypt, wrote in the century following Censorinus. They seem to have agreed about the time of the beginning of a Sothic period, but it is not proven that this originally related to Sirius.[9]

Even assuming that it was, there are numerous problems attendant with correlating the Sothic period to known Egyptian events. First a name is needed that is associated with a Sothic period and is found in one of the dynasties listed by Manetho. The name Menophres has been provided by Theon. It is commonly thought that this name refers to Ramses I. If this were true, and if the ancient Egyptians used a Sothic period for a time reference, then finding a basic chronology would be relatively easy. However, the first is questionable and the second is only a device used by historians to try to develop this "certain" history.

Actually, Theon did not say that Menophres was a king. He could have been a sage, seer, scientist or former spiritual advisor to the Pharaoh. The idea has also been considered, with much logical support, that Menophres was not a person but the city of Memphis, an ancient capital of Egypt.

If you are willing to accept the assumptions that Menophres was a person and a king, there are at least six possibilities from Manetho's list of kings who have names which sound similar to, but are not quite the same as, Menophres. Some of these have no substantial evidence to prove their existence other than that they appear on the padded list of Manetho.

One possibility was Merneptah, who succeeded Ramses II. The name was similar, and some historians were willing to place his dynasty in the time period of -1321. However, he was rejected because the historians did not want to place Ramses II before about -1300.

Thus, the man ultimately selected, supposedly because of a name similar to Menophres, was assumed to be Ramses I, also called Menpehtire which is similar to Menophres. But this identification is from the inscriptions on the monuments and not from the king's list. (Seti I was once thought to have been identified as Menophres, but this identification was based on a circular argument.)[10]

There are at least two other references to Sothis. One is on a papyrus found in the precinct of the Illahum Temple at Fayum. This gives the time of a rising of Sothis during the reign of an unnamed king. Assumptions can be made about the king, but then the exact astronomical calculations depend on these assumptions. Another reference was found on a stone in Elephantine. This is *assumed* to be a reference to a heliacal rising of Sothis, and the king has been identified as Thutmose III. However, the year of reign of Thutmose III is not given, so additional error can arise.

Velikovsky effectively argues that so-called astronomical support for conventional chronology is, at best, highly speculative. The nebulous fit of astronomical information, *even assuming no changes in the solar system* (which is in itself, an unfounded assumption), could be caused by three things. The Sothis period may not refer to Sirius; it may refer to Sirius but no reference is actually made to heliacal rising; or it is Sirius and was used as a reference, but no substantiating data is extant. Either of the first two would eliminate the accepted astronomical support, and the third indicates that there is considerable room for error.

With so little actual support, it is not surprising to find that others before and after Velikovsky challenged the so-called "Sothis" theory. However, as Danelius points out, *Velikovsky offered a substitute chronology.*[11]

THE REVISED CHRONOLOGY

The outline for Velikovsky's revised chronology was first published in 1945 in the booklet *Theses for the Reconstruction of Ancient History* which contained 284 basic points of his reconstruction. By 1972, Velikovsky had discovered new evidence which led him to change his mind about three or four of these points, but the overall reconstruction was still maintained as being valid.

In 1952, Velikovsky published *Ages in Chaos* which contained a more detailed explanation and support for the various points made in the *Theses*. *Ages in Chaos* was only the first of a now-projected four-volume work; and therefore covered only the time period from the Exodus to the reign of the Pharaoh Akhnaton. Portions of that text will be reviewed here, although the reader is again referred to Velikovsky's own work for an intriguing detailed discussion.

IPUWER

In the *Theses*, Velikovsky stated that the Papyrus Ipuwer "comprises a text which originated shortly after the close of the Middle Kingdom; the original text was written by an eyewitness to the plagues and the Exodus." Gardiner, who translated the Papyrus Ipuwer, also called *The Admonitions of an Egyptian Sage*, originally ascribed this document to the First Intermediate Period.

Professor Lewis M. Greenberg has pointed out that, since Gardiner's work, only John Van Seters, other than Velikovsky, had subjected the Papyrus to close scrutiny.[12] [13] Greenberg quotes Van Seters as saying that "taking all the pieces of evidence together, there is one date which seems to fit all the requirements, and that is the late Thirteenth Dynasty. Not only has the orthography and linguistic evidence always pointed toward this later date, but our present knowledge of the social and political history of the period confirms this opinion. The last word has certainly not been said on the subject, and it is hoped that more learned authorities will enter into a re-examination of this important literary work. If this later dating should stand, then the (admonitions) will, in fact, aid our understanding of the Second Intermediate Period and the Hyksos problem. To the present writer, it seems the burden of demonstration rests on those who would still maintain an early date."

THE HYKSOS

The Hyksos have only briefly been mentioned before, so a reasonable question is who were the Hyksos? This question is also of some concern to historians[14] and is discussed in detail by Velikovsky in Chapter II of *Ages in Chaos*. Again many of the clues to this identification are found in the writings of people who quoted the Egyptian priest Manetho whose work is no longer extant.

Scholars disagree as to the origin of the Hyksos. There appears to be little information available about them. They left no artistic or literary works, and few references, by Egyptians, exist concerning Hyksos rule.

According to some ancient sources (Manetho, and Josephus), the Hyksos were barbarians who knew only how to destroy and the Egyptians might have been happier with another natural plague. One source refers to the Hyksos as a group of "...ignoble origin from the east...", who took possession of Egypt with no difficulty.[15] If the Hyksos were, as Velikovsky claims, the people who entered Egypt after the Exodus, it would not be surprising that they would have no problem in taking control. The country had not only been devastated by a natural catastrophe, it had also lost a major section of its army in a "whirlpool". This would explain the lack of opposition in Egypt but not really who the Hyksos were before they sought employment as rulers of Egypt, or, equally important, where they went after being driven out of Egypt.

As mentioned in Chapter II, physical conditions were apparently in a state of upheaval everywhere and many groups of people were forced into migrating about this time. The Israelites were already on the borders of the Sinai Peninsula when they encountered a part of this heavy traffic in the form of the Amalekites. They had at least two major battles and many minor battles with the Amalekites, whom Velikovsky equates with Hyksos. These were probably also the same people called Amu by the Egyptians.

The Hyksos, or Amalekites, had occupied southern Palestine only a short time before this. This is where the Israelites hoped to go; however, they were discouraged by their encounters with these nomadic hordes. The Hyksos-Amalekites were fierce and more powerful than most other tribes of the area. The Israelites lost heavily in the battles with them and decided not to attempt to enter Palestine. This was the beginning of the time of the wandering in the desert. The battles with the Hyksos-Amalekites left a strong impression with the Israelites, and the word Amalek is still associated with deep-seated fear.

The Egyptians also had distasteful remembrances of the Hyksos. To the Egyptians, the Hyksos were among the worst of a series of bad events of a time when nothing seemed to go right. There is an indication from the scriptures that this last "plague" in Egypt was known to the Israelites. In a discussion of the plagues in Egypt, the writer of Psalms said, "He cast upon them fierceness of his anger, wrath and indignation, and trouble, by sending evil angels among them." [16] The term "evil angels" has created considerable discussion among Biblical historians. Velikovsky suggested that since there is no other mention of "evil angels" and the phrase is not only unusual Hebrew, but is grammatically incorrect Hebrew, perhaps the text was corrupted. [17] By the change of only a silent letter "aleph", the "sending of evil angels" becomes "invasion of king-shepherds". Manetho said of the Hyksos, "Their race bore the generic name of Hycsos (Kyksos), which means "king-shepherds". It appears that the last plague was the invasion of the king-shepherd Hyksos. In this case "evil-angels" was probably a proper description, though not as informative as the original.

In addition to a description of upheaval and invasion, the Papyrus Ipuwer also contains the statement that the public offices were entered and the census-lists were removed. Hebrew legend has a description of the Amalekites acquiring the genealogical information of the Israelites from the Egyptian Archives. This lends additional support to the suggestion that the invaders of the papyrus were the Hyksos-Amalekites. Under conventional chronology, the Egyptians were still strong after the Exodus and would have been unlikely to allow the theft of their government documents.

Ancient documents indicate that the Hyksos ruled Egypt for just over four hundred years. According to accepted chronology, based on the Sothis theory, the Hyksos ruled in Egypt for only 120 years. However, there is not enough time between the Twelfth and Eighteenth Dynasties to house the Hyksos and any cultural changes that must fit this time span unless the Hyksos actually ruled for a far greater period than one hundred years. This possibility was considered by Flinders Petrie who suggested an extra Sothis period should be added for the time of Hyksos rule. This would add 1460 Julian years, thereby allowing enough time for Hyksos rule and a sufficient duration for significant cultural changes. Unfortunately, this leaves twelve centuries too many to fill. Thus, the idea of adding an extra Sothis period between the Twelfth and Eighteenth Dynasties was rejected in favor of the "shorter version".

Under the revised chronology, the Hyksos ruled over Egypt for the time period between the fall of the Middle Kingdom and the rise of the New Kingdom. This lasted about 400 years. This would also be the time period described in the Book of Joshua and in Judges. These books do not mention any Egyptian rule over Canaan. This is reasonable under the revised chronology since the Egyptians themselves were under foreign domination. However, under the conventional chronology, Egypt would be ruling Palestine which creates the problem of why there is no mention of Egyptian control in Joshua and in Judges.

During their four-hundred-year rule, the Hyksos created a sequence of Hyksos Pharaohs. They were callous rulers of Egypt and their power and bestiality were known in many countries. In the scriptures, it said that Amalek was the first among nations. This is understandable under the revised chronology where they are identified as the Hyksos. It is not reasonable under conventional chronology. This chronology suggests that the Amalekites must have been a small band of guerrillas because no slot in history is available for them as a powerful group.

The Bible records that the name Agog (Agag) was applied to two of the Amalekite leaders. Part of this record also indicates that the Israelites thought the Amalekites were more than a fly-by-night nomadic band of thieves. Agog ruled about the time of Joshua. A sorcerer's wish for Israel says: "...and his king shall be higher than Agog, and his kingdom shall be exalted". [18] The Israelites' rulers would have already considered themselves above what is the accepted opinion of the Amalekite rulers. Why then the desire to become "higher than Agog"? Agog was among the first of the Amalekite rulers, and another Agog was the last of the Amalekite rulers. Among the first of the Hyksos Pharaohs was Apop, and another Apop was the last of the Hyksos Pharaohs. This correlation is among the myriad coincidences which Velikovsky suggested are not coincidences, but are logical consequences of the revised chronology. Agog was Apop, and the Amalekites were the Hyksos.

Velikovsky pointed out that the similarity between Agog and Apop is even greater in the early written Hebrew. [19] The size of the angle between two oblique lines was the only difference between p (pei) and g (gimel). Also, there is some freedom in translating the Egyptian hieroglyphics into modern consonants, thus the difference may have occurred during this process.

Greek legends relate a story of a time of upheaval when an important king by the name of Ogyges ruled. However, Ogyges was not the king of Greece. Some of the legends say Ogyges lived in Egypt and the Thebes of Egypt has been referred to as "the Ogygian Thebes" to distinguish it from the Greek Thebes. [20] This, and other indications, led Velikovsky to suggest that the time of Ogyges was the time of Agog since the latter would be one and the same as the former.

The Hyksos built a capital-fort at Avaris. This was one of the main strongholds of the Hyksos rulers. From here, they gave orders to the figure-head native Egyptian princes. The eventual overthrow of Avaris is what led to the resurrection of Pharaonic Egypt and the start of the New Kingdom of Egyptian history. The description of the battle for Avaris has been found in Egyptian records. This took place during the time of the vassal pharaoh Kamose. One of the better descriptions was found on the wall of the tomb of one of the officers involved in the conflict. This, of course, extols the virtues of the officer in the battle, but it also gives major credit to an unnamed foreign power. The ally who apparently was the deciding factor in the expulsion of the Hyksos was referred to as "One". "One" did this and "One" did that and eventually "One captured Avaris". [21]

It is not unusual to attribute great acts to "one" when you are not the one doing them. This may be an ancient custom, but it will probably always be stylish. The Egyptians had perfected "oneing" by the end of the Hyksos period and did not even mention the king of the "ones". If the Hyksos were the Amalekites and ruled for about 400 years, their ejection from Egypt with the aid of a foreign power would coincide with the capture of "the city of Amalek" and the Amalekite king Agog by the Israelite Saul. The "city of Amalek" has caused some comment because the conventional chronology requires the Amalekites to be a small nomadic tribe with no great city.

After the defeat of the Hyksos-Amalekites and the capture of Avaris, Saul allowed Agog and some others to go free. This turned out to be a great political mistake. The remaining Hyksos fortified a city named Sharuhen and Joab's army and the Egyptian army "besieged Sharuhen" for several years before its fall. The extra years of war were costly enough, but the moving of the Hyksos to Sharuhen eventually would cause problems for the Israelites even until today. The later historian Manetho possibly did not have access to the Egyptian documents which clearly stated that the Hyksos went to Sharuhen, or he misquoted them intentionally or inadvertently, but he did say the Hyksos built a city in Judaea and called it Jerusalem. Velikovsky suggested that this false identification of the Jews as the hated Hyksos has been responsible for certain prejudices ever since.

The explusion of the Hyksos was beneficial to the entire Middle East. Egypt began to revive its greatness and Israel continued to prosper. After David, Solomon came to power and created a great kingdom. This presents certain problems, since conventional chronology indicates that Solomon must have been almost an unknown ruler to the Egyptians while no great female rulers can be identified as the Queen of Sheba, an otherwise obscure ruler from a minor principality.

THE QUEEN OF SHEBA

The story of the Queen of Sheba has always had a somewhat mysterious air. From the Biblical narrative, it appears that a majestic queen heard of the wisdom and power of the king in Jerusalem who was named Solomon. She went to Jerusalem to determine if all the things she heard about Solomon were true, and she took some gifts for him. They were mutually impressed and Solomon also gave her some gifts. They engaged in intellectual conversation, played around a little, and she returned from whence she came. This story is described in more detail in two locations in the Scriptures. [22]

Josephus, an historian of the first century, said *the Queen of Sheba* was "queen of Egypt and Ethiopia". [23] Under the conventional chronology, there were no female Pharaohs during this time. Ethiopia is willing to claim her as its own and would not object to having signs around saying "The Queen of Sheba Slept Here". Also, Southern Arabia (Yemen) is thought to be the homeland of the queen.

However, Yemen is 1400 miles from Jerusalem across perilous desert, and a queen only of Ethiopia does not meet all the qualifications. Despite the geographical difficulties, the land of the Queen of Sheba is still sought in relation to standard chronology.

Under conventional chronology, some six hundred years before Solomon was entertained by this mysterious visitor from the West, there occurred, in Egyptian history, a possible inverse of this story. Queen Hatshepsut, a female Pharaoh of Egypt, went to a land called Punt and took some gifts. After visiting with the ruler of Punt and receiving some gifts, she returned to Egypt. There she built a temple and initiated cermonies not unlike what she had observed while on her trip. If Velikovsky's correlation of the Hyksos and Amalekites is correct, this would also make Hatshepsut a contemporary of Solomon. Instead of one story with a lot of mysteries and its inverse, with as many unknowns, we are left with two complementary stories describing the same event. [24]

What are called the Punt reliefs relate the story of Hatshepsut's journey to the land of Punt. The land of Punt, the Divine Land, God's Land, or Retenu, should have easily been recognized as Palestine; however, some of the people pictured seemed to have a different hue and some of the plants were not thought to be indigenous to Palestine. This, plus the idea that, under conventional chronology, Palestine would not have been worth the visit for Hatshepsut, made historians seek elsewhere for the land of Punt.

It has been argued that the trip was a regular commercial trip, but one would not go to a lot of trouble to memorialize a standard event and suggest that it was the experience of a lifetime. Some scholars even suggested that Hatshepsut did not actually make the trip since she is not actually depicted on one of the expeditionary boats. However, in line with the Egyptian custom of that day, she is not pictured with the commoners, but is drawn queen size beside the ship. This conforms to the statement that she led the expedition by land and by sea.

Correlating the details of the two stories led Velikovsky to conclude that Hatshepsut traveled along the Nile from Thebes to Coptos and then overland to el-Qoseir which was, in ancient times, considered to be the embarkation point for trips to the Divine Land. From there, the ships went across the Red Sea to the Gulf of Aqaba and up the gulf to Ezion-Geber where Solomon had built a great harbor. From there, the journey was made overland to Jerusalem. This corresponds to the record of the trip to Punt being partially by sea and partially by land. The return trip originated from a Mediterranean port and went up the Nile to Thebes. This also corresponds to the record.

When Hatshepsut returned, she built a temple patterned after the one she had seen in Punt. She even referred to the construction as building a "Punt"; and the reliefs on one wall were devoted to describing the trips to Punt. The temple was called "The Most Splendid of Splendors" and the remains are still located at Deir el-Bahari near Thebes. Many comments have been made concerning the apparent fact that the architecture does not fit the standard traditional Egyptian style.

Solomon's temple was destroyed, but the record indicates a strong similarity between his temple and "The Most Splended of Splendors". Among the features of the temple in Punt that most impressed Hatshepsut were its terraces planted with Algum trees. This botanical feature was also in her own temple. The three to one ratio of the main hall of Solomon's temple was used, and portions of the Hebrew religious ceremony may have been instigated by Hatshepsut. Many of the "marvels" pictured in the reliefs were items which were known to have been accumulated by Solomon, and he gave the Queen of Sheba any of these she desired.

SHISHAK-THUTMOSE III

Hatshepsut's successor was Thutmose III. Velikovsky contends that this Pharaoh was the Hebrew Shishak. Toward the end of Hatshepsut's reign, they apparently were co-rulers, and Thutmose III was a young prince at the time of the trip to Punt. He may have been with Hatshepsut on the trip or heard of it later, but it is evident that Thutmose III knew of the richness of the Divine Land. Greed and possibily revenge played a large part in his desire to conquer this territory.

After the death of Solomon, Palestine (specifically Judah) was indeed sacked by an Egyptian Pharaoh. The records from Karnak and from Hebrew history both indicate this event. Conventional chronology, however, places the Sinai in a sort of time warp which would have Thutmose III conquer a place that was not there until hundreds of years later. Yet, it would appear, from the evidence, that it was Thutmose III who did, in fact, despoil the temple of Solomon in Jerusalem.

Under the revised chronology, two great empires, Israel and Egypt, emerged from the former Hyksos-Amalekite empire. Jerusalem was the ruling center for the area from the Euphrates to Egypt which included Syria, Canaan, Edom and part of the Arabian peninsula. This encompassed an area of diverse customs. As is standard political practice, Solomon tried to please everyone in unimportant matters and catered to self-interest on the important issues.

Solomon made enemies who found personal satisfaction and financial gain by siding with Thutmose III. Thutmose III encouraged the internal conflict in order to aid in the ease of the overthrow of Palestine. When Solomon died, rivalry for power resulted in internal hostility. Thutmose III recorded this fact which supports the view that he encouraged it. Otherwise he would not have mentioned it since it would have reduced the greatness of his victory.

After making the most of the internal fighting, Thutmose III invaded Palestine. After the final campaign there, a list of one hundred and nineteen conquered cities was prepared. At the head of the list, where the most important city should be, was the name Kadesh. This creates two questions under the conventional chronology. Where was Kadesh and why should it head the list?

There is a Kadesh in Syria, but in this campaign Thutmose III did not go that far. Also, he would not have mistaken a town in northern Syria for the capital of Palestine. There was a minor Kadesh in Galilee, but listing it first would be like listing Bugtussle, Texas, as the most important city in the United States. In many ancient Hebrew and Arabic writings, Jerusalem is called Kadesh. These are not vague inferences. Obviously, Kadesh was Jerusalem and should be listed, since it was the capital of Judah. Unfortunately for the conventional chronology, David did not establish Jerusalem as the capital until after it was conquered by Thutmose III. In the case of other names on the list of cities conquered by Thutmose III, some which are mentioned (for example, Etam-Itmm, Beth Zur-Bt sir) did not have the courtesy, under conventional chronology, to exist at the time of their conquest, but were established later by the Hebrews. Supposedly, the Hebrews came to this region hundreds of years after Thutmose III.

Under the revised chronology, the Hebrew record states that the capital city of Palestine, Kadesh, was ruled by Rehoboam and was conquered by Shishak, king of Egypt. This corresponds to the Egyptian record which says Thutmose III conquered Kadesh. Velikovsky demonstrates that the two accounts, by the different nations, are astoundingly similar in details, and points out that this would be a fruitful area for additional investigation.

In particular, Velikovsky claims that a detailed comparison of the spoils of war taken by Thutmose III with the contents of Solomon's temple should prove highly informative; and Velikovsky does give part of an analysis of this type. [25] It is not exhaustive, but is enough to identify some of the objects listed on the wall at Karnak as being originally from Solomon's temple.

Many of the objects were made by highly skilled crafts-men. Under the conventional chronology, it is surprising to find the work of these great artisans in relatively un-cultured Canaan. However, under the revised chronology, the work can be seen to have been done by the skilled tech-nicians of David and Solomon. Since conventional chro-nology credits the uncultured Canaanites with highly skilled artistic work, the statements of investigators actually pro-vide an unbiased evaluation of the Israelite capabilities during this period. A typical evaluation of the people who made the objects captured by Thutmose III was that they "stood at a higher stage of civilization than even the wonder-fully gifted race of Egypt." [26]

The following are a few of the comparisons made by Velikovsky: The bas-relief at Karnak depicts many objects that Thutmose III took from Solomon's temple and put in the temple to the god Amon. The objects are described in the Hebrew record in the Book of Kings and the Book of Chronicles. Three main metals are described: gold, silver and bronze. (Bronze is an alloy of copper, tin, and zinc. Brass is an alloy of two parts copper and one part zinc. Some of the translations seem to use these terms inter-changeably. In the following commentary, the word bronze will be used to describe those objects made of bronze or of brass, in order to simplify matters.)

In Karnak, the upper five rows of the Temple bas-relief represent objects of gold. Then come several rows depicting silver, followed by drawings of bronze objects. Precious and semiprecious stones are included in some items. The objects also have a symbol which indicates how many of a certain object were captured. Coincidentally, Solomon had some objects of solid gold and others of wood with hammered gold overlay. In Karnak some items were called "gold" and others indicated as "overlaid with gold".

The Ark of the Covenant was used to transport religious objects during the years when Israel had no permanent location. Replicas of Ark-shaped chests are found in Kar-nak. On many objects there is a design called "lily work".

Velikovsky notes that this is "a very unusual type of rim ornament" and appears to be found only in the scriptural account and on the bas-reliefs of Thutmose III. [27] Lions and oxen were used as decorative figures in Solomon's temple, and these figures are seen in the drawing at Karnak.

A magnificent gold altar was used for burnt offerings in Solomon's Temple. Another altar was bronze. In Karnak one of the gold objects is labeled "The (a) great altar". Another item is called "One great altar of Bronze".

A metal object mentioned in Hebrew history was called "showbread". In Karnak a cone-shaped replica of a silver object is labeled "white bread". Also unique, fountain-like fluid containers are described in Hebrew history and depicted on the wall. Gold chains are also described in both places.

Representations of idols to the various gods of Egypt were common in Egyptian inscriptions. The spoils of the foreign temple, which were dedicated by Thutmose III to one of his gods, were obviously not sacred objects of an idolatrous cult. This non-idolatrous aspect of the objects would be expected if the objects were from the temple of Solomon.

Something not located in the temple, but mentioned in Hebrew history, was a group of three-hundred shields. A shield is drawn in Karnak, and the symbol for three hundred is located by it. The type of metal is not given.

The walls of the temple at Karnak also contain drawings of the great zoological and botanical collections of Solomon. There are rare and exotic birds, plants and animals which Solomon spent years collecting from many parts of the world. They are not the result of Thutmose conquering lands to which these items were indigenous.

Before Solomon died, Jeroboam plotted to make part of Solomon's territory an independent country. Solomon discovered this and thus Jeroboam went to Egypt for protection by the Pharaoh.

Later, the Pharaoh saw a chance to create internal conflict in the Divine Land by sending Jeroboam back after Solomon died.

According to the Scriptures, Jeroboam married Ano while in Egypt. She was the eldest sister of Thelkemina, wife of Shishak, identified by Velikovsky as Thutmose III. Furthermore, Velikovsky drew attention to an ancient Egyptian visceral jar in the Metropolitan Museum of Art in New York. This jar was intended to preserve the viscera of the deceased; and the deceased in this case was a princess named Ano. The jar was established to have been of the time of Thutmose III. No other princess by the name Ano is known in Egypt.[28]

RAS SHAMRA

If the Egyptian chronology is incorrect, then problems should occur in the histories of countries whose absolute chronology is determined from the Egyptian standard. In *Ages in Chaos*, Velikovsky provides several impressive examples of this.

One of the examples concerns the relationship between Cyprus and Ugarit, the ancient city of Ras Shamra on the Syrian coast. It is thought that layer I of Ugarit was dated by two independent methods. Some Egyptian items were found which were dated to the Eighteenth and Nineteenth Dynasties of Egypt, (about -1600 to -1200). Some Mycenaean styles of pottery were found supposedly dating from the fifteenth through part of the thirteenth centuries B.C., thereby confirming the Egyptian correlation. These are *not* two independent dating methods that confirm one another, however, but only *one* since the Mycenaean pottery dating depends on Egyptian chronology for its dating. Therefore, the dating of Ugarit depends solely on Egyptian chronology for its absolute dates. Certain periods of Cypriot art can be dated independently of this standard.

On Cyprus and at Ugarit there are unique tombs which, because of conventional chronology, are thought to have been built about five hundred years apart. Cyprus is about sixty miles from the coast of Syria. On a clear day you can see Cyprus from Ugarit. It is reasonable to assume that the occupants of each location knew of the other, traded with each other and influenced the life styles of each other. With Velikovsky's revised chronology, the tombs become contemporary and it is not surprising to find that these two locations had the same type of uniquely styled tomb in their respective cemeteries. Not only was the architectural style the same, but the tombs on Cyprus and in Ugarit had tubes for providing fluids to the departed.[29]

It is also reasonable to assume, under the revised chronology, that the chambers in Ugarit were patterned after those in Cyprus. However, conventional chronology has those in Ugarit existing before Cyprus. This means that about   five hundred years supposedly elapsed before one culture influenced the other. If the indications that Ugarit was influenced by Cyprus are correct, then conventional chronology would require Ugarit to have architects who could look five hundred years into the future. Even if the influence was from Ugarit to Cyprus, it is still a strained hypothesis to suggest that such direct influence could occur after Ugarit had been buried for nearly five hundred years.

Some tablets were found in a library in layer I of Ugarit. (The dating of the layer was done before the tablets were analyzed.) At least four different languages were found on these tablets. They were Sumerian, Akkadian, Khar, and an early form of Hebrew. When some of these were translated, a number of identifications of people and locations would have been relatively easy were it not for conventional chronology.

On one tablet, the expulsions of a king and groups of foreigners is discussed. The king's name was Nikmed. Nikomedes is a Greek name thought to have originally been Ionian. One of the groups of foreigners were called Jm'an and identified as the Jaman, which means Ionians.

A city mentioned in connection with the Jamans had the name Didyme. This was deciphered as the Ionian city of Didyme, famous for the workmanship of Apollo Didymeus. Other inscriptions from Ugarit were translated "Aplon Didymeus". Unfortunately, these obvious connections are not allowed by conventional chronology. The Ionians, their Ionian city of Didyme and the god Apollo were not around until after the demise of Ugarit, if Ugarit's end is dated to the thirteenth or fourteenth century B.C.

Finding ancient Hebrew in a location supposedly buried sometime around the thirteenth or fourteenth century B.C. was surprising, since there should have not been any Hebrew writing there at that time according to conventional chronology. Nor was it not a rough early Hebrew language that was found; it was an advanced alphabetical form of writing. Under conventional chronology, it appears that the crude Canaanites used Hebrew before the Hebrews arrived in that part of the world. It also appears that the barbarian Canaanites were quite advanced culturally and had the same religion as the Hebrews. Unusual expressions and linguistic styles are found to be the same in regular Hebrew and the supposed Canaanite Hebrew of previous centuries. In addition to accurately duplicating the customs and idioms of a place that had been buried for five to six hundred years, the Hebrews also duplicated the earlier jewelry and system of weights and measures. Under the revised chronology, those scripts become an early form of Hebrew dipicting the life of the early Hebrews.

The language called Khar also produced some surprises because of the conventional chronology. Previous information indicated that there were some people who spoke Khar, but because of the timing they were assumed to be a type of barbaric cave dwellers mentioned in the Scriptures as Horites. The reasonably advanced state of the Khar writing eliminated this identification with the Horites since evidence of the Khar language was found in a number of other locations. The people who spoke Khar were, therefore, given the name Hurrians. Giving them an identity is not easily compatible with conventional chronology. The Hurrians traveled extensively and accomplished much, but exactly who they were is difficult to determine. Velikovsky suggested that five to six hundred years later the Carians went to similar places and accomplished similar things, and that, under the revised chronology, the Hurrians were the Carians. [30] (Robert H. Hewsen suggested that a comparison of the Hurrians' language with Urartian should also be considered.) [31]

On one of the tablets at Ugarit an epic poem was found which has become known as the Poem of Keret. Keret was the hero in the poem which told of the hero's exploits in leading various groups against an invading army. Asher and Zebulun were two tribes also mentioned in the poem, although it is not definitely known on whose side Zebulun fought. An individual named Terah led an opposition force of three hundred thousand men against Keret. The encounter took place in Negeb, south of Palestine.

Again, conventional chronology presents problems in identifying the characters and locations. Asher and Zebulun are known tribes in the area; however, they did not exist until long after the poem was written, according to conventional chronology. There was a Terah, the father of Abraham, who was once in this part of the world. But there is no reason to place him in the Negeb. Neither could the family of Terah be described as an invading army of three hundred thousand men.

An Edomite city called Serirot (singular of Sarira) was also mentioned in the poem. Sarira was the mother of Jeroboam after whom he named a fortress which was built about -920. Under the revised chronology, one generation after the building of the fortress, the name Edom-Serirot is used in a poem describing events of the area. Under conventional chronology, the poem uses a name for the city hundreds of years before it even had the name, or it was a different city which no one seems to have encountered.

Problems of identification became so complex that, at least, one investigator decided that it was not a war poem about real events at all but rather an esthetic love poem. Terah was translated as *bridegroom*, Asher as *after* or *behind*, and Zebulun as *sickman*. [32]

Under the revised chronology, the identifications of the Poem of Keret are discernible without undue strain. Under either chronology, it is accepted that the Egyptian Pharaoh Amenhotep II, also called Okheperure, threatened the Phoenician coast, including Ugarit. The key then is to compare the Poem of Keret with the invasions of Amenhotep II and then match that with the Hebrew record for the time period of Amenhotep II under the revised chronology. Velikovsky has done this, and shown many similarities in the three accounts which cannot be easily explained as mere coincidence.

The Ugaritic poem said that the invader had bronze and copper daggers. Amenhotep II's men had bronze and copper daggers. Even more impressive, though, is the fact that the poem found in Ugarit used the Egyptian word for copper dagger and the Egyptian word for bronze dagger.

AMENHOTEP II

Amenhotep II succeeded Thutmose III, who had conquered the Palestinian and Syrian areas and taxed them heavily. When Thutmose III died, these people recognized a chance for independence. They revolted, giving Amenhotep II an opportunity to demonstrate his power. He was successful in a couple of campaigns, but one of the last that is listed as a victory does not appear to have the attributes of a victory.

The first battle of this campaign took place at a location called Moresheth, which was one day away from where he started. After the battle he headed home, which is not the usual action of a leader starting on a glorious military adventure. On the way home, the vassal cities created disturbances and were disrespectful to Amenhotep II and his army. This is usually not done to a powerful victorious army passing through town.

When he arrived home, he had his scorekeeper chalk up one victory, but the spoils he listed indicated otherwise. He won a chariot, two horses, a coat of mail, two bows, a full quiver and a suit of armor. Another item which cannot be deciphered was listed, but since it was listed after the full quiver it could not be momentous. It sounds as though Amenhotep II made a strategic exit by absconding with an enemy chariot, and the other items happened to be in the vehicle.

Another indication that the battle was not a victory is the fact that the record keepers did not stress that a great victory was won, but glorified Amenhotep II's battlefield heroics and mentioned his single-handed combat experiences. The winning team does not leave the king to fend for himself. Moreover, Amenhotep II's successor referred to himself as the conqueror of Syria, which would not have been necessary if Amenhotep II had, in fact, retained complete control.

It is thus apparent that Amenhotep II was defeated in this battle. This coincides with the conclusions drawn from the Poem of Keret and the Scriptures. Velikovsky is not the only one to conclude that Amenhotep II was defeated. Velikovsky referenced Sidney Smith who, in 1949, independently reached the same conclusion. Velikovsky did, however, identify Amenhotep II as Zerah the Ethiopian who is then seen to be one and the same as Terah of the Poem of Keret.

THE FOURTH GENERATION

Up to this point, Velikovsky had worked through three successive periods in Egypt and demonstrated a detailed analogy to three successive periods in Palestine. (Hatshepshut, Thutmose III and Amenhotep II in Egypt and Solomon, Rehoboam and Asa in Palestine.) [33] With conventional chronology, however, the historical periods under consideration are separated by about five to six hundred years. It is difficult to explain the correlations between them as mere coincidence, while Velikovsky's study of the reign of Amenhotep IV (Akhnaton) is even more impressive.

During the reigns of the Pharaohs Amenhotep III and IV, important people of neighboring countries wrote to and received letters from these rulers of Egypt. Names and details of the correspondence can actually be correlated in two extant records. One record is to be found in what are called the el-Amarna letters, and the other account may be gleaned from the Scriptures, supposedly written over five hundred years after the el-Amarna letters. A few details of this correlation follow.

Some tablets were found at the site of the capital of Akhnaton (Amenhotep IV). This archaeological site was designated Tell el-Amarna, and some of the tablets found there were called the el-Amarna letters. These tablets were correspondence between the Egyptian Pharaohs Amenhotep III and IV, and kings of other lands. Some of these lands, such as Syria and Canaan, were under the rule of Egypt. The language was mainly Assyro-Babylonian (Akkadian) with a number of words being a Syrian dialect similar to Hebrew. Letters addressed to Amenhotep III were probably brought from Thebes when Akhnaton moved the capital. The revised chronology would place these letters and their associated events around -870 to -840 as opposed to their present placement of around -1410 to -1370.

One of the cities mentioned in the letters was easily identified as Jerusalem. It existed under that name in both chronologies. However, conventional chronology encounters the problem of determining why it was referred to by an Israelite name years before the Israelites were there to provide that name.

Two other cities are not so easily identified. They are Sumur and Gubla, and are mentioned numerous times. Many clues point to the identification of these two cities as the two capitals of Israel-Samaria (Sumur) and Jezreel (previously Gubla). Unfortunately, according to conventional chronology, these cities did not exist at the time the letters were written. Postal service being what it is, you might not be surprised at receiving a letter from a defunct town, but letters from a city to be built five or six hundred years in the future would not be expected.

The naming of Jezreel can be linked with the time of Ahab, which was after the time the tablets were written, according to conventional chronology. Ahab was married to the infamous Jezebel. In the Jezreel Valley he built a city which was to later take the name of the valley. However, at one time, the city may have been called Gubla. Velikovsky points out that there could have been at least two possibilities for the origin of the name. Jezebel was Phoenician, and she may have wanted it named after a Phoenician locale, or it could have been named after her. Jezebel or Jzebel in the Biblical record would be Jebel or Gubla in cuneiform. [34]

Many of the Egyptian pharaohs had several names. The names of the pharaohs mentioned in the el-Amarna letters were not Amenhotep III and IV, but this identification was made from other Egyptian documents. The other rulers mentioned in the el-Amarna correspondence also had several names. This reduces the probability of finding the same or similar names in the letters as well as the Scriptures.

Random substitution is, of course, not permissible, but unlike the conventional chronology, the revised chronology leaves less doubt as to the identification of the various kings. Not only are events relating to the kings found to be similar in both the Scriptures and el-Amarna letters, but other involved historical personages, who usually had only one name, have similar names and the same occupation in both sources. Also, the names of Syro-Palestinian

rulers are recorded in the annals of the Assyrian king
Shalmaneser, who was a contemporary of Jehoshaphat
and Ahab. Many of these names square with those of the
el-Amarna letters, and both were written in cuneiform.

Five kings are often mentioned in the letters and in the
Scriptures relating to the time in which the revised chronology places the letters. Of these, even with a low chance of
finding the same name in both sources, two do have similar names. Hazael, king of Damascus, was referred to in
the letters as Aziru, Azira, or Azaru. Velikovsky quotes Gelb
as saying that removal of the H in Hazael is also in ac-
cordance with the facts observable in other cases while the
l and r are interchangeable. [35] The Moabite, Mesha, is
called Mesh in the letters. The other identifications of kings
made by Velikovsky, also after intricate correlations of
events in both sources, are that Jehoshaphat of the Scriptures was Abdi-Hiba of the letters, Ahab was Rib-Addi and
Ben Hadad was Abdi-Ashirta.

Velikovsky extensively analyzed the el-Amarna letters
and compared them to Hebrew sources and Assyro-
Babylonian sources. Part of the results of this comparison
are found in Chapters VI, VII, and VIII of *Ages in Chaos.*
This comparison reveals, if one accepts the conventional
chronology, that on two occasions, about five hundred
years apart, there occurred the same series of events, during the same unusually dry weather, and enacted by people
with the same political office with identical or similar names
in different languages. Furthermore, under the conventional chronology, there is no record in Hebrew history matching the events and names that are found in the Egyptian
record, and about five or six hundred years later there is no
record in the Egyptian history matching the description
of events by the Hebrews. However, under the revised
chronology, these two records are seen to be describing
identical events and the one-to-one correlation of minute
details is not unexpected.

These intricate correlations can be found in *Ages in
Chaos*, and a brief review is presented in Appendix II. An

analysis of this and Velikovsky's other writings about ancient history indicate that Eva Danelius was correct in stating that there is "no objective argument against an attempt to take up the challenge and test the so-called 'revised' chronology of Velikovsky by applying it to a specific historic event." More historians are now doing this and finding that the revised chronology is a useful model for a proper reconstruction of ancient history. [36]

Danelius analyzed a specific case related to the revised chronology and summarized: "In the special case made the object of this study, the most recent archaeological discoveries not only do not discredit Velikovsky's 'revised chronology' but, to the contrary, events observed by the archaeologists, who had no explanation for them, may find an acceptable interpretation the moment this 'revised chronology' has been applied.

"The one great hindrance for a re-evaluation of the accepted chronology seems *purely psychological.* It was best formulated by a well-known Biblical scholar with whom this writer discussed a different interpretation of a Biblical text: 'But how can I discard a theory which has taken 25 years of my life to build?!'

There is no answer to this." [37]   (emphasis added)

Chapter IV

THE COMMON QUESTIONS

The preceding chapters have provided a basic review of Velikovsky's suggested reconstruction of the recent history of the solar system. Now we will look at questions that have been raised about this model. One of the first and most frequently asked questions concerns the association of the word comet with the planet Venus.

COMETS AND EFFECTS

In *Worlds in Collision*, Velikovsky repeatedly refers to the "Comet Venus". The question is often asked: "Why did Velikovsky call Venus a comet when it could not, by definition, be a comet?" There are really two answers to this—the short form and the long form. The long form involves the physical details of comets, but both answers are partially contained in the wording of the question itself: man's "definition" of any phenomenon changes with his understanding of it.

SHORT FORM

The ancients did not have the same physical parameters for a comet that the moderns do. The word "comet" is derived from *coma*, a Greek word for "hair". When the ancients looked into the sky and saw an unfamiliar object with a diffuse, "hairy" atmosphere, they called it what we would translate into English as "comet", but not because the word itself implied any "scientific" definition.

Translated literally, the ancient terms often involved hair or smoke or fire. They were anciently applied to what became the planet Venus, although they no longer apply. The Peruvian name for Venus is still "Chaska", the wavy-haired. Early traditions of Mexico described Venus as the "star that smoked", which is also their term for a comet. They also called it the "mane".

It is thought that the ancient cultures did not understand the nature of Venus because they regarded it as once having been a comet. Perhaps it was not they who misunderstood. But whether or not the ancients actually saw Venus with an extended atmosphere or were hallucinating, they described it as a "comet". Velikovsky writes about what the ancients discussed and hence is justified in his terminology. His reasoning is clearly stated in *Worlds in Collision*, and people really interested can detect this. Complaining about his use of the word "comet" is not unlike complaining about someone calling a Volkswagen a "bug".

LONG FORM

Although in the context of *Worlds in Collision* Velikovsky makes proper use of the word comet, some people still irrationally insist that Velikovsky leads a "comet cult" and that he must be wrong, since in no way can Venus be imagined as a comet under the strict, modern definition of that term. Actually, there is no "strict" definition of a comet, and the exclusion of Venus even today may be arbitrary.

Many people think that a comet is defined by a highly eccentric orbit, a long gaseous tail, and a small mass. They say, therefore, that Venus cannot be remotely considered as comet-like since it has a near-circular (low-eccentricity) orbit, has no tail (diffuse atmosphere), and has a large mass.

How circular may an orbit be before an object is no longer classed as a comet? Comet Oterma III and Comet Schwassmann-Wachmann have planet-like (near-circular) orbits. They are said to be "exceptional comets"; however, Stromgren suggested that there is a large group of comets of this type, orbiting the Sun beyond the range of detection by present instruments.[1]

Astronomers admit that some comets cannot be determined as such on the basis of orbit alone. When Comet Arend-Rigaux was designated a comet, it was because it, on occasion, showed some diffuseness, although it has an orbit similar to that of a minor planet.[2] When W. Baade discovered Hidalgo, he was undecided whether to call it a comet or a minor planet. He decided to call it a minor planet (asteroid) for the very scientific reason that minor planets were more popular than comets among astronomers at that time, so he thought it would receive more attention as a minor planet.[3]

At the Tenth Lunar and Planetary Exploration Colloquium in 1961, D. Alter, who was then Director Emeritus of Griffith Observatory, said that a comparison of the orbits of comets and some asteroids indicates that there is a relationship between the two types of bodies. He also claimed that when a comet or asteroid is discovered, it is often difficult to tell which it is.[4]

The ancients called a diffuse celestial object a comet, and we see that even in modern times diffuseness (or a "hairy" appearance) remains the basic criterion for calling an object a comet.

The mass in the definition of a comet is even less strictly defined. The masses of comets are difficult to determine, but they are generally thought to range from 10^{17} to 10^{20} grams[5], whereas, the mass of Venus is on the order of 10^{27} grams. Some definitions of comets include masses of up to only 10^{21} grams.[6] However, Bobrovnikoff calculated that one comet may have had a mass on the order of that of the moon (10^{24} grams).[7] So it appears that the maximum mass of a comet is entirely arbitrary and is set in terms of modern experience.

Odd as it may seem after the reaction to Velikovsky's wording, certain features of Venus have recently been called "comet-like" by a modern scientist. Max Wallis of the Division of Plasma Physics, Royal Institute of Stockholm, prepared in 1970 a report titled *Comet-Like Interaction of Venus with the Solar Wind.*[8] Later, Mariner 10 results led to the use of this same terminology. A number of people from several well-known research organizations helped prepare an article in which it is stated that downstream (in the direction of flow of the solar wind) of Venus there are indications of "the presence of a comet-like tail" that was extensive.[9]

I am not suggesting that we start calling Venus a comet, but it seems clear that a lot of name-calling in the name of science has been not science but semantics. One need not be anti-semantics, so to speak, to notice that people who did (and still do) raise the "Venus is not a comet" argument are not approaching the issue objectively.

After all the complaining by various astronomers about the use of the term comet in connection with Venus, one of these same astronomers, W. C. Straka, brought to the attention of *Pensee* readers an article entitled "A Cometary Venus". He said that looking it up would be of interest, since it was published in 1948 and "this predates Velikovsky by a couple of years".[10] Since Straka was trying to support his own unfounded opinion that "in no case was any" confirmed hypothesis of Velikovsky "exclusively his or first suggested by him", his reference to the 1948 article is essentially a way of saying that there is no justification for Velikovsky's statement about Venus once having been a comet, but just in case, he was not the first to suggest it.

By saying "you may be interested in looking at" this article, Straka tries to leave the impression that he would be happy to have the reference checked. However, if he really did feel this way, he would not have mentioned the article, since it has almost nothing to do with the subject he alleges to be discussing. What is reported is that toward the end of the 17th century a citizen of Westminister, named Gad-bury, noted on two occasions that Venus appeared "like a comet", due to an unusual optical phenomenon caused by conditions in Earth's atmosphere.

Obviously there was nothing unscientific about Velikovsky noting that the ancients referred to Venus as a comet; however, the reaction of scientists was unfounded. As we shall see, this was not the only case where this happened relative to Velikovsky's work.

ORIGIN OF COMETS

Dr. S. K. Vsekhsvyatskii is a noted Russian astronomer who is the director of the Kiev Observatory. For a number of years he has investigated comet properties and orbits. He concludes that comets originate in or near the giant planets, particularly Jupiter. His work is generally ig-nored in the United States since it does not coincide with accepted views here. (Velikovsky does not propose the same mechanism for the ejection of Venus from Jupiter as Vsekhsvyatskii proposes for the ejection of comets, but other portions of his work fit well with the concepts dis-cussed by Velikovsky).

It is not only people who are interested in Velikovsky's ideas who realize that sometimes an accepted theory is stressed while reasonable alternatives are neglected. Re-cently, a Nobel Prize winner co-authored an article about the nature and origin of comets. In this article it is stated that texts and review articles tend to emphasize only the accepted theory while not even mentioning alternative theories, and "even sweeping under the rug those observa-tional facts which are adverse to the dominant view". [11] Vsekhsvyatskii's work not only is adverse to the domin-ant view, it relates to Velikovsky's proposals in at least two ways: First, the orbital calculations performed by Vsekhsvyatskii and others investigating his ideas tend to support the possibility of the type of orbit-acquisition and changes suggested for Venus; second, Vsekhsvyatskii's work has long indicated that there is considerably more activity in the region of the giant planets than one would expect from the "cold, dead planets" concept. (Recent space-probe data tends to support this, also.)

About 160 years ago, Laplace and Lagrange express-ed opposing suggestions concerning comet origins. Then, there was very little data about comets except some ob-servations related to their orbital motions, so these hypo-theses were mainly speculative. Laplace was intrigued by the newly discovered wandering nebulae and centered his ideas around comet origins external to the solar system; in his view, the observed comets were captured bodies. As-teroids were also newly discovered objects, and Lagrange expressed ideas about comet origins which coincided with the proposed origin of the asteroids by the explosion of a former planet.

The choice was not simply wandering nebula versus exploded planet. It was comet-origin outside the solar system and distant in time, or inside the solar system, with the possibility of relatively recent origins. In keeping with attitudes of that time, the most widely accepted idea was the one that put comet origin "long ago and far away". The same applies to theories of comet-origins which are widely accepted in the United States today. According to Vsekhsvyatskii and a number of other investigators, this acceptance is based mainly on faith.

The most commonly accepted opinions about comet origin are those of Kuiper, Whipple, and Oort, and, of these, probably the best-known is Oort's comet-cloud the-ory. [12] Oort assumes that comets formed about the time everything else supposedly formed, and that they accumu-lated into a vast cloud just outside the solar system. At various times perturbations by other bodies in the galaxy send individual comets into the planetary system. Since the undisturbed comets remain in cold storage, they do not disintegrate. Only those comets that enter the inner solar system and become heated by the Sun begin to de-teriorate.

About speculations of this nature, Vsekhsvyatskii says: "It should be taken into consideration that these hypotheses explain absolutely nothing, they only remove the comet-problem decision into indefinite past time and rather remote regions of the solar system. One can but wonder how such hypotheses possessing no intrinsic logic and no required efficiency, nevertheless could satisfy some investigators, while at the same time numerous arguments are available that the processes of creation as well as development of small bodies, comets among them, occurred quite in another way." [13]

Vsekhsvyatskii gives several areas of support for the ideas that comets originate in the planetary system. His greatest support, however, derives from quantitative analyses of known cometary orbits. [14] In a summary article in *Soviet Science Review*, July, 1972, Vsekhsvyatskii says that these analyses of comet parameters confirm "beyond any doubt, that the comets and their disintegration products were formed within the solar system (and, on average, much later than the planets)".

COMETS AND PETROLEUM

Scientists have recently postulated and experimentally supported the suggestion that petroleum might result from the interaction of a comet and the Earth. In *Worlds in Collision*, Velikovsky suggests that the ancients observed this process in action during the first encounter between Earth's atmosphere and the comet-like atmosphere of Venus. In 1950 scientists insisted that nothing of this nature could ever have occurred.

Then, it was assumed that all petroleum was formed many millions of years ago. Two processes were considered: the abiogenic origin, where petroleum is supposedly formed from hydrogen and carbon under great heat and pressure; and the organic theory, where petroleum forms from plant and animal remains.

A Yale geologist, C. R. Longwell, in the August 1950 issue of the *American Journal of Science*, which he then edited, scorned the idea that petroleum might have a cosmic origin and maintained that the assumption that petroleum was millions of years old negated Velikovsky's claim that *some* oil deposits were of recent origin. (He did not claim a cosmic origin for *all* deposits or that all those which might be of cosmic origin were attributable to the Venus-Earth encounters.) An Indiana University geologist, J. B. Patton, also argued that the fact that liquid hydrocarbons were never found in recent sediments proved Velikovsky wrong.

When Velikovsky wrote to W. F. Libby, the originator of carbon dating, to ask about the possibility of carbon-dating petroleum deposits, Dr. Libby referred Velikovsky to a paper by P. V. Smith. [15] Smith had carbon-dated petroleum from *recent* sediments in the Gulf of Mexico area.

The assumptions of this dating method would probably not be valid during the conditions under which the petroleum may have been formed. Therefore, the absolute date is not significant, although it was on the order of 9000 years. The important point is that carbon 14, the chemical isotope used in this method, decays to undetectable amounts in about fifty thousand years. Petroleum that has not acquired carbon 14 from the atmosphere in millions of years should not yield a carbon date.

By 1961 Oro had suggested that an important consequence of interactions between comets and the Earth "would be the accumulation on Earth of relatively large amounts of carbon compounds which are known to be transformed spontaneously into amino-acids, purines and other biochemical compounds." [16]   Later, Oro and Han stated that "aromatic hydrocarbons and other organic compounds may have been formed as a result of collisions of large meteorites with planets containing reducing atmospheres." [17]

Oro and Han further state that "it is also possible that the formation of these compounds is occurring presently in localized areas of Jupiter". They also quote Nobel

Prize winner Libby as having suggested, at the 1966 Special Seminar on Aerospace Engineering and Science in Houston, that "oil" is raining on Jupiter. If this is true, it supports Velikovsky's suggestion that a Jovian origin should not be ignored in seeking an explanation of the hydrocarbons acquired by Earth during the Venus encounter.

This type of activity brings to mind present-day oil spills and the problem of ancient pollution. In 1969 a Union Oil Company well ruptured off the coast of Santa Barbara, California. Before being repaired the well gushed crude oil into the channel for eleven days. Later, a study was conducted by the Allan Hancock foundation of the University of Southern California. Although the project was co-sponsored by the taxpayers and the Western Oil and Gas Association, there was no restriction on the type of research or publication. The major findings were unexpectedly optimistic. The overall damage was "much less" than expected, and the area was recovering. Much of the oil had adhered to silt washed into the channel and had settled to the bottom of the basin.[18] (Although there was some contradiction between this and a similar study done by the Woods Hole Oceanographic Institute, the latter study concerned a spill of refined instead of crude oil.)

This is not mentioned in advocation of oil spills. The environment is damaged too much even with people trying to protect it, so it would certainly be insane not to have restrictions. However, the above finding does tend to suggest that any oil spilled in the oceans several thousand years ago should not be expected to be floating on the seas today.

There is, of course, the question of how petroleum came to be in its present locations. This is just as much of a problem for geologists and for Oro and Han as for Velikovsky, but an "in" group is asked questions out of curiosity instead of malice. Recent Earth Resources Satellite photographs may provide a clue to the answer. Evidence of past cracks in the Earth appears in some oil-rich areas.

Saunders, *et al* evaluated ERTS-1 imagery of the Texas-New Mexico area for indications of known mineral and hydrocarbon deposits. They were surprised by their results. Structural lineaments and geomorphological evidence, visible in the images, clearly define the petroleum-productive Central Basin Platform in West Texas.[19] Also, Rich analyzed data of the Northern Coast Ranges and Sacramento Valley, California, and reported a potentially important fracture system which "appears to be associated with some of the oil and gas fields within the Sacramento Valley". He even suggested that subsequent ERTS imagery might delineate areas for ground-truth evaluation.[20]

Velikovsky also mentioned the possibility that hydrocarbons could be formed by electrical discharges acting in appropriate gas mixtures.[21] Later Urey, presumably independently, made essentially the same suggestion. That this is true has been demonstrated a number of times, and recent work along these lines has been performed by Zeitman, Chang and Lawless.[22]

PETROLEUM MAKES FOOD

Since we are on the subject of petroleum, it may be surprising to discover what can be done with this substance besides making plastics and fuels. Scientists have demonstrated that petroleum can be changed into edible carbohydrates. Velikovsky noted that the ancients seemed to have taken advantage of this process after the first Earth-Venus encounter. In 1950, many scientists felt that food could not be made from petroleum.

Velikovsky suggested that one possibility for the formation of the edible material discussed in the ancient histories would be microbial action on the petroleum, as discussed earlier. Astronomer Cecilia Payne-Gasposchkin, introduced in Chapter I, claimed that it was ridiculous to think that food could be produced from petroleum. Otherwise, she claimed, all the starving people of the world could be fed.

Alan C. Nixon, past president of the American Chemical Society, recently proposed doing exactly what astronomer Payne-Gaposchkin said was impossible. He noted that the technology exists for producing protein and fats directly from petroleum. He also noted that this would not be as wasteful as it sounds, since food-production presently consumes almost as much energy in the form of petroleum as it produces as food. [23]

In 1971 the British Petroleum Company started production in a plant capable of producing 4000 tons of food from petroleum each year. [24] A second plant near Marseilles, France, started later that same year with a planned annual capacity of 16,000 tons. By 1976 the production of protein from petroleum had undergone more than eleven years of rigorous testing.

The trade name for this product is Troperina. It is mixed with other ingredients to provide a high-protein feed more nutritious than common animal feeds and at comparable cost. Plans are being made to manufacture protein from petroleum for human consumption.

In addition, Wong Kee Kuong has shown that there are at least six other possibilities for producing carbohydrates from hydrocarbons through reactions in the Earth's upper atmosphere. [25] For example, the hydrocarbons could mix with the hydrogen and oxygen layers. Combustion and cosmic irradiation could produce a mixture of carbon dioxide and hydrogen, carbon monoxide and water vapor. Irradiation of this mixture could produce formaldehyde, from which various types of sugars and starches could be generated by polymerization and aldol condensation.

According to the ancient sources, the order would even be correct. The mixture would receive radiation during the day, and polymerization would occur in the cooler night, particularly on dust particles. The end product would fall to the ground in the early morning.

STONEHENGE

Some people have been led to believe that Stonehenge was built as an intricate computer designed to keep track of important celestial objects. This was supposedly done before the last catastrophe. An important question then is, if catastrophes occurred, why does Stonehenge still work, if it does?

Stonehenge is a stone arrangement on the Salisbury plain not far from Oxford, England. Huge monoliths weighing many tons were arranged and stacked in a design for which the original purpose is not definitely known. The area has probably been used for everything from Druid religious ceremonies to seances and Halloween parties, but these activities were by people who found Stonehenge already in existence. What the builders used it for is still debatable.

The main circle of stones is about 120 feet in diameter. The circular system comprising the stones, two inner circles of holes called the z and y holes, an outer circle of holes called the Aubrey holes, and the surrounding ditches and mounds is about 340 feet in diameter. Extending from the circle toward the northeast is a lane about 80 feet wide called the avenue.

What is called the heel stone is now to one side of the center of the avenue and about 75 feet from the outer ditch of the circular system. There are indications that this stone was located elsewhere in the avenue or that other stones were in the avenue.

Some of the other stones are not in their original positions. Within the last century, a few stones were replaced to what is assumed to be the proper location, but others are not where they stood when the system was erected.

Stonehenge became better known with the introduction of a book, *Stonehenge Decoded*, by Gerald S. Hawkins. A television documentary program based on the book was shown repeatedly in the United States. The basic conclusion of *Stonehenge Decoded* was that the builders were exceptional astronomers who, after having spied on the stars for years, skillfully coded intricate astronomical data into the stone arrangement. Using a computer, Hawkins claims to have decoded Stonehenge, so that it is as if he can take us back to those thrilling days of yesteryear when the stone arranger spies again.

It is generally believed that the originators of Stonehenge had abandoned it before 687 B.C., the time of the last Mars-Earth encounter, and probably had built it sometime around or before 1500 B.C. The obvious question then is: if Stonehenge has really been decoded and works today according to uniformitarian assumptions, how could any major changes have taken place?

Velikovsky published a reply to the Stonehenge question in the April 1967 issue of *Yale Scientific* Magazine. [26] Some of his comments are reviewed below.

DECODING REFUTED

One of the initial assumptions of Hawkins' theory is that, when viewed from the central position of Stonehenge on the summer solstice, the Sun rises directly over the Heel Stone. It is also thought that when this happens the shadow of the Heel Stone is cast on the Altar Stone. Professor of Archaeology, R. J. C. Atkinson, a noted authority on Stonehenge, said: "Neither of these widely held beliefs is correct". He further states that, at the summer solstice now, the Sun rises to the left of the Heel Stone and on uniformitarian calculations would have risen even further to the left when Stonehenge was built. He adds that it will not rise *over* the Heel Stone for more than a thousand years. (Even if the Sun did now rise over the Heel Stone at summer solstice, it would not have done so 3000 years ago.)

Hawkins also argues that we have no record of just what moment the ancients considered as sunrise. This allows him to introduce an additional source of error by using the first ray of sunlight in some calculations, but waiting until the Sun's full diameter is above the horizon for other calculations. Velikovsky notes that records from many ancient cultures do specify the moment of sunrise as being that at which the first ray becomes visible.

Atkinson published several articles critical of Hawkins theory, but Hawkins later answered some of those points. [27] However, Hawkins still had a margin of error larger than normally considered as useful for precise astronomical calculations.

Even by allowing large limits of error (and then exceeding these limits), and with 27,060 possible alignments associated with 165 positions, there appears to be no detectable correlation with any of the planets or fixed stars. The only significant correlation was with what Hawkins called a 56-year lunar-eclipse cycle. However, in 1967, Colton and Martin pointed out that there is no 56-year lunar-eclipse cycle; it is actually a 65-year cycle.

Although most of the lunar eclipses in a cycle are not visible from Stonehenge, Hawkins argues that it is better to call out the troops for an eclipse that does not occur than to have an eclipse of the Moon occur as a surprise. Those which prove to be not visible can be said to have been averted by the great powers of the magician.

It was important to be able to predict these events, Hawkins says, because they were "most frightening things". Yet if one could not accurately predict them, then everyone might sleep through one of those most "frightening" events.

In July of 1973, during the reading of a paper at a conference in Mexico City, Hawkins stated that his work *had probably not decoded Stonehenge*. [28]

Analyzing Hawkins' work is still important, although Stonehenge has not been decoded. With all the possibilities and all the computer analyses, no significant astronomical associations have yet been found for this monument thought to have been constructed to keep track of astronomical movements. However, this null result is significant in itself.

STONEHENGE SIGNIFICANT

Stonehenge is generally thought to have been an observatory, but nothing works. This may be a result of apparent changes in the orbits of objects Stonehenge was designed to observe. It is significant that Stonehenge was repeatedly reordered and rebuilt; hence, the various designations such as Stonehenge I, II, IIIA, IIIB, etc. It is possible that even the Heel Stone was moved. In the "Avenue", a hole exists which is large enough to hold a huge stone, which is nevertheless missing. If Stonehenge was actually used for observations of the stars or planets and needed to be changed, could it have been because the apparent motions of the observed objects changed? Hawkins notes that one of the arrangements appears to have been abandoned suddenly and suggests that this happened because the builders discovered that the device did not work as expected. Perhaps they discovered that suddenly it no longer worked the way it had previously worked.

OTHER STRUCTURES

Many other attempts at explaining megalithic monuments similar to Stonehenge have been made. The most notable is probably the work of Alexander Thom. The work of Thom and others is available in the literature, as are discussions offering counter-arguments to these ideas. Entire books can and have been written about this subject, and analysis of each of these theories is beyond the intended scope of this book. However, some quotes from an article by Andrew Fleming demonstrate that we would be acting purely on faith if we considered these theories as "proof" of uniformity before the 7th century B.C. Fleming's article was titled "Megalithic astronomy; a prehistorian's view".[29] Some of his comments follow:

Thom's work is probably the best known of recent work concerning accurate measurements of megalithic sites. His work seems to imply that a standard unit of measure was known in a large region where there was once thought to be little cultural interaction among the various groups. In some cases drastic modifications of concepts of pre-history would be required to fit Thom's suggestions. Fleming says: "It seems likely, however, that any model of European prehistoric processes which changes to accomodate Thom's ideas would itself strain credulity". This, of course, is only an opinion and may not be correct. Luckily, many of Thom's conclusions, if correct, will not affect Velikovsky's conclusions.

The suggestions that would bear on uniformity are those concerning astronomy. About this Fleming states the following, which is not merely opinion: "Unfortunately, prehistorians are now faced with all manner of claimed astronomical directions, involving rugged skylines, broken, recumbent menhirs, excavated pot holes, stone alignments, cairns and barrows, unexplained humps and bumps, and even in one case straight, presumably modern tracks. Standing stones can be interpreted as general pointers or precise indicators; at various times their tops, lower portions or flattened sides can be considered as significant".

Fleming mentions that there does seem to be a rough correlation indicating the builders had a basic knowledge of the Sun's behavior, but then he notes that some birds build their nests with orientations indicating they are also familiar with the Sun's movements. Some major changes could occur in the apparent motions of the Sun and planets without necessarily affecting the general alignments of such nests. The same could be true for the monuments. Significant alignments may then be results of the desire to find them.

THOM'S DATA

This desire may be noticed in some of Thom's work. [30] He *assumes* that certain megalithic structures can be used to determine the angle between the Earth's axis and the ecliptic plane at the time of construction of the monuments. His results fit the uniformitarian theoretical curve. However, data that are independently *known* to be measures of this angle do not agree well with the theory. [31]

The plane that passes through the Sun and contains the orbit of the Earth is called the *ecliptic*. The axis about which the Earth spins is not perpendicular to this plane, but is tilted about 23.5 degrees from the perpendicular. The exact angle, however, changes slightly with time. On the basis of uniformitarian assumptions, de Sitter and Newcomb derive formulas by which one may calculate this angle as a function of time. The results from each calculation are the same except for before 1000 B.C., when there is a very slight difference in the results.

The data acquired from what Thom assumes that the ancients tried to measure fit the theory perfectly. Other data, acquired from what the ancients claimed to have measured, diverge from the theory, and the difference between measurement and theory increases the further back one goes in time. So it appears that if you do not know what the ancients measured, it is easier to make your solution fit the uniformitarian theory.

TITIUS-BODE: THE MNEMONIC "LAW"

Bode's rule is an empirical formula that provides an easy way to remember the approximate relative distances of the planets from the Sun. It is commonly called Bode's law, but it is not really a law and was not even discovered by Bode. It was originally discovered by Titius and is more properly called the Titius-Bode formula.

The formula is generally given as $r = .4 + .3 \times 2^m$. The letter r represents the distance from the Sun to the orbit of the planet, and m represents the order number of the planet. m does not start with zero or one for Mercury, as might be expected; it starts with negative infinity. The sequence for m is $-\infty, 0, 1, 2, 3, \ldots$ for Mercury, Venus, Earth, Mars, ... respectively. The distances are given in AU, or Astronomical Units. One AU is the distance from the Sun to the Earth. Table I contains the results of the Titius-Bode law and of the actual distances. [32] You can see that the actuals versus the predictions diverge quickly beyond the orbit of Uranus.

SIGNIFICANCE TO VELIKOVSKY

Schatzman mentioned that many cosmological theories assume that the Bode equation reflects the conditions of the Solar System at the time of formation of the planets, approximately five billion years ago. [33] This assumption has been used as an argument against the idea of recent changes in the Solar System. For example, in 1975 Sklower described some mathematical relationships about the Solar System and the motions of the planets. She said that although she did not dispute Velikovsky's general theory, she questioned if the order of the Solar System was disrupted. One of her reasons was that Bode's law works. [34]

The use of the Titius-Bode law in arguments against Velikovsky's work began as early as 1951, when astronomer John Q. Stewart of Princeton University argued that Venus could not have entered into its present orbit after the creation of the Solar System because this would contradict Bode's law. [35] More recently (1974) Bass described a conversation with Lloyd Motz, Chairman of the Astronomy of Columbia University: "Dr. Motz told me that one of his reasons for not accepting Velikovsky's postulate is its obvious glaring conflict with Bode's law, which has to its credit since 1781 at least three valid major predictions (orbits of Uranus, Ceres, and Saturn's seventh satellite, Hyperion), but which is seemingly spoiled if Venus should be removed from the solar system". [36]

MODIFIED RULE

Because of this attitude, I began to wonder what would happen to the form of the Titius-Bode law if a planet were removed from the interior but no other change occurred. (It is obvious that no change of form would occur if the outermost planet were removed, or a new one added at the end.) A trivial mathematical analysis revealed that if the .3 in the common form of the formula were changed to .6, all the orbits for planets would remain identical, *except that the orbit for Venus disappears* (see Table I). Therefore, the Titius-Bode rule does not appear to offer valid support for the opinion that no change has ever occurred in the original Solar System.

This effectively demonstrates that the Titius-Bode rule does not eliminate the possibility of occurrence of the events described by Velikovsky, but a look into a possible physical mechanism behind the formula reveals additional information related to his theory.

TABLE 1

PLANET	ACTUAL DISTANCE	TITIUS-BODE EQUATION	MODIFIED EQUATION
Mercury	0.39	0.4	0.4
Venus	0.72	0.7	
Earth	1.00	1.0	1.0
Mars	1.52	1.6	1.6
Asteroids	2.80	2.8	2.8
Jupiter	5.20	5.2	5.2
Saturn	9.55	10.0	10.0
Uranus	19.20	19.6	19.6
Neptune	30.10	38.8	38.8
Pluto	39.50	77.2	77.2

Values given in AU. Column 1 contains the measured orbital distance from the Sun. Column 2 contains values calculated from the normally used Bode's formula. Column 3 has values computed with the modified equation.

THE PHYSICAL MECHANISM

As mentioned, the simple form of the Titius-Bode rule does not fit well beyond Uranus. A number of investigators have attempted to improve the correlation between the predicted and actual values by modifying the equation, using various mathematical techniques. Nieto discusses these works in detail.[37]

Some of these attempts have been successful. One equation has been designed that accurately describes the orbits of the planets as well as the orbits of the moons of Jupiter, Saturn and Uranus. But it should, since the equation was developed to do just that. If one performs a mathematical analysis to fit a formula to the data, one should not be surprised if it works. However, these curves do not provide an understanding of the physics behind what is happening, and in no way imply anything about the arrangement of the original Solar System. This was the basis of Velikovsky's reply to Stewart in 1951.[38]

Bass, Ovenden, and Hills have independently performed investigations which may provide an understanding of the basic physical reason for the planets having acquired a distribution which is easily expressed in a Bode-type formula. Their works also indicate that the Titius-Bode relationship does not preclude the possibility of the events described by Velikovsky.

At the Eleventh International Astronautical Congress at Stockholm in 1960, Dr. Robert W. Bass presented a paper about a new variational principle for solving the N-Body problem.[39] In part III of this paper, Bass introduces what he calls the *Principle of Least Mean Potential Energy.*[40] It is Bass' mathematically reasonable suggestion that bodies in a central force field, such as the planets in the gravitational field of the sun, tend to acquire positions where they interact with each other the least. These orbits can then be described by a Bode-type formula.

Later Ovenden, without knowledge of Bass' work, noted that intuitively one would feel that a system of bodies orbiting a central force would change its configuration slowly when the planets are far apart and quickly when they are close together. This was confirmed by computer simulations done by Hills and by Ovenden. Ovenden generalized this conclusion to what he called *The Principle of Least Interaction Action.* [41] Ovenden demonstrated empirically what Bass had proven mathematically.

Their conclusion is basically that the planets can be thrown into orbits around a central force and interact until they reach a point of minimum interaction, at which time their orbits can be described by a Bode relationship. This is also the conclusion reached by Hills, and he calls this process "dynamical relaxations".[42]

Whatever the name given to the process, there is mathematical and empirical evidence indicating that the Bode equation, *however refined for precision*, does not prove that all the planets were formed in their present orbits. Ovenden specifically stated that his results suggest "...that the present distribution of planets gives no information concerning the origin of the solar system". These three investigators have demonstrated that the physical process underlying the Titius-Bode rule indicates that planetary interactions could have taken place after the origin of the planets and that the present arrangement could be a result of these encounters.

TITIUS-BODE IGNORED

At times astronomers claim that the Titius-Bode rule indicates that nothing has changed since the origin of the Solar System, and they claim that the system has been proven to have been stable for billions of years. However, they do not let this stop *them* from postulating orbit-changes similar to those suggested by Velikovsky.

An example is related to recent ideas about the moon. In an article about tidal friction, MacDonald argues that certain information "is not consistent with the hypothesis that the earth-moon system has existed throughout geological time".[43] Singer later published an article titled "Where Was the Moon Formed?"[44] He mentions some of the properties discovered about lunar rocks and a previously published opinion about how these properties might have occurred. He then makes some calculations relating to the accretion process for material in Earth-orbit and for material accreting elsewhere and later being captured as one body by the Earth. He states that "the conclusion can be drawn that the moon accumulated not in earth orbit but as a separate planet. and that it was later captured by the earth".

Cameron has expanded on this concept.[45] He reasons that the natural place for the Moon to form with described characteristics would be inside the orbit of Mercury, and that the relative difference of the orbital radii of the Moon and Mercury would be less than for other adjacent planets. "Thus gravitational perturbations of the orbits of the two bodies would probably accumulate until a close approach took place, at which a very large modification in the elements of the moon's orbit would become possible. If the modified orbit of the Moon were sufficiently great to allow it to approach the Earth, then gravitational capture of the Moon by the Earth would become possible, even if improbable." Cameron continues with an "illustrative" energy analysis of the same type used by Rose and Vaughan, where they considered orbit changes of Venus, Mars, and Earth.[46]

Rose and Vaughan considered possible orbit changes specifically related to the events described by Velikovsky. They calculated a scenario that fits reasonably well with the description of the ancients and with conventional celestial mechanics. They do not claim that their postulated orbits are *the* orbits of the past, but they demonstrate that it is possible to obtain a reasonable fit.

In their set of orbits, Mars is originally in an orbit between the earth and the sun. Rose suggested this independently.[47] This unique suggestion was a result of being able to clear the mind of preconceived ideas about where the planets should be, and letting the physics of the situation determine the most advantageous position. As Rose pointed out, from this position a large portion of the orbital angular momentum lost by Venus could be acquired by Mars.

Many astronomers have also recently freed their thinking of old assumptions about the origin of the Solar System. These assumptions are sometimes still used as "proof" that Velikovsky is wrong, but it is becoming more obvious that these assumptions are not being supported by the latest information.

Additional evidence revealing that astronomers are becoming less upset at the thought of changes in the Solar System is found in a 1974 paper by Harrington and Van Flandern, who write: "Thus contrary to expectation, there is no counter evidence to the hypothesis that Mercury might once have been a satellite of Venus".[48] It may be just slow in coming, but so far there has not been any violent outcry that this does not fit Bode's law.

There is even a physical example demonstrating that orbit changes once thought to be impossible can actually occur. Fokin states that during a near approach to Jupiter, the comet Oterma III, which before 1938 had an orbit entirely between the orbits of Jupiter and Saturn, changed its orbit so that it was entirely between Mars and Jupiter.[49] After 1965, its orbit was again between Jupiter and Saturn.[50] "In the peculiarities of its motion the comet Oterma III is one of the most remarkable comets discovered in the present century."

Bass notes that in the case of a three-body problem involving the Sun, Jupiter, and a third body with a mass about that of Venus or smaller, the motions of the three bodies are essentially independent of the mass of the third body. This is commonly known and accepted. Since, with negligible error, one may substitute a mass smaller than that of Venus, one may obtain a possible orbit change for Venus by comparing the effect to the orbit change of a smaller body such as a comet.[51]

TITIUS-BODE USED TO SUPPORT CHANGES

After the claim by some astronomers that the Titius-Bode rule proves the planets formed in their present orbits and after this was ignored by other astronomers when they postulated changes, other astronomers used the physical basis of the rule as support that changes have occurred in the Solar System. For example, Ovenden concluded that a planet once existed near the asteriod belt.[52] This planet was calculated to have been about ninety times as massive as the earth and to have existed until about sixteen million years ago.

Ovenden's hypothesis received additional support from Thomas C. Van Flandern of the U.S. Naval Observatory. At the April 1976 meeting of the American Geophysical Union in Washington, D.C. he reported the preliminary results of his calculations about the orbits of a number of comets. The calculations indicated that there is a tendency for many of the orbits to intersect at a point in the asteriod belt about six million years ago. (Vsekhsvyatskii's work and Van Flandern's work challenge the Oort theory of the origin of comets.)

Ovenden mentioned several problems to be considered about his theory. Two of these are related and are of interest because the major problem is identical in form to one of the questions concerning Velikovsky's work. (See Chapter V .) The problem Ovenden mentioned is where did the energy come from to dissipate the planet, and what happened to the mass of nearly ninety times the mass of the earth? Ovenden was not ostracized because this question was not answered before he published his work, and his hypothesis is still being openly investigated. The problem of the energy required for the ejection of Venus from Jupiter should be much less difficult to solve.

STABILITY OF THE SOLAR SYSTEM UNPROVEN

Another question relates to the stability of the Solar System. Some scientists have the opinion that certain work in celestial mechanics proves that the Solar System has been stable for billions of years and that orbit changes of the type described by Velikovsky are impossible. Dr. Robert W. Bass has performed an astute analysis of this question and has demonstrated that such opinions are unfounded. [53] His articles contain a number of complex mathematical statements, so only his conclusions will be reviewed here. His original work should be consulted for details.

Bass is a Professor of Physics and Astronomy at Brigham Young University. He was a Rhodes Scholar and obtained his doctorate in 1955 under the late Aurel Wintner, then the world's leading authority on celestial mechanics. He undertook three years of post-doctoral research in non-linear mechanics at Princeton under Solomon Lefschetz. This does not guarantee that his analysis is perfect, but does disprove the statement that no one with a background in celestial mechanics would consider investigating Velikovsky's work.

Bass devoted one article to an examination of why many astronomers have the misconception that the solar system has been rigorously proven to have been stable for millions of years. Part of the problem is that they actually did what they accused Velikovsky of doing. They used out-of-date sources and did not read far enough in the sources they did use.

In 1773 Laplace published a theorem which supposedly demonstrated that the Solar System is stable and that planets could not have near-collisions or interchange their orbits. Poisson improved on this theorem and later Laplace used techniques developed by Lagrange and published another theorem which added to the support of stability. However, because of the work of Poincare in 1899, authorities have known that their results are valid at most for only limited lengths of time. The question to be investigated then became how long might stability prevail? Laplace previously guessed ten million years without proof.

The presently accepted and widely acclaimed opinion of some experts is that the valid time interval is hundreds of millions of years. Their justification, they claim, comes from the other experts who actually performed the calculations. One of the most-often-quoted experts is E. W. Brown. In particular, pages 152 and 249 of the book *Planetary Theory* by Brown and Shook are often cited as authoritative evidence that the Solar System is stable. In Kopal's recent book, *The Solar System*, he even refers to Brown, who Kopal agrees "could speak to this subject with the greatest authority" as claiming a time of stability of hundreds of millions of years. Bass states that actually, in their book, Brown and Shook did say things "which on first reading could be misinterpreted...., but which upon careful study are far less categorical". Further reading shows that they were hedging the question of time and knew that certain conditions invalidated their results suggesting a long time span.

Brown himself drastically reduced his own estimate of the length of time of stability of the solar system. In 1895 Newcomb estimated one hundred billion years. Later estimates brought this down to one hundred million years, and then Brown went to one million years. These times, involving changes by a factor of one hundred thousand, did not derive from rigorous calculations; they merely reflected what various investigators "felt". "estimated", "thought", and "assumed" were reasonable time periods. Brown cites problems with resonance phenomena as the main reason for thinking the times should be reduced.

In 1953, Dr. W. M. Smart, Regius Professor of Astronomy at the University of Glasgow, published a book titled *Celestial Mechanics*. In it he indicates that the Laplace-Lagrange-Poisson type "stability" calculations can be trusted at most for time spans of *three hundred years*.

Yusuke Hagihara has published four parts of a planned five-volume treatise on celestial mechanics. Bass notes that "... it is evident that this will be the most exhaustively thorough and definitive treatment of celestial mechanics of decades to come." Hagihara is one of the highest authorities, and it is one of his publications in *The Solar System* (ed. by Kuiper) which is most widely cited by astronomers to support their claims of stability for time spans of over ten billion years. Bass notes, however, that the equations used in these estimates are coupled to the equation which led Smart to restrict the time to "a century or two". Bass remarks: "Thus, the system of six coupled equations is not valid for more than a few centuries (for the second approximation fails after 300 years and so *a priori* the third approximation cannot be considered over a long interval".)

From some of the other considerations and quotations given by Bass, it is apparent that Hagihara is aware of the lack of rigor in estimates of time spans of stability. About the question of the time interval, Hagihara says "Present mathematics hardly permits this question to be answered satisfactorily for the actual solar system". He also explicitly admits that conclusions about orbital changes cannot be drawn from his discussion of invariant mean distances. Many misconceptions about the stability of the solar system arise because Hagihara's qualifying remarks are often overlooked.

Bass briefly reviews why the mathematical analyses do not produce proof of stability and also recalls that "Three of the greatest contemporary mathematical celestial mechanicans" have indicated that presently accepted celestial mechanics cannot be used to conclusively prove that Velikovsky's hypothesis is forbidden. Bass also claims that the results of his review provide "proof that the astronomers who have asserted that Velikovsky's central hypothesis is incompatable with Newtonian dynamics have been laboring under a radical misapprehension of the objective facts". He concludes "The life's work of a sincere and dedicated scholar, who has published all of his sources for critical scrutiny by everyone, should not be dismissed hastily upon mere *group consensus* about the validity of obsolete ideas, which true experts have long ago dismissed as illusion".

So the next time you hear an authority claim that it has absolutely been proven that the Solar System was stable in the past, is now, and shall be forevermore, amen, perhaps you can detect just a hint of faith in the expression. There is no such rigorous proof, and this is so noted by many authorities.

GRAVITY VERSUS ELECTROMAGNETIC FIELDS

Velikovsky notes that the ancients observed electrical discharges between the Earth and external bodies during close encounters between them. It was then natural to conclude that the bodies were not at the same electric potential. He also noted that the tilting of the Earth's axis could be most easily accomplished by electromagnetic interactions between Earth and another body. A number of other effects associated with the close encounters could be explained by electromagnetic interactions. However, some astronomers claim that gravity cannot explain the events, and electromagnetic fields are too weak. They then make calculations about charged planets in their present locations. This does not help clarify the problem, since these are not the conditions under discussion.

The discussion about Bode's rule, orbital changes and stability were all related to standard gravitational mechanics. This is because, at present distances, gravitational theory is a working model and should be used as a first order explanation for as many events as possible. It is apparent that Velikovsky realized this in 1950 when he wrote that his theory "...can, if required to do so, conform with the celestial mechanics of Newton." [54] However, it is also apparent that he understood that electromagnetic fields played a greater part in solar-system affairs than was accepted at that time. (See Appendix 1B) For example, he suggested that the Earth's magnetic field extended beyond the Moon. Astronomers considered this impossible at the time, and Menzel even used this suggestion as a point to support his claim that Velikovsky was wrong; however, this suggestion has since been verified.

The influence of electromagnetic fields in the past events needs to be referenced to what can be attributed to gravity. To clarify this, a distinction needs to be made between a working model and a *true* model. A working model may provide very accurate results for the conditions where it is applied; however, the model may not be an accurate description of what is actually occurring, and the model may not work outside these conditions. Engineers and physicists sometimes use what is called a "black box" approach. Formulas are devised to compute a measured output of a black box for a given input. The exact circuit in the box is not known, but a number of circuits can be devised to give the proper output with a given input. Anyone of these circuits would be a working model, but none would necessarily be the *true* model of the contents of the box.

Gravity is a working model at the presently observed distances of the planets and other bodies in the solar system. The gravitational force exerted by one mass on another mass is equal to a constant times the two masses divided by the square of the distance between the masses.

(Recent investigations indicate that this may not be strictly true. [55] Long performed experiments with small masses and small distances. He found that at small distances– less than 100cm–the gravitational constant changes with distance. Continued experiments may indicate that the *constant* is not only related to distance, but to mass *and* distance. No recent observations have been made on planetary masses at relatively small distances. Since unexpected results were found at the small mass - small distance condition, it is reasonable to assume that we do not know exactly what would happen, even gravitationally, with planetary masses at distances of only a few planetary radii. When electromagnetic fields are added, it is certain that we do not know exactly what would occur in close interactions of the type observed by the ancients.)

The motion of many celestial objects can be predicted by means of the standard gravitational model. This does not mean it is a *true* model, and it certainly does not mean that this model gives us any real understanding of what gravity is. Gravity does not explain *all* of the motions of the solar system, and this is obvious from the accepted scientific literature. However, astronomers are justified in claiming that at the present distances it is a useful working model and should be used, if possible.

Unfortunately, what is strictly *known* about orbital calculations using gravity and what is *assumed* about these calculations are often lumped into one category of "known facts". Because of this, astronomers themselves are responsible for part of the misunderstanding related to the importance of gravity versus electromagnetic fields. They overburdened the load required of electromagnetic fields and then complained that Velikovsky could not justify his theory in terms of their mistake.

Astronomers in 1950 *incorrectly* assumed that most of the orbital changes described by Velikovsky were completely contrary to all known laws of gravity. Because of the discharges between planets and other features of the ancient observations, it was obvious to Velikovsky that electromagnetic fields were important. He naturally concluded that what was not due to gravity must be due to other forces. This conclusion is still correct. However, it may not be a matter of less than 10% gravity and over 90% electromagnetic effects, as astronomers forced themselves to believe in 1950; it is probably largely gravity with electromagnetic perturbations. (This still does not mean that gravity is anything other than an empirical model.)

Chapter V

THE PLANETS AND MOON

When pointing out what they consider to be flaws in Velikovsky's hypothesis, many scientists suggest that not only is Velikovsky wrong about the points under discussion, but no "real" scientist would ever have considered the possibility of such events. However, since 1950 nearly every major idea advanced by Velikovsky has been re-advanced by a noted scientist. Some instances of this have already been discussed, but there are some noteworthy ones related to the planets.

In this discussion I will try to distinguish between theoretical speculations and interpretations and actual findings. Also, I do not necessarily claim agreement with theories which may be brought up in connection with various points; they are mentioned primarily to demonstrate that authorities now discuss, in the open scientific literature, certain postulates for which Velikovsky was ridiculed before, during and even after these same discussions by the experts. Although the explanations offered may be incorrect, the fact that theories continue to be advanced in explanation of such phenomena does demonstrate that the "authorities" now consider them subjects worthy of study.

FORMATION AT DIFFERENT TIMES

In 1950 most scientists firmly believed that all the planets were formed in their present orbits; many of them ridiculed

Velikovsky for suggesting otherwise. However, by 1960 W. H. McCrea, who at the time was President of the Royal Astronomical Society, published a theoretical argument that no planet could originally have formed from a solar nebula any closer to the Sun than the orbit of Jupiter.[1] Later J. G. Hills attempted to show that no planet could initially have formed outside the orbit of Saturn.[2] Between the appearances of these papers, H. Alfven, who later received the Nobel Prize in physics, theorized that the giant planets may have been formed before the "terrestrial (smaller) planets".[3] He also presented arguments for the inverse order of events. Either way, within a very few years at least three respected scientists argued that all the planets need have been formed neither at the same time nor in their present orbits.

If no planet initially formed inside Jupiter's orbit or outside Saturn's, then major orbital changes must have taken place since most of the planets were formed. Hills explicitly suggests that the planets now outside the orbit of Saturn may have been knocked into their orbits by encounters with other planets. We have already seen that events of this type have recently been explained theoretically. As early as 1953, R. A. Lyttleton, a noted British cosmologist, explained an orbital change of the type which some of his colleagues had, for at least three years, been claiming to be impossible.[4]

ORIGIN OF LATER PLANETS

In addition to planet-formation at different times, scientists have discussed various processes of formation for different planets. Probably the most widely held view is that they all formed, whenever they formed, through "accretion". By accretion is meant that fine debris aggregates into small objects, which grow by colliding with other objects until great balls are formed. The bigger the ball, the greater its gravitational attraction; hence, the greater its ability to attract more debris. Eventually, planet size is reached.

Other methods have also been discussed. Theoretical work by N. D. Suvorov led him to conclude in 1971 that planets could be individually expelled from the Sun. [5] The previous year, Sarvajna discussed the possibility of a charged body ejected from the Sun acquiring an orbit around the Sun. Later, I. P. Williams reinvestigated this proposal and concluded that Sarvajna's estimates of charge values were too high, but that the mechanism still had possibilities. [6]

Historical evidence indicates that at least one planet may not have been formed in this manner. Velikovsky points out that the ancients taught that Venus erupted from Jupiter within the memory of man. In 1950, many critics of *Worlds in Collision* ridiculed the idea that such a thing could ever happen, and especially in historical times. However, some credentialled scientists do consider such possibilities, not to support Velikovsky, but simply in the course of investigations into what could have occurred in the past.

In 1961 Lyttleton published his own conclusion that the terrestrial planets must have erupted from the giant planets. [7] He said that under certain conditions a large planet formed near Jupiter's present orbit would rotate very rapidly as a consequence of conserving the angular momentum of all accreted matter. As it increased its mass, it would rotate faster and faster. It would eventually become unstable and be forced to disrupt "into two very unequal pieces".

Most cosmologists like to assume that the major events in the Solar System took place hundreds or thousands of millions of years ago. However, by Lyttleton's theory, the more time that has elapsed since the origin of a large planet, the more likely it is to suffer disruption.

ENERGY FOR FORMATION

An exceedingly high rate of rotation could supply most or all of the energy needed to expel a large body from Jupiter. Jupiter is about 318 times as massive as the Earth, and its radius is slightly over 11 times that of the Earth; so, having Jupiter rotate "in a few hours" sounds impressive. That much mass spread over that much area and rotating that fast sounds impossible. However, Jupiter now rotates in just under 10 hours. If this were not a measured quantity, a suggested period of 10 hours would probably sound impossible, also.

Numerous astronomers and physicists have calculated the energy needed to eject Venus from Jupiter. In doing so, most of them have made mistakes for which they would fail members of their freshman physics classes. [8] However, such major mistakes make only minor differences in the answer. With all the necessary corrections and refinements, the energy still amounts to about 10^{40} ergs. This is a lot of energy. (Suvorov's theory also requires a lot of energy.)

Velikovsky notes that, according to the ancients, Saturn and Jupiter were at one time involved in a near-collision. It also appeared that this event was related to the ejection of a large body by Jupiter. Velikovsky points out that if these ancient observations were valid, then the energy needed to eject Venus from Jupiter would be reduced by the magnitude of whatever influence Saturn may have had during the near-encounter.

People like to compare this ejection energy with the energy received from the Sun in a year, or with the number of times you might bicycle around the equator on the same energy, as if to say that so much energy could never be available. Actually, such remarks do not show it to be unavailable; they merely emphasize that it certainly is a lot of energy.

If a sudden event involving this much energy occurred in the Solar System today at 5 p.m., an *ad hoc* explanation would be available for the 6 o'clock news, and three weeks from now an abundance of theoretical papers would be appearing in the literature.

Theories exist for many things in the universe which require more than 10^{40} ergs expended over a short time. Some of these theories existed before the phenomena in question were even observed. Mostly, however, such events occur at great distances from the Earth. All this is in keeping with the principle that one may respectably theorize about anything of any magnitude, so long as it is held to have taken place "long ago and far away".

Perhaps Lyttleton's speculations are not discordant with some other recent ideas about Jupiter. As Jupiter accumulated mass and started rotating faster to conserve angular momentum, it may have also decreased its radius because of the increased gravitational force. This decrease in radius would also increase the spin rate in the same way that the pulling-in of a skater's arms makes her spin faster.

A continuing, present-day decrease in the radius of Jupiter through gravitational contraction has been considered by several investigators. In an article about the findings of Pioneer 10, McDonough cites that probe's confirmation that Jupiter emits more energy than it receives from the Sun. He adds: "The source of this radiation is a major theoretical problem".[9] Smoluchowsky noted earlier that some theorists believe this emission can be accounted for by a gravitational shrinkage of Jupiter amounting to about one millimeter per year.[10] As in Lyttleton's theory, this phenomenon would increase Jupiter's spin rate with time.

DENSITIES OF LATER PLANETS

How might Jupiter, a body of very low mean density, produce terrestrial planets all of which have high mean densities? The mean density of Jupiter is 1.334 grams per cubic centimeter, and the average mean density of all the inner planets is close to 5 grams per cubic centimeter.

The answer to this question is almost a matter of the definition of the term "mean density". The question is similar to asking why one would expect to find a large volume of water on the Earth when the mean density of the Earth is 5.52 grams per cubic centimeter and that of water is only 1.0 grams per cubic centimeter. Actually, though, the situation is somewhat more complicated than this. Some theoretical models of Jupiter deny the existence of a core of materials which might retain high density without the high pressures near the center of Jupiter. Other models requiring a core of rocky materials do exist, however.

Determining an accurate model for Jupiter should help answer the question about the different mean densities. Before 1965, according to Hess and Mead, most models of Jupiter and Saturn were "based on the assumption that they are completely cold planets.."[11] This assumption made replying to Velikovsky easier. In 1974, Anderson noted that the main problem in constructing accurate models for Jupiter and Saturn is the fact that they emit more energy than they received from the Sun.[12]

Although there was this complication even before 1974, until then the "solid hydrogen core" model for Jupiter was popular. This non-rocky-core model made it difficult to imagine Jupiter ejecting part of its interior to form a high-mean-density planet. However, in 1972 A. H. Cook published his conclusion that "it would be possible for all planets to have cores of similar composition to the earth's, surrounded by mantles of different sorts, silicates for the terrestrial planets and mostly hydrogen for Jupiter, Saturn, Uranus and Neptune".[13] Such construction, if correct, would make more plausible both Lyttleton's theory of inner-planet formation and Velikovsky's explanation of the origin of Venus.

I once mentioned Cook's paper at a NASA research center where several investigators were engaged in research to support one of the solid-hydrogen-core models of Jupiter. They informed me that they were working on *the* correct model. I asked if they had read Cook's paper, and they replied that they had never heard of it until then. However, they were certain Cook was wrong, this on the basis of the assumption that they were right. No doubt their approach would have been slightly more scientific had Velikovsky's work not been the main topic. Which, if either, theory is on the right path may not be known for awhile. Until one or another model is actually confirmed, objections based on mean density should carry little weight against Velikovsky's work. (For additional support of the idea that there is no density problem, see an article by Ralph Juergens in KRONOS II, #1, 1976.)

CHARACTERISTICS OF THE PLANETS

In 1950, various planets were thought to have certain "known" characteristics. Velikovsky noted that many of these characteristics were not consistent with what one would expect if events really occurred as described in *Worlds in Collision*. He then postulated some planetary characteristics that would be consistent with those events, and these suggestions have become known as "advance claims".

These "advance claims" by Velikovsky are not results of mathematical analysis or physical theorizing. Nor are they predictions arrived at through ESP or any other conjuring technique, as is sometimes suggested. (Although the word "prediction" is often used in scientific discussions, some scientists have tried to give it overtones of the supernatural when used in connection with Velikovsky. This is perhaps why he prefers to speak of "advance claims".)

Velikovsky's advance claims result from considering what one would expect to find in the Solar System today if the events described by the ancients actually happened. Mathematical ability and agility have nothing to do with the matter. The conclusions were reached through deductive reasoning; so, refusing to consider these claims because Velikovsky has no degree in mathematical physics is inane.

JUPITER

In 1950, Jupiter was thought to be a cold dead planet. Even in 1961, many people discounted observations suggesting that Jupiter's temperature might be higher than the theoretical value, arguing that such evidence could be due to "imperfect measures" or "faulty estimates" of certain quantities. [14] As late as 1964, Asimov, in what he intended as a non-fiction book, wrote that Jupiter does not develop enough heat to warm its surface and that any warmth there is due to solar radiation. [15]

RADIO NOISE

However, Velikovsky maintained that Jupiter must be more active than accepted theories would lead one to believe and that, indeed, the giant planet would be found to be emitting radio noise. Both of these characteristics of Jupiter have been confirmed.

Radio noise from Jupiter is a subject about which Einstein and Velikovsky had many discussions. Einstein was convinced that space must be free of magnetic fields and plasmas and that there would thus be no reason for Jupiter to emit radio waves. Most astronomers shared this viewpoint, and no attempt was made to examine the possibility of radio noise from Jupiter.

However, in 1955, Burke and Franklin discovered radio noise from Jupiter. As F. Graham Smith states in a book on radio astronomy, "but for a fortunate accident, nothing might have been known of Jupiter's radio flashes". [16] Einstein was so impressed with the discovery that he offered to assist Velikovsky in having other investigations performed. But it was too late; Einstein died the next week. A copy of *Worlds in Collision* lay open on his desk. [17]

A Doubleday editor wrote to the discoverers of the radio noise and mentioned that Velikovsky had anticipated such a result. One of them replied that even Velikovsky is entitled to a "near miss" once in awhile. [18]

Dr. James Warwick, now a noted authority on the radio emissions from Jupiter, is more generous. He credits Velikovsky with a valid prediction, although at the same time he concedes that he will make no attempt to have Velikovsky merited for this prediction. This action (or inaction) is understandable in light of past and present events.

Warwick also points out that Velikovsky is not the only one inadequately recognized for a noteworthy suggestion. This is not in defense of the scientific community; it is offered simply as a statement of fact. [19]

RED SPOT

If Jupiter ejected a large object, this would lead one reasonably to expect that a structural defect would be left in the planet. Velikovsky suggests that one of the most prominent characteristics of Jupiter, its red spot, is an atmospheric effect related to the scar where Venus was ejected.

Hide has suggested that the red spot could be the result of an anomaly in the structure of Jupiter, and that the disturbance this creates manifests itself in the heavy cloud layer at the top of the atmosphere.[20] He has since expanded this explanation in terms of a "Taylor Column" and performed experiments which further support the ideas.[21] Recent probe data, however, is interpreted in terms not requiring a surface anomaly.

LIFE

At a NASA news conference in 1973, Sagan spread a fabricated story to the effect that Velikovsky "explicitly" predicted that frogs would be found in the atmosphere of Jupiter. It is impossible to see how Sagan might have reached this conclusion from an ethical examination of Velikovsky's work.

Velikovsky actually wrote, concerning frogs, that during the Venus encounter, "The internal heat developed by the earth and the scorching gases of the comet were in themselves sufficient to make the vermin of the earth propagate at a very feverish rate. Some of the plagues, like the plague of the frogs ("the land brought forth frogs") or of the locusts, *must* be ascribed to such causes".[22] (emphasis added)

He does note, however, that because of ancient traditions the question arises whether or not Venus infested the Earth with vermin, which may have been transported in the trailing atmosphere of Venus. He presents this as a question to be considered and not as a fact. He emphasizes that, since conditions are so different on other planets, "it seems incredible that the same forms of life exist there as on the Earth; on the other hand, it is wrong to conclude that there is no life on them at all".[23]

"Whether there is truth in this supposition of larval contamination of the earth is anyone's guess. The ability of
many small insects and their larvae to endure great cold
and heat and to live in an atmosphere devoid of oxygen
renders not entirely improbable the hypothesis that Venus
(and also Jupiter, from which Venus sprang) may be
populated by vermin".[24]

Velikovsky mentions that he was not the first to hypo-
thesize life on other planets, and obviously he was not the
last. Recent planetary probes have included experiments designed to detect life, while other experiments have been performed on earth to help in evaluating the possibility of life
on other planets. In particular, Koch has performed experiments from which he concludes that some terrestrial
organisms could survive in Jupiter's atmosphere.[25]

VENUS

As early as 1946 Velikovsky offered for investigation
three of his expectations for Venus. All concerned characteristics which would not be surprising if events had
actually occurred as described in *Worlds in Collision*, but
none of them would be expected on the basis of uniformitarian concepts of the origin and evolution of the Solar
System.[26] These expectations were related to the rotation,
the temperature, and the cloud-composition of Venus.

ROTATION

When viewed from north of the plane of the Solar System, any planet rotating about its axis in a counter-clock-
wise direction has what is called prograde rotation, or
direct rotation. The concept that all the planets formed in

the same manner at about the same time from a solar nebula suggests that all the planets should rotate in the same direction and have about the same degree of tilt in their rotational axes. This sounds so logical that one must almost feel sorry in stating that such conditions do not exist.

Both Earth and Mars have axes tilted about 23 degrees, and this was long considered to be the standard, since the axial tilts of several other planets are not greatly different. The 3-degree tilt of Jupiter was considered close enough to satisfy uniformitarian requirements. However, Uranus was considered a bad datum point, since its more-than-90 degree tilt actually meant that it had retrograde rotation. Still, most scientists believed this could be ignored because, as Sagan has argued, this may be considered a "marginal case" of retrograde rotation. [27]

So, in 1950, it was thought that the planets fit the idea of uniformity and that Venus was no exception. It was thought that Venus had a prograde rotation, and early investigators assigned it a tilt close to 23 degrees, although studies by Kuiper had yielded inclinations as high as 32 degrees. [28] Velikovsky, however, suggested that Venus would probably exhibit anomalous rotation because of its recent violent interactions with other planets.

Space-probe data and Earth-based radar studies have confirmed that Venus does have rotational properties quite out of keeping with uniformitarian theories. The tilt appears to be near zero degrees, and the spin is *retrograde* rather than prograde; Venus spins "backwards".

After this latter discovery, many attempts at an explanation, some of a catastrophic nature, were published. Sagan blamed tidal friction, but without offering any supporting evidence. [29] Singer suggested that a retrogradely orbiting moon nearly collided with Venus and reversed its spin from the normal spin it *must* have had originally (under uniformitarian theories). [30] Retrograde satellite orbits are known in the Solar System, but they, too, are difficult to explain by accepted theories. Singer leaves the origin of the retrograde moon to people interested in retrograde-moon problems. He seeks to explain only the retrograde rotation of Venus.

Some evidence suggests that Venus' rotation may be even more exceptionally odd, but this is still debated. Venus appears to present the same face to the Earth every time it passes between Earth and the Sun. How precisely this is true depends on whose measurements one accepts. Lewis, then with the M.I.T. Department of Earth and Planetary Science, stated in 1971, "How Venus could find its rotation locked on to Earth despite the fact that the sun's tidal force on Venus is some 10^4 times larger than Earth's is far from clear".[31] Kopal called the mechanism of the Earth-Venus coupling "obscure".[32] Goldstein has said: "Thus we are led to consider twin anomalies of Venus' rotation; a retrograde direction and at least near synchronism with the earth".[33] The reason for the cautious "near" is that the earth-synchronous period is 243.16 days, while his observational limits of error put Venus' rotational period at 242.6 ± 0.6 days.

Bass has noted that "Nonlinear resonant oscillators can become *locked in resonance* in a manner which is orbitally stable and therefore is only slightly disturbed by subsequent perturbations".[34] If the phenomenon dates from a time when Earth had stronger gravitational interactions with Venus, subsequent close approaches of Mars to both of these bodies may not have been influential enough to break this coupling.

On the other hand, Rose thinks the Mars-Venus interactions would probably have erased any Earth-Venus coupling dating from before the Mars-Venus and Mars-Earth interactions.[35] If so, the phenomenon, if it really exists, may have nothing to do with the events described by Velikovsky.

The near-resonance conditions of a number of bodies in the solar system have been used as a uniformitarian argument to support the assumption that the solar system has been stabilizing for billions of years. Rose noted that measurements are not precise enough to distinguish between various possible resonance conditions for most bodies. He said: "The fact is that almost any conceivable state of affairs is relatively close to *some* state of commensurability."[36] He also convincingly argued that "the existence of numerous near-commensurabilities is hardly proof that the solar system has not undergone any drastic rearrangements within historical times."

Whatever the outcome of this question, it is obvious that the spin of Venus is difficult to force into a uniformitarian frame.

TEMPERATURE

In 1952, Harold Urey wrote that the histories of Earth and Venus "should be very similar". [37] On this basis, many of the then-accepted opinions about the properties of Venus were not unreasonable. It was thought that Venus had an average surface temperature only slightly higher than that of the Earth and an atmosphere largely composed of nitrogen. The clouds were thought to consist of water vapor and Menzel and Whipple even extended this idea into the suggestion that the surface of Venus ought to be covered with water. [38] (All this in spite of the fact that spectroscopic studies had given no evidence of water; but again it was argued that the data could be misleading.)

In 1940 Wildt predicted that the temperature at the surface of Venus might be as high as 135 degrees C. [39] Kuiper re-evaluated this estimate, using data available in 1952. His estimate for the temperature *at the tropical midday surface* was 77 degrees C. This would imply an average surface temperature for the entire planet of about -23 degrees C. [40]

Velikovsky expected the temperature to be found much larger than the accepted values. His researches indicated that "Venus experienced in quick succession its birth and expulsion under violent conditions;" and later had near-encounters with both Earth and Mars. "Since all this happened between the third and first millennia before the present era...", Venus simply has not had enough time to cool. Velikovsky also stated that Venus might still be hot enough to have vaporized petroleum in the atmosphere. It is quite apparent from Velikovsky's book that he did not expect Venus to be found only slightly warmer than the Earth. It has since been determined that Venus is *considerably* hotter than the Earth.

Actually, data available in 1950 supported this conclusion. But in attempts to make the information fit accepted theories, it was interpreted in a way which created confusion.

Interpreting data is a common scientific task, one that is useful and necessary. But there is a large step between acquiring facts and correctly accounting for them. That Menzel and Whipple were wrong does not in itself make their endeavor unscientific. Every scientist misinterprets data at some time or other. The unfortunate event associated with these data is that a reasonable interpretation was ignored because it was suggested by Velikovsky. When he provided this alternative explanation, he was accused of being unscientific and of not admitting the "facts". Actually, he was only disagreeing with the "official interpretation" of the facts.

Up to 1950, the two basic observations relating to the heat of Venus involved actual cloud-top temperature measurements and indirect evidence about the spin rate. It was found that considerable heat radiated from the dark side of the planet. The bright part of Venus did not seem much hotter than the dark side. If the planet rotates slowly, the sunlit side should be hotter than the dark side. Therefore, some people suggested that Venus must rotate so quickly that the dark side does not have time to cool before it is again heated by the Sun.

This information, however, seemingly conflicted with data which indicated a slow rotation rate for Venus.

The unbroken cloud cover of Venus makes it impossible to see its surface. Spectroscopic determinations of the radial velocities of points on opposite sides of the disk of Venus, as seen from the Earth, seemed to show that the rotational velocity was too small to measure by this method. This meant a probable rotation period of greater than 20 days. If the rotation period were comparable to an Earth-day, Venus should be perceptibly flattened at the poles, i.e. oblate. Numerous precise measurements of Venus showed no oblateness, so on this basis also it appeared that the planet rotated very slowly. This has since been confirmed.

There appeared to be a conflict. Some people said that Venus must rotate slowly, while others claimed that it must rotate quite rapidly, since it does not cool on the night side. (As late as 1959, in a study performed for the U. S. Air Force, Shaw and Bobrovnikoff reiterated the argument that the rotational period of Venus must be no longer than a few weeks, since both the dark and the bright sides emit about the same amount of thermal radiation.) Each view had its supporters, and the discussion was at this point in 1950 when Velikovsky said that *there was no conflict*; Venus rotated slowly, but it was extremely hot.[41]

Velikovsky's suggestion was logical, no matter what explanation might be given for the heat. Not only was it logical; it also turned out to be correct. When this fact was discovered, opponents objected that Velikovsky had failed to specify an exact temperature. They argued that "hot" was a relative term, and since they, too, had expected Venus to be warmer than the Earth, they had also said it would be "hot". However, from what has already been discussed, it is apparent that both sides in the controversy made their positions clear from the start, and no astronomer expected Venus to be extremely hot. If any had, he would have readily accepted Velikovsky's reasonable (and later proven correct) resolution of the apparent conflict between data on rotation and temperatures.

Microwave observations first suggested that Venus did have a high surface temperature, and this has now been confirmed by space probes. It is now thought to be on the order of 750 degrees K. [42] An explanation was needed which would fit the uniformitarian concept, so in 1960 Sagan revived the Wildt suggestion of a greenhouse effect. [43] Sagan estimated the necessary water vapor on Venus to make the greenhouse effect successful. In 1963 Moroz analyzed the reflection spectrum of Venus in the 2-to 2.5-micron range and concluded that this analysis "contradicts the notion of a greenhouse effect due to water vapor". [44]

A number of other scientists objected to the greenhouse theory and demonstrated that the conditions on Venus were not as required for an effective greenhouse mechanism and that the temperatures produced would not be as high as those actually found on Venus. Since the only other theory to consider was Velikovsky's, a "runaway" or "enhanced" greenhouse theory was postulated. [45] The exact physical cause of this was inexplicable, but scientists felt nevertheless that this *must* be the explanation for the high surface temperature of Venus.

CLOUDS

Velikovsky reasoned that if the Venus-Earth encounters left hydrocarbons on the Earth, then the source of the hydrocarbons was probably Venus. Since Venus still has not lost all of its natal heat, its hydrocarbons could still be in a vapor state, and hence some of its clouds may consist at least partly of hydrocarbons. Of all his suggestions about Venus, Velikovsky considered this one to be possibly the most revealing. However, although it has been the most discussed of his ideas about Venus, so far the most revealing results have had to do with human nature.

Although the issue is important, Velikovsky does not rest his entire theory on its outcome, as some scientists have people believe. This was yet another suggestion about what one might reasonably expect to find on Venus if the events he described had actually occurred. It was expressed as an *assumption*: "On the basis of this research, I assume that Venus must be rich in petroleum gases" [46] Also, he said (in 1950) that after certain spectroscopic techniques were developed "the spectrogram of Venus may disclose the presence of hydrocarbon gases in its atmosphere, if these gases lie in the upper part of the atmosphere where the rays of the sun penetrate". [47] (If Oro and Han, as described in Chapter IV, are pursuing the correct path, the hydrocarbons may not have been indigenous to Venus, but caused by the atmospheric interactions. If this is the case, the abundance of hydrocarbons on Venus may be less than Velikovsky originally anticipated.)

Some people will complain about anything; therefore, some have complained that Velikovsky stated this idea as an assumption. However, it seems more logical to call one's assumptions "assumptions" instead of labeling them as facts.

In 1955 Hoyle speculated that hydrocarbons might be abundant on Venus. Many scientists replied that this seemed improbable, but they attempted to follow his line of reasoning. [48] Perhaps this was an attempt to cover all bases: If hydrocarbons are discovered on Venus, Hoyle is right; if hydrocarbons are not found, then Velikovsky is wrong. Either way, "science" has upheld uniformity.

The atmosphere of Venus is composed largely of carbon-dioxide. But this does not tell us much about the clouds. Saying that the clouds cannot contain hydrocarbons because we have detected carbon dioxide in the atmosphere of Venus is like saying that the clouds of Earth cannot be water vapor since the terrestrial atmosphere consists largely of nitrogen.

The clouds of Venus were once firmly believed to be composed of water ice or water vapor. This was partially because of the assumed similarity between Venus and Earth. Even after several dissimilar characteristics became evident, the ice theory survived and eventually came to be regarded as "proven". Sagan once wrote that "..., it has recently been established that the clouds of Venus are indeed made of water". [49]

"Establish" means to make stable or firm, to confirm, to prove, to verify or substantiate, but it also means "to enact or decree by authority". Evidently Velikovsky investigators are not the only ones who believe that Sagan sometimes relies too much on the latter definition, since after his decree several other models for the clouds of Venus came into existence. Two of them were the hydrochloric-acid and the carbon-suboxide models. Hansen and Arking then re-examined the evidence and determined that although these models were not absolutely excluded, the probable validity of either was not very high. They suggested that a new investigation of the cloud composition would be in order. [50] They also noted that the index of refraction eliminates pure water, a point which Velikovsky had made earlier. [51]

One new investigation was by Hapke, who proposed "A Dirty Hydrochloric Acid Model". [52] Rea re-affirmed the deduction that the upper clouds might be of a hydrochloric acid solution. [53] Also, perhaps because of stomach problems related to such clouds, it was then suggested that they contained bicarbonates. [54]

In 1969, Dr. William Plummer, then a member of the Department of Physics and Astronomy at the University of Massachusetts and now a Senior Scientist at Polaroid Corporation, published a report in *Science* in which he concluded that the evidence still supported the idea that the upper clouds consist of ice particles. [55] In the same article, Plummer graciously admitted that Velikovsky had made some successful advance claims, but felt that he had been proven incorrect about the hydrocarbons.

Velikovsky submitted a reply to Plummer, but it was not accepted for publication by *Science*. The reason given was that several reviewers had objected to one of Velikovsky's remarks about the oxidizing properties of Venus' atmosphere; however, the same remark appeared in *Science* the week after Plummer's article. (The idea of an oxidizing lower atmosphere has recently been revived by Rossow of Princeton University. [56]) Velikovsky's reply was later printed in *Pensee* along with Plummer's article. [57]

Velikovsky showed that Plummer's argument was inconclusive for a number of reasons. First, the investigation concerning hydrocarbons was based on three incorrect assumptions about Velikovsky's claims. These are that he stipulated condensed hydrocarbons, that he considered them the only constituent of the clouds, and that the hydrocarbons formed the upper cloud layer. However, Velikovsky's original statement in *Worlds in Collision* makes it clear that he suggested vaporized hydrocarbons which are not necessarily the only constituent and may not be in the upper layers.

Second, Plummer's discussion of the near-infrared, 2.4-micron-wavelength region did not cover all the relevant data, some of which, cited by Velikovsky, would have modified Plummer's conclusion. Velikovsky also noted that during the previous year even Pollack and Sagan had written that the region between 1 and 3 microns in the spectrum of Venus could not be interpreted in terms of a definite compositional makeup.

Third, Plummer's conclusion about the clouds being ice crystals contradicts the evidence from the refractive index of the clouds, which is higher than that of ice. A number of hydrocarbons, however, do have the observed refractive index. Water ice does not explain the yellowish color, but this color is compatable with hydrocarbons. Finally, the low content of water vapor in the atmosphere above the clouds seems incompatible with the ice theory.

The issue of *Pensee* which contained the reprint of the Plummer article and Velikovsky's reply also contained a paper in which Dr. Albert Burgstahler reviewed all available evidence (August, 1973) concerning the clouds of Venus. He mentioned that the measured index of refraction of the clouds is about 1.45 at 0.55 microns, which is too high for water (1.33) or ice (1.31). This value is also incompatible with the hydrochloric acid-solution model, which also fails to explain the absorption bands found in the 9.5 to 11.2-micron region of the spectrum of Venus' atmosphere. Burgstahler pointed out that several other proposed cloud constituents also fail to meet these conditions.

Burgstahler concluded that the then-popular view of the upper cloud layer as being composed of about a 75-percent solution of sulfuric acid was most probably correct. This theory had been advanced by G. T. Sill and developed in 1973 by A. T. Young. The index of refraction matched, and the spectral features in the 7 to 11.5 micron region matched reasonably well.

Burgstahler's paper was followed by one written by Velikovsky reviewing the controversy. Velikovsky included a table composed of quotations from Burgstahler's article. He tabulated remarks about hydrocarbons and sulfuric acid under various subjects treated by Burgstahler. Each column cited evidence which *could* be attributed to hydrocarbons. On the other hand, sulfuric acid *could not* account for certain features in the ultraviolet or *any* of the features of the near infrared region of the spectrum. Burgstahler's article, a representative review of then-accepted opinion, supposedly "proves" that no hydrocarbon exists on Venus. Not only does it fail to do this, but it even more convincingly proves that the upper cloud layer is *not* composed of sulfuric acid.

The following February at the AAAS meeting Sagan said that he had read Velikovsky's reply to Burgstahler and was unimpressed. Sagan still supported the view that the clouds consist of sulfuric acid. (Apparently he no longer felt they were "established" as being water.) However, the next year A. T. Young, whom Burgstahler had mentioned as one of the developers of the sulfuric-acid model, again reviewed the physical and chemical properties of the clouds of Venus and wrote: "none of the currently popular interpretations of cloud phenomena on Venus is consistent with all the data. Either a considerable fraction of the observational evidence is faulty or has been misinterpreted, or the clouds of Venus are much more complex than the current simplistic models." Also: "A sound understanding of the clouds appears to be several years in the future."[58]

Young does not appear to be the only scientist with this view. On April 11, 1975, the Royal Astronomical Society held a joint meeting with the Royal Meteorological Society and the Geological Society to discuss the Mariner 10 results concerning Venus and Mercury. Although one of the participants (Hunt) discussed the possibility of sulfuric acid in the cloud tops, it was clear that it is definitely not known what is closer to the surface.[59]

The question of hydrocarbons is still disputed; however, one of the side issues is not. Referring to the possibility of petroleum fires in Venus' lower atmosphere, Velikovsky noted that such fires would yield water as one product, following which the water would be dissociated in the upper atmosphere, and some of the hydrogen would escape. Therefore, claimed Velikovsky, one would expect to find free oxygen in the upper atmosphere of Venus.

To this Sagan replied that "there is none, as has been clearly shown by ground-based spectroscopic observations."[60] The following month, *Science* carried reports on the findings of Mariner 10. One of the reports contained the following: "The data revealed the presence of significant concentrations of hydrogen, helium, carbon, and oxygen atoms in the upper atmosphere of Venus."[61] The origin of the oxygen may be debatable, and this is not mentioned as support for Velikovsky. This is just another example of Sagan being wrong.

Sagan repeatedly backing the wrong assumption and claiming it as fact can possibly be understood as a misguided attempt to advance science, but it is easier to believe that the advancement he has in mind is personal instead of scientific when he fabricates and perpetuates falsehoods about opposing theories.

APPEARANCE

Russian probes recently soft-landed on Venus and took photographs. These photographs reveal sharp-edged rocks, which were classified as young-looking. The Venera 9 and 10 photos show a young-looking surface that inspired speculation that Venus is in an "*early cool-down phase of evolution rather than in a final stage of suffocation in a thickening atmospheric greenhouse*" (emphasis added). It was suggested that on the evolutionary scale, Venus should be classed with the "young, still living planets."[62]

(In a *Nature* article, Sagan said that the rocks should look young because there should be very little erosion.[63] He also provides a possible explanation of erosion for those rocks that might look old, and he describes a source for rocks that might look young and actually be young. The only case he did not cover was old rocks eroded to look young. It is wise to consider as many cases as possible, but choosing one of the diverse possibilities is not proof that the young looking rocks are not young.)

In 1968 Jastrow and Rasool noted that Venus has many theoretical resemblances to the Earth, but in actuality it is a strikingly different planet.[64] The same year Nobel Prize-winner Libby urged that "only with the greatest reluctance should we relinquish the idea that Earth and Venus, so similar in size and average density, could have similar composition and hence similar volcanic history". [65] We should not, however, be overly reluctant to consider that the histories of the two did not start at the same time. Books are filled with speculations about conditions and events in the early history of the Earth, while we may have been ignoring a laboratory example of early Earth conditions just one orbit over.

MARS

Mars had at least one major encounter with Venus and several more with the Earth-Moon system. Mars is considerably smaller than Venus or Earth; therefore, Mars should have special surface features attributable to these encounters. Velikovsky specifically discussed certain likely features, and there are other characteristics of Mars which are reasonable under his model but which he did not mention explicitly. Some of these characteristics are not easily explained in terms of uniformitarian concepts.

ANGULAR MOMENTUM AND LINEAMENTS

Angular momentum is a relationship between the mass and the distribution of mass in a body and the spin rate of that body. At the 1974 AAAS meeting, as additional evidence allegedly attesting to a long and stable history of the solar system, J. D. Mulholland mentioned "a smooth sequence of angular momentum as a function of mass which is satisfied by nearly all of the planets... (and) can

only be related to the formation of the entire system..."[66]
Here is an opinion stated as fact. A review of current literature reveals that the smooth function is only smooth if
certain information is thrown out in order to make it
smooth. Even Mulholland admitted that Mercury, Venus,
the Moon and Mars were not considerate enough to conform to the theory. Colombo observes that although Mercury, the Moon and several satellites of Jupiter have odd
angular momenta, the behaviors of Venus and Mars are
much more difficult to explain.[67]

Surface cracks which tend to be straight for extended
distances are called lineaments. Analysis of Mariner 4
photographs of Mars reveals a well-defined system of
lineaments. In only eight frames sent back by the early
Mars probe, about 160 lineaments are apparent. Binder
remarked: "The presence of these lineaments may indicate
that Mars has lost appreciable angular momentum during
its history."[68] Later, Fish noted: "The means by which
Mars could have decelerated presents a problem."[69]

Mariner 6 and 7 supplied additional evidence of lineaments. In contrast to the Mariner 4 data, these later photographs contained great numbers of readily discernible
linear features. Binder and McCarthy say that these data
"demonstrate that the lineaments are expressions of real
elements of surface structure that have systematic, pre-
ferential trends."[70] These structures are also found on the
Moon and Earth, and on all three bodies they are similarly oriented with respect to the axes of rotation. Binder suggests that all of them may be due to the loss of rotational
angular momentum. Additionally, he notes that the loss
for Mars cannot be accounted for by tidal interactions
between Mars and its satellites Phobos and Deimos, or
with the Sun, and other mechanisms must be sought.

CANALS

These lineaments, which are too small to be seen with Earth-based telescopes, should not be confused with the so-called "canals" of Mars. Schiaparelli, in 1877 and 1879, announced the discovery of a great number of fine, dark, straight lines crossing portions of Mars. He called the lines "canali" (channels) and in 1881 he announced that many of these became double at times, like the parallel tracks of a railway. In 1892 and 1894, Pickering and Douglass also reported canals on Mars. Later, doubt began to arise about the existence of the canals. At one extreme was Lowell, who saw a complex network of over 400 canals extending with geometrical precision over both the ruddy and the darker regions of Mars. At the opposite extreme was Barnard, who, during years of observation with some of the then-greatest existing telescopes, never saw any trace of such a system of fine geometrical lines, although at times he saw a few short, diffused, hazy lines and a couple of long, hazy, parallel streamers. There were some observers in between who saw a few canals and a few hazy lines. All of these accounts represent the mature judgments of trained and experienced observers after long and careful study of Mars under favorable viewing conditions. However, their conflicting interpretations cannot all be correct. *Science* refers to the period of discussion of the "canals" as an "embarrassing epoch for American science..."[71]

Many people liked to think of the "canals" as evidence of extinct or extant higher life forms on Mars. Although this view was often expressed in popular stories, probably most serious investigators by 1950 no longer considered this as the most reasonable interpretation. Velikovsky was among those who felt this way. He reasoned that since Mars is less than two tenths the size of Venus, the Venus-Mars encounter would have been more destructive to Mars. He wrote in *Worlds in Collision* that if there were any "canals" on Mars they were not constructed by intelligent beings, but rather were "... a result of the play of geological forces that answered with rifts and cracks the outer forces acting in collisions".[72]   Sixteen years later, Opik said: "The canals may be cracks in the crust, radiating from the points of impact of colliding materials."[73]

SURFACE BLEMISHES

Close approaches by other planets could also be expected to produce large perturbations of the surface of Mars. Velikovsky did not explicitly suggest large mountains on Mars, but it is interesting to note that opponents to his work explicitly suggested just the opposite. Lowell estimated that no mountain as high as 750 meters was present on Mars.[74]   Later Slipher, an astronomer at Lowell Observatory, said that certain observations "... prove conclusively that there are no high mountains on Mars, and that the surface is surprisingly flat."[75] (Notice the use of the word "high". Is this any more definite than "hot"? As with Velikovsky's "hot", some indication of a lower limit was discernible from consideration of other available information.)

Later radar studies by Goldstein indicated that 13,000-meter variations exist between peaks and valleys on Mars.[76] Also Mariner 9 photographs of Mars displayed a "super Volcano" some 24,000 meters high. It is nearly 500 kilometers (310 miles) wide at the base and 65 kilometers (24 miles) wide at the top. Slipher, however, was in good company in the matter of inaccurately determining the morphology of the Martian surface. According to *Sky and Telescope*, the Martian surface relief deduced by Sagan and Pollack was quite "uncorrelated with the actual Martian topography."[77]

Again Velikovsky did not explicitly predict the discovery of volcanoes on Mars, but their presence is not surprising considering the circumstances he described for Mars' recent history. Also, continuing activity on Mars even today would not be surprising, and Mariner 9 data indicate that "weathering and volcanic activity are taking place on Mars to a significant degree."[78] This was unanticipated by uniformitarian theorists.

Dale R. Hankin, the editor of *Modern Astronomy*, writes: "as recently as the 1950's and early 1960's persons who proposed that *any* volcanic activity on Mars *may* exist were treated as 'oddies' of the astronomical community". He further states that records of observations of Mars during the last 100 years contain evidence which may easily be interpreted as indicating possible volcanic activity on Mars. Since much of this work was done by amateurs, professionals preferred to ignore it; it did not readily coincide with uniformitarian theory. However, when professionals did study Mars seriously, they made the same observations as the amateurs.[79]

HEAT

Some scientists have claimed that Velikovsky predicted that Mars would be found to emit more heat than it receives from the Sun. They further argue that his theory must be wrong, since Mars is "known" to be at its equilibrium temperature.

First, Velikovsky made no such prediction; second, his entire theory cannot be made to depend on this point; and third, it is questionable that Mars is actually at equilibrium.

In *Worlds in Collision* Velikovsky referred to certain astronomical measurements which indicated that Mars emits more heat than it receives from the sun. This would not be expected if Mars had actually been at peace in its present orbit for billions of years. He reasoned, however, that *if* the measurements were correct, then Mars must have acquired so much heat during its recent encounters that it still radiates excess heat. This was not a prediction, but simply an explanation proposed for a reported observation.

More recent data tend to indicate that Mars may emit more heat than it receives from the Sun, while other measurements seem to indicate otherwise. Unfortunately, Mars seems to be near enough to an equilibrium point that the measurements are not sufficiently precise to settle the issue. To illustrate the problem, let us assume that the equilibrium temperature for Mars is exactly -46 degrees C.[80] If the actual temperature is -45 or -44 degrees C., then Mars is emitting more heat than it receives from the sun. However, the measurements are rarely better than plus or minus a few degrees and are sometimes plus or minus as much as 30 degrees.[81] So measurements which are claimed to demonstrate that Mars is in thermal equilibrium really only demonstrate that it is close to equilibrium. If nothing had happened to Mars in several billion years, then it would be quite reasonable to expect it to be at its equilibrium temperature, but rough measurements cannot be used to prove that Mars has been untouched for billions of years.

When depth probes become possible on Mars, it should not be surprising to find heat flowing out of Mars.

RED

The reddish atmosphere of Mars may be caused by an iron oxide called limonite. Binder says that this mineral could not have formed under present conditions on Mars, and conditions must have been different in the past.[82] Perhaps the Red Planet acquired this characteristic by the same process that brought about the name change to the Red Sea (see *Worlds in Collision*).

Dollfus proposed that the red material was limonite.[83]
Sharonov agreed that large portions of Mars are covered
with silt consisting of very fine particles of limonite. He
also noted that "The broad abundance of sizable masses
of limonite silt on the surface of Mars, of course, is itself
a circumstance that demands explanation."[84] Moroz analyzed the 0.4 to 4-micron region of the spectrum of Mars
and concluded that the data were in agreement with the
reflection spectra of limonites.[85] Binder and Cruikshank
also performed infrared analysis which supported this
suggestion.[86] Fish mentions that certain polarization
studies indicate that a significant part of the Martian surface material is limonite.[87] Later, Binder conceded that
the dust may be limonite (and this is supported by the
Viking lander), but repeated that it could not form in the
present Martian atmosphere. He concluded that the atmosphere must have been different in the past.[88]

The atmosphere of Mars probably was different in the
past, but the limonite may not have originally formed on
Mars.

ARGON

In 1946 Velikovsky suggested that the atmosphere of
Mars might contain large amounts of argon and neon.
This basic suggestion was repeated in *Worlds in Collision*.
It was widely used as "proof" that Velikovsky was wrong,
until 1974. Then Soviet Mars probes indicated that the
Martian atmosphere may contain "tens of percent" of argon. Later Kaplan said that the presence of argon could
be inferred from pressure broadening of carbon-dioxide
lines.[89] Also, Levine and Riegler revived Harrison
Brown's suggestion about radioactive decay producing
argon and claimed that as much as 28 percent argon
could be produced in the Martian atmosphere by this
method. Even more striking is that Moroz, a Russian

astronomer, conducted a combined analysis of infrared and ultraviolet spectrometic observations and other measurements of the Martian atmosphere and concluded that "all these data indicate an argon abundance of 25% to 35% in the Martian atmosphere." [90] All of this occurred after it was claimed for over twenty years that there was no justification for expecting the atmosphere of Mars to contain argon.

While some scientists were claiming that there was no justification for this suggestion, other scientists were making the same suggestion. Harrison Brown discussed the argon content of the atmosphere in relation to the radioactive decay of potassium into argon. He stated, "In the case of Mars, it might well be that argon is the major atmospheric constituent." [91]

Some people repeated the idea of Mars possibly having a large percentage of argon, but the suggestion was not widely accepted. In 1952, Urey said, "Mars has a substantial atmosphere, probably of argon and nitrogen." [92] No reference was given, so it is difficult to determine if this was a guess on his part or if he had read the works of Velikovsky or the later work of Brown. (It is hard to tell what Urey meant by substantial. It is also hard to tell whether the argon was supposed to be a substantial part of the substantial atmosphere, or nitrogen the substantial part, with argon as a minor constituent. All this from someone who complains that Velikovsky fails to provide exact calculations and numerical estimates.)

Soviet measurements indicated that the polar regions of Mars may contain large percentages of the argon, causing a depletion in other regions of the planet. Viking I measurements indicate one to two percent argon at its location. It is not now known if this is the average percentage in the Martian atmosphere, or if the Soviet measurements are correct and this is one of the depleted areas.

Velikovsky did not discuss the origin of the argon on Mars. He only suggested that some of the original argon on Mars was removed by the Earth and Moon. Some scientists have recently suggested that theortically Mars should have more than one or two percent argon in its atmosphere. If it does not now, perhaps it did only several thousand years ago. (See KRONOS II, #1, p. 105, 1976 for more details about the Martian atmosphere.)

LIFE

It has long been fashionable to speculate about life on Mars. Velikovsky did not really venture into this area, but it is clear that if life does exist there, the life is not necessarily indigenous to Mars.

Experiments support the possibility of life on Mars. In 1963, some experimentalists investigating this concluded that complex organisms could exist on Mars. In some cases they noted that "very high levels of ultraviolet radiation were required to suppress the growth of higher plants."[93] (In their experiments, they used gaseous mixtures containing very high percentages of argon.) In 1965, Abelson concluded that abiogenic synthesis on Mars is extremely unlikely.[94] Life not originating on Mars does not mean that it does not exist there.

PHOBOS AND DEIMOS

Mars has two satellites, Phobos and Deimos. Velikovsky noted that the orbital revolution rates of these moons were very close to the rates described in a fictional narrative written before the moons were seen with a telescope. He suggested that the author, Jonathan Swift, may have had access to writings containing information from ancient texts and that some ancients may have determined the rates from actual observations. The data would have been taken when Mars approached Earth after Mars was damaged by Venus and its elongated tail.

Mariner and Viking photographs reveal that the moons are irregularly shaped, heavily cratered objects. They appear not to be composed of unusual material, though Sagan, in 1966, said that the idea that they may be artificial satellites "merits serious consideration." [95]   Certainly Velikovsky's careful research about the recent history of the Solar System has always warranted more serious consideration than idle supposition about spacemen.

Viking Orbiter photographs of Phobos show pronounced striations covering more than half of the area of the part of the satellite visible in the pictures. The cause of the striations is unknown, but a member of the Jet Propulsion Laboratory *speculated* about various possibilities. Two of the suggested causes of the striations were Phobos passing through a *cloud of debris* and a large part of Phobos *breaking off in some ancient cataclysm.* [96]

MERCURY

In an unpublished book, Velikovsky describes pre-1500 B.C. events. Stories from that time are more fragmented and nebulous than later ones; hence, there is more theorizing about what actually took place. Because of this, Velikovsky decided to publish the work after the ideas expressed in *Worlds in Collision* had been more adequately investigated. However, the conclusions he reaches are not based on material so vague that each investigator will obtain totally different opinions about what happened during that time. Other researchers have independently arrived at some of the same conclusions. [97]

Mercury was involved in some of these pre-1500 B.C. events. Since this area is opening more for discussion, some characteristics of Mercury will be mentioned.

The history of man's understanding of just one of these properties demonstrates that *although scientists may agree among themselves on a given conclusion, that conclusion may still be erroneous.*

ORBIT

Since Velikovsky believes that Mercury was involved in certain of the Earth's recent catastrophic events, he naturally concludes that Mercury has occupied its present orbit only since recent times. This may never be proven one way or the other, but it is worthwhile to re-emphasize that recently (1975) astronomers also suggested that Mercury is not in its original orbit. (Chapter IV) These investigators probably do not believe Mercury acquired its present orbit recently, but as Bass has shown, the long time span normally assumed necessary for orbit changes is open to question.

SPIN

Mercury goes around the Sun in 88 days. Before 1965 the period of rotation of Mercury about its spin axis was also thought to be 88 days. This would give Mercury a resonant orbit in which one side of the planet always faced the Sun. The Moon is in a similar situation, in that it always turns the same face toward the Earth. This was thought to be the case for Mercury since the last century, when Schiaparelli concluded that it had an 88-day period.

The planet's surface is visible in photographs, and identifying land marks appear to exist. The 88-day period of rotation fit nicely with the uniformitarian concept, and since it was officially blessed, later photographic studies appeared to confirm the result. However, recent radar investigations have indicated that Mercury's period of rotation is actually only about 58.65 days. Since then, the photographic evidence has been *re-interpreted* and, surprisingly, the analysis confirms a 58.65 day period.[98]

It has also suddenly been discovered that the 88-day value was only one solution to an equation used in the analysis; another, previously ignored solution fits the 58.65 day period.

ASYMMETRIC CRATERING

Another surprising observation about Mercury, although one not at all inconsistent with Velikovsky's ideas, is that the planet exhibits a hemispherically nonuniform distribution of surface features. With this evidence it becomes apparent that the Moon, Mars and Mercury all have both cratered and lava-flooded hemispheres. This coincides well with the idea of near-encounters among these planets. However, it has been pointed out that this requires re-evaluation of theories about the Moon, since the asymmetry there is attributed to its orbital resonance with the Earth.[99]

HEAT

Because of its near-contact with other planets in the

past, Velikovsky suggested that Mercury could have undergone some heating during these encounters, and if it has not had enough time to come into equilibrium with its surroundings, its night side could be unexpectedly warm. Results to date are inconclusive. If Mercury actually had recent near-encounters with other planets, it may have been heated so little that it quickly radiated away the excess heat. If it still has some residual heat from those encounters, the measurements may not be refined enough to reveal it.

ATMOSPHERE

A suggestion by Velikovsky about Mercury that appears to have been confirmed is that Mercury has an atmosphere. This was unexpected from the uniformitarian standpoint, because Mercury, which is even smaller than Mars, does not have enough mass to retain an atmosphere. However, Mariner 10 data indicate that Mercury does have an atmosphere, extremely thin, but greater than expected. It is interesting to note that Velikovsky was not the only one to expect an atmosphere on Mercury. Many amateur astronomers reported an atmosphere on Mercury before the Mariner 10 results. However, since they were only amateurs and could not be expected to understand physics, it was explained to them that "theory" does not allow an atmosphere. What was thought to be an atmosphere by a non-professional observer was called an optical illusion by those who understood the theory.

Numerous *ad hoc* explanations have since appeared for the existence of this atmosphere. The first Mariner reports about Mercury having an atmosphere appeared early in 1974, and soon after, *Nature* published a theoretical explanation for the existence of the atmosphere.[100] The author concluded that there *should* be a tenuous atmosphere on Mercury and that it should be basically composed of hydrogen. He also said, "any helium and argon released by radioactivity would become trapped in this atmosphere and should be detected."

Consequently, in a few short weeks we went from the *proven* conclusion that Mercury "could have retained no atmosphere"[101] to observation of an atmosphere and having a nice theoretical explanation for its existence.

EFFECT FROM CHARGE ON THE SUN

In 1952, Menzel calculated that for certain of Velikovsky's suggestions to be valid, enough excess charge for a surface potential of 10^{19} volts would be needed on the Sun. For this discussion, it does not matter if Menzel was correct in his assertions.[102] What is important is that Menzel said this much charge on the Sun was impossible, and he implied that no sane physicists would make such a suggestion. Others have stated that if the Sun possessed this much charge, the orbit of Mercury would be drastically affected.

In 1960, Bailey, a physicists from Australia, said that several astronomical phenomenon could be explained by assuming stars had a net negative charge. Further, he calculated that there may be enough charge on the sun to give it a surface potential of around 10^{19} volts. Bailey did not know of Menzel's work or of the Velikovsky controversy. Bailey and Menzel both obtaining the same figure was coincidence. However, Menzel asked Bailey to retract his theory since it was hurting the efforts of Menzel and other American scientists to discredit Velikovsky.[103]

Bailey did not appreciate being asked to abandoned his theory merely to accomodate anti-Velikovsky forces. Bailey died before his scheduled trip to the United States where he hoped to perform experiments to test his theory. Later, Burman, who was familiar with the work of Bailey, considered what effect a solar charge of this magnitude would have on the perihelion motion of Mercury. He concluded that this amount of charge would have no significant effect.[104]

THE MOON

The Moon, because of its proximity to the Earth, was also involved in the catastrophic events of the past as described by Velikovsky in *Worlds in Collision*. The observations of the ancients suggest that the Moon may have been affected by the passages of both Venus and Mars. Velikovsky, believing that he had reconstructed an accurate account of what the ancients actually observed, made a number of suggestions concerning evidence of these encounters to be found on the Moon.

All of these suggestions were made before the first manned lunar landing, and many of them before anyone thought seriously of going to the Moon.[105] Velikovsky maintained that remanent magnetism would be found in the lunar rocks, that there would be a measurable outflow of heat from the interior to the surface, and that an excess of argon would be found in lunar materials. Additional observations involved dating results by certain dating methods, bubbles formed at the surface, moonquakes, traces of carbides, and areas of localized radioactivity. Each of these ideas defied prevailing opinion about the Earth's natural satellite.

REMANENT MAGNETISM

A remanent magnetic field is a field induced in a rocky material by an external magnetic field and left in it after the external field has decayed or been removed. When the temperature of molten rock drops below its Curie temperature, while the rock is in the presence of an external magnetic field, certain molecules which have been lined up by the field are frozen into alignment. (If ferromagnetic materials are raised above a certain critical temperature called the Curie temperature, the magnetic alignment is disturbed and the materials become paramagnetic. The paramagnetic susceptibility aligns the particles with the existing external fields, if any are present, and upon cooling below the Curie temperature the new ferromagnetic ordering is frozen in as an artifact of the disturbing fields. The Curie temperature for iron is 1043K.) After cooling reaches the Curie temperature, the external field can be completely removed, and the frozen-in magnetism will be retained almost indefinitely. Hence, proper measurements can give an indication of the direction and strength of the external magnetic field at the time of cooling.

Several months before the first manned lunar landing, *Nature* published a note stating that no remanent magnetism was expected in the lunar rocks.[106]Velikovsky held the opposite view. He felt that if the Moon had been involved in catastrophes during historical times and earlier, some of its melted rocks would have cooled below their Curie temperatures while still immersed in magnetic fields. Therefore, he suggested that the orientation of the rock samples, with respect to the lunar cardinal points, be marked. However, this was not done, since remanent magnetism was not expected under accepted theories.

Researchers were quite surprised when they discovered remanent magnetism in the first rocks returned to Earth from the Moon. Diverse theories for the origin of the effect were suggested. They were based on postulates which included an internal lunar field, a time in the past when the Moon and the Earth were close together, fields in the transporting spacecraft, and fields in the laboratory.[107]It was eventually concluded that the magnetism actually was indigenous to the Moon and not an artifact due to the environment or handling of the rocks after they were picked up from the lunar surface.

In a letter sent to Harold Urey, Nobel laureate and geochemist, friends of Velikovsky mentioned that the latter had expected such a finding. Urey, in reply, said that conventional scientists had expected everything that Velikovsky had suggested.[108]

Urey's statement is incompatible with those of other scientists, and even contradicts his own later remarks. In May, 1973, Urey coauthored an article with E. K. Runcorn, opening with this sentence: "One of the most unexpected discoveries of the Apollo program has been that the returned rocks, both crystalline and breccia, possess a stable remanent magnetic field."[109]

In an unsigned *Nature* article (1974) about the changing views of the Moon's magnetism, Fuller's review of the subject was mentioned. It is stated in this article that it is "historically quite correct to suggest," as does Fuller, that before the manned lunar landings "the Moon was generally regarded as 'magnetically uninteresting'." Furthermore, it is recalled that most measurements made during the ten years before the landing indicated that the Moon was magnetically inert, and this was "a result entirely in accord with preconceived ideas about the nature of magnetism in planetary bodies in general and about the nature of the Moon in particular."[110]

By the time the Fourth Lunar Science Conference convened in 1973, the problem still existed. One report stated: "How the lunar rocks came to be magnetized, however, is not easily explained." And later: "It is very hard to rationalize the existence of this field." (The field in this case being the one required to produce the remanent magnetism.)[111]

The dynamo theory is often called upon to explain the origin of a magnetic field on the Moon. This is the same theory used to explain the Earth's present magnetic field. It should be remembered that even the experts do not agree that the dynamo process has properly been explained. Therefore, when one reads a statement concerning the dynamo theory, e.g., "if the moon had an internal magnetic field produced in the same way as the earth's," it should be kept in mind that we do not really know how the Earth's is produced. Even invoking this theory, however, has resulted in the suggestion that "a lunar dynamo is not a tenable explanation for the magnetic remanence observed on the moon."[112]

In 1976, Gold and Soter even proposed that the magnetism in the lunar rocks was created by *cometary impacts* on the Moon![113] The fields on Mercury and Mars were also attributed to encounters of this nature.

Whatever the eventual explanation, large amounts of paper have been consumed in printing explanations of something that was not generally expected from theories other than Velikovsky's.

THERMAL GRADIENT

Because of the cosmic violence to which the Moon was subjected in historical times, Velikovsky suggested that heat should still be flowing strongly from the interior to the surface. This was not the generally held view, although one Russian measurement from space indicated this possibility. [114] Urey, at best, tended toward exaggeration when he insisted that this, too, was what everybody expected. [115] Urey's own theory of the origin of the Moon, which lunar research has now shown to be invalid, would not necessarily indicate this either. Some theorists expected a

slight heat flow due to internal radioactivity but the measured heat flow is much greater than expected even from
this process.

ARGON

Velikovsky's work led him to believe that argon may
be an important component of the atmosphere of Mars.
(On argon in the Martian atmosphere, see KRONOS, Vol.
I, No. 3, Fall, 1975, pp. 88-90.) Assuming this conclusion
to be valid, he reasoned that interactions of the Moon with
Mars could have left argon in excessive amounts on the
Moon; and this would then yield anomalously high ages
for samples dated by the potassium-argon method.

In fact, this very problem did arise concerning the
lunar samples. It has since been relegated to near-obscurity,
but investigators were initially shocked at the "unexpected"
excess argon.

The first manned lunar landing was in July of 1969.
By September of the same year, reports indicating that
argon was creating problems in dating the last major
activity on the Moon were already appearing in print.
It was found that the breccias and fines held extremely
large quantities of rare gases. It was conceded that "the
age determined from K-Ar (potassium-argon) dating is
both intrinsically and experimentally uncertain."[116]

Later, it was noted, in connection with a sample designated as a type C breccia, that "this material contained
very large quantities of both 36Ar and 40Ar and consequently it has not been possible to calculate a realistic
age for the sample..."[117] Remarks about "embarrassingly
high" (more than 7 billion years) K-Ar ages were published.[118]

Eventually came recognition of a new puzzle about the
Moon - the origin of the Argon 40. Some evidence seemed

to indicate that at least portions of the rare gases "appear to be surface-correlated in the soil fragments" -- the greater the ratio of surface area to volume for a given sample, the greater would be its "excess" of argon as a fraction of its total mass.

It was suggested that the most likely origin of these absorbed, or trapped gases, was the solar wind or solar cosmic rays; however, it was also noted that in some cases the "ratios of elements in the sample differ significantly from the solar values..." Funkhouser and his colleagues stated: "The large amounts of rare gases found in the soil and breccia indicate that the solar atmosphere is trapped in the lunar soil, as no other source of such large amounts of gas is known."[119] So, although its composition was incorrect, the solar wind shouldered the blame by default.

The solar-wind theory, however, was short lived. By July, 1970, the solar wind had become only a secondary aid in explanations dealing with an excess of rare gases on the Moon. Scientists tended to veer toward the suggestion that the argon 40 was a result of potassium decay inside the Moon. The argon 40 supposedly had diffused outward, escaped into the tenuous lunar atmosphere, and then been driven back into the soils by the force of collisions with particles in the solar wind.

Measurements have indicated that argon 40 varies in concentration in the thin lunar atmosphere. It is recognized that some of the trapped argon 40 is gas from the lunar "atmosphere". But the original source of most of the argon 40 on the Moon can still be debated. It is noteworthy that "the ratios (^{40}Ar/^{36}Ar) vary in such a way as to suggest that Ar 40 was more abundant in the ancient lunar atmosphere than it is now."[120]

The greater abundance of argon 40, suggested for the past, is consistent with Velikovsky's reconstruction of the recent history of the Solar System.

AGE OF THE MOON

It may seem that the previously discussed character-istics of the Moon are individually ignored, though Veli-kovsky accurately anticipated each of them. Actually, they are not individually ignored; but they are collective-ly ignored because of interpretations of other lunar data related to the age of the Moon.

According to conventional thinking, nothing important has happened to the Moon in several billion years; hence, some conclude that it does not matter how many individual lunar discoveries Velikovsky predicted, since these features, however surprising, could not have been acquired recently.

Two things make this conclusion questionable. First, the *age* of the Moon is often confused with the time that something last happened there. Second, the dating methods and the interpretation of the results are assumed to be un-assailably accurate. As we shall see, there is good reason to re-evaluate the basic assumptions of radioactive dating.

Velikovsky has never ventured to conjecture about the actual *age* of the Moon. Two accepted dating methods (uranium-lead and rubidium-strontium) give such an *age* (accurate or not) for the Moon. Approximately the same "age" is indicated by still a third method (potassium-argon) supposedly capable of determining when something cata-strophic last happened there. Collectively, then, results of these dating methods are misinterpreted as three indepen-dent demonstrations that nothing has happened on the Moon for at least three and a half billion years.

(In the 19th century, the great Lord Kelvin "had three arguments for the age of the earth: the first argument was based on the supposed age of the sun, the second was based on the time required for the earth to cool to its pre-sent temperature from a molten state, and the third was based on the secular acceleration of the moon and the accompanying slowing of the earth's rotation caused by the friction of the tides. All three methods employed *un-proved assumptions* and very shaky estimates; neverthe-less they *conveniently agreed on the age of the earth"* (emphasis added). Many notable scientists worked very hard to bring their figures into agreement with the "ac-cepted" value put forth by Kelvin; and "even if it was not a case of 'fudging', it still took a lot of lively imagination for all those different scientists using different dubious methods to come up with the same erroneous results.")[121]

The methods most commonly applied to lunar dating involve determinations of uranium-lead, rubidium-stron-tium, and potassium-argon ratios. The last, however, is the only method which yields an estimate of the time since a sample was *last heated or shocked*. Should heating or shock occur, all of the decay product - argon - may escape, and the radioactive timer may then be turned back, or reset, to zero.

Conversely, a later addition of argon can make a sample appear older. This problem has been encountered on the Earth. Hypothetical *ages* of millions of years have been "found" for materials with known ages of mere hundreds of years. [122] York, for one, has admitted that the excess argon on the Moon "complicated" the potassium-argon method, but claimed that if you assume the "correction" factors to be correct, then all three methods give about the same ages. [123]

Consequently, there is only *one* method for determining the elapsed time since the last catastrophe on the Moon, and this method is given credence only because it gives results similar to two methods which reputedly give the *age* of the Moon. Unfortunately, in addition to the general problems associated with radioactive dating, the two other methods also have specific problems similar to that men-tioned about potassium-argon dating.

If the abundance ratio of the elements in question is changed, a different *age* is indicated. Such a change can be effected by either decreasing or increasing the abundance of one of the elements with respect to the other. For example, if a sample is heated, some fraction of one of the elements may vaporize and escape into the environment.

Were a sample containing uranium and lead heated to a temperature where the lead would vaporize, some of the lead would leave the sample, to recondence elsewhere. At the site of recondensation, there would be a deposit of lead without apparent uranium antecedents. A sample from such a deposit would appear much older than it actually was. Lead, with no associated uranium (or thorium) is called parentless lead.

Parentless lead has been found on the Moon. [124] This has been attributed to "an important thermal episode" on the Moon about 850 million years ago. This is still a long way from the recent; however, the date is not guaranteed, and it is also a long way from three and a half billion years, the figure generally invoked as the time when the Moon was last significantly active. Apparently, statements to the effect that there is no evidence for anything important happening on the Moon for more than three billion years are based on ignorance of such findings and selective acceptance of laboratory results.

Wright has discussed the vaporization problem with respect to the rubidium-strontium dating technique. [125] He noted that the vapor-pressures of rubidium and strontium differ greatly. The high temperatures reached during the long lunar days easily surpass that at which rubidium would vaporize and migrate to cooler places. Therefore, even normal conditions on the Moon necessarily make dating the formation of the Moon by this method highly questionable.

In fact, all lunar dating techniques are so questionable that the collective rejection of Velikovsky's correct predictions about the Moon is entirely untenable. One questionable method of dating the last major lunar event is not enough to refute a theory which successfully anticipated several important discoveries that were totally unexpected by uniformitarian thinkers.

One dating method not yet mentioned is that based on "thermoluminescence". If carefully applied, and if the quality of the material is suitable, this technique can give an estimate of the time that has passed since the material was last heated or shocked. Even the normal variation in temperatures on the lunar surface is enough to affect material to a depth of around six inches. Therefore, samples must be taken from cores collected at greater depths in the lunar soil. Methods of extracting cores may affect test results, thereby rendering them inconclusive. However, some tests do indicate that a disturbance may have occurred on the Moon on the order of ten thousand years ago. [126] The exact nature, cause, and extent of this event are not known.

BUBBLES

Velikovsky made several other suggestions about the Moon, but these are not so uniquely associated with his cosmological theory. The domes on the Moon are a case in point.

It has been proposed that some of these domes may have resulted from outgassing and bubbling on the lunar surface when it was heated. Many of these domes have been observed on the Moon, although their origin is still in doubt. Two small domes are shown in a NASA photograph of the Alphonsus and Fra Mauro area. [127] Another Apollo photograph reveals a "smooth dome" in the center of crater Behaim. [128]

Several scientists have discussed the formation of craters on the Moon by a bubbling effect. Sukhanov stated that a number of craters evidently had this type of origin. [129] Ronea proposed that craters range from impact craters, through impact craters changed by volcanism, to completely volcanic craters. [130] Mills discussed a process called fluidization, whereby craters are formed by an upward flow of gas or liquid. [131] This process requires less heating than the volcanic model.

Velikovsky had claimed that the existing domes would be found to have been caused by bubbling and, although the domes were known to exist, he was in good company in offering his explanation for the domes (unburst bubbles) and certain craters (burst bubbles).

Juergens discussed an alternate proposal for the origin of some of the craters, but he noted that the concept that *some* craters are burst bubbles is of entirely peripheral importance to the ideas presented in *Worlds in Collision.*[132]

Whatever the origin of the craters, there appears to be no question that the Moon once had "a heat problem". "Evidently the part of the moon we have access to has been completely melted at one time or another."[133] In discussing the heating of the outermost layers of the Moon (hundreds of kilometers in depth), the Lunar Sample Analysis Planning Team noted that "the source of heat for such an event is poorly understood." This heating "is thought to have occurred during or immediately after the formation of that body, *chiefly because of the difficulty of accounting for extensive near-surface melting at a later time*" (emphasis added). [134]

The same team has also discussed the chemical content of the lunar rocks and a possible explanation for the distribution and percentage of the various components. It was duly noted, however, that their "solution of the chemical problem creates a difficulty in the area of heat generation." Calculations based upon uniformitarian models indicate a particular type of cooling distribution, and "temperatures would not rise again in a sub-crustal layer or zone unless some external source of energy was involved."

MOONQUAKES

Velikovsky also suggested that moonquakes would still be frequent as the lunar body continued to recover from the recent violence in the Solar System. However, he said only that quakes would be numerous and did not suggest that they would be of great magnitude; indeed, the quakes are exceedingly small, and most would not be detectable on the Earth. Their magnitudes are easily within the limits expected by Y. Nakamura and others. [135] Some are, however, attributed to the release of strain, and the origin of some of that strain would have been due to the encounters described in *Worlds in Collision.*

(Because known periodic meteoroid showers are not detected, a writer for *Nature* recently raised the question about whether the seismometers are actually measuring what they are intended to measure.) [136]

CARBIDES

If, in addition to the Earth, hydrocarbons also rained on the Moon from the proto-planet Venus, during close encounters with that body, Velikovsky reasoned that remnants of this material would later have been heated, possibly forming carbides. In fact, both hydrocarbons and carbides have been found on the Moon. [137] While the amounts detected were relatively small, the actual sources of this material are still open to debate.

RADIOACTIVITY

Velikovsky suggested that electrical discharges between planets and the Moon were powerful enough to have produced localized hot-spots of radioactivity. In particular, he anticipated that one hot-spot should be in the vicinity of Aristarchus. It has been shown that lightning discharges in the Earth's atmosphere produce radioactive carbon, so it is reasonable to assume that stronger discharges can produce other radioactive materials.

Localized hot-spots of radioactivity have been found on the Moon, and one of these locations is indeed the region of Aristarchus. Gamma-ray spectrometer measurements made by Apollo 15 and 16 instruments indicated that the Aristarchus region was one of three locations showing enhanced radioactivity. In addition, the alpha-particle spectrometer on Apollo 15 detected a high count rate in this region. The alpha spectrometer was designed to detect radon decay and identify regions of "unusual activity".[138] After considering various possibilities, the investigators attributed the alpha-particle activity to increased emanation of radon-222.

Radon-222 has a half-life of 3.8 days and is a daughter of radium-226, which has a half-life of 1620 years. Juergens has pointed out that "if the radium were produced by an electric discharge to the Aristarchus site some 2700 years ago, more than 25 percent of it would still be there, emitting radon-222."[139]

Chapter VI

DATING METHODS

AND

MISAPPLICATIONS

We have already seen that problems can arise with various dating methods (Moon section, Chapter V). If one assumes that a given element decays at a constant rate, there are still numerous ways that the data can be misinterpreted, and there are many conditions which can arise that make the data meaningless. To complicate the situation even more, recent investigations have led to the questioning of the validity of the assumption of a constant decay rate. This rate is assumed to be constant over billions of years, but it actually may be effectively constant over a much shorter period of time.

This problem appears to cause only a small percentage of the error that arises in carbon dating, so for the first part of the discussion of carbon dating, it will be assumed that the decay "constant" is a constant. The technique of carbon dating will be discussed, and then some applications of the method will be given. Also included, is a review of the ASH correspondence, a series of letters concerning Velikovsky's attempts to have carbon dating applied to Egyptian artifacts. After the discussion of carbon dating, other techniques will be mentioned with respect to the "constant" that may not be constant.

CARBON DATING METHOD

In 1952, Dr. W. F. Libby published an account of the development of a new technique for dating the time since the death of previously living matter. In 1960 he, very deservingly, received the Nobel Prize for his pioneering efforts in this field. Libby reprinted a review article about this method in *Pensee*.[1] Some of his major points will be given in the next few paragraphs.

Carbon 14 is a radioactive form of carbon, and it is produced by cosmic rays in the atmosphere. Living matter assimilates carbon 14 along with regular carbon 12. If the ratio of carbon 14 to carbon 12 in the atmosphere remains constant, then the ratio will also remain constant in living material. When an organism dies, radioactive carbon 14 no longer enters the system. As the carbon 14 decays, the ratio of carbon 14 to carbon 12 decreases. If the rate of decay is known, then the measured ratio of radioactive carbon to normal carbon can be used as an indication of when the organic material died. The original ratio is very small, about one in a million million atoms, but it can be fairly accurately measured with the use of sensitive instruments. The method is, however, tedious and expensive, and requires burning the artifact material for an ash sample to analyze.

The half-life of radiocarbon is 5,730 years. This means that, after 5,730 years, half of a sample of carbon 14 has decayed. After another 5,730 years, half of the remaining half will have decayed, leaving a fourth of the original amount. For example, if you started with 100 carbon 14 atoms you would have 50 left after 5,730 years and 25 left after 11,460 years. The ratio becomes too small to measure after about 50,000 years. (We have discussed in Chapter V various radioactive dating methods which are good for different spans of time. This is because each radioactive material has a different half-life. Some half-lives are thousands of years and some only fractions of seconds.)

To obtain accurate dates from this method, it must be assumed that the decay constant for carbon is actually a constant. Also, the rate of production of carbon 14 in the atmosphere must be constant and the mixing of carbon 14 must be uniform throughout the atmosphere in order that, as an example, northern latitudes do not have less carbon 14 than central regions and thus appear to be younger. Even if those assumptions are valid, which is not necessarily the case, samples can become contaminated and give incorrect dates. So what is billed as an unbiased scientific tool actually leaves considerable room for "interpretation" of the data.

If events similar to those described by Velikovsky did occur, then one would expect the production rate of carbon 14 to have varied. It might vary even during uniformitarian periods, but variations during catastrophic times should certainly be expected. Some of the catastrophic events were of short duration, so the change in carbon 14 production caused by these events may not be large compared to changes caused by a process of longer duration. If the catastrophe produced a major permanent change in the rate of carbon 14 production, an increasing deviation of real time and calculated time would be expected the farther back one goes on the time scale. The data give a deviation of this nature, but this can also be interpreted in another manner. Some say a deviation of this type was caused by some presently unexplained gradual change. (This gradual change appears to have occurred rather quickly as far as geological time goes.) This explanation is not inherently better than other explanations, but does fit the uniformitarian concept.

The bristlecone pine is considered the oldest living thing on earth. By using this tree, a calibration curve of real time vs. calculated time can be made for thousands of years. The process is based on the techniques and theories of tree-ring dating (dendrochronology) which have been developing since the early part of this century. Most people are familiar with this process. Anyone who ever chopped down a small tree or picked up a log to toss into the fireplace may have noticed the rings and counted them to estimate how old the tree was. The process is generally the same as the one used with the bristlecone pine except, in addition to counting each ring, wood from each ring was carbon dated. Theoretically, a new ring is grown on the tree every year. The old ring, for the purpose of assimilating radioactive carbon, is essentially dead. Therefore, each ring can be carbon dated to give a radiocarbon age. If it is known when the tree was cut, the outer ring should give a radiocarbon age corresponding to the time since the tree was cut. Each inner ring should give a radiocarbon age of a year earlier than the previous ring. This process has demonstrated that the carbon 14 age deviates from the actual age, but the process also provided a calibration curve by which the actual age could be determined by use of a radiocarbon age.

The results of a calibration of this type are reproduced from Libby's article. (Fig. 1) The graph contains a horizontal straight line which represents perfect agreement between the true ages measured by counting the tree rings and the radiocarbon age given by carbon dating the individual rings. The data presented show the deviation from perfect agreement. Radiocarbon dates are given in years B.P. which is Before Present and are referenced to 1950. Therefore, a date given as 1000 B.C. would be a radiocarbon date of 2950 B.P.

Deviations to both sides of the perfect agreement line are observed from the present to about 300 B.C. These can possibly be explained as normal fluctuations in an otherwise uniform environment. However, before 300 B. C., there is a distinct trend in the data toward a deviation to one side of perfect agreement. All radiocarbon dates start making the dated material appear younger than its actual age. By 6850 actual years B.P. the radiocarbon date is too young by about 850 years. There appears to have been a major change in "normal" conditions before

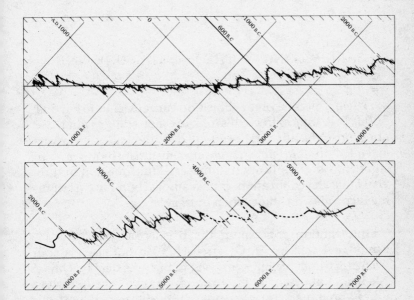

Figure 1. If the carbon date year matched the counted tree-ring year, the point would lie on the horizontal line. Carbon dates are given in years before the present (B.P.) and the counted tree-ring dates are in calendar years. Example: A carbon date of 6000 B.P. corresponds to a tree-ring age of 4900 B.C., or 6850 B.P. (after Libby) Divergence to only one side of the ideal horizontal line begins sometime before about 300 B.C.

300 B.C. and these conditions were probably stabilized by around 300 B.C. A seemingly reasonable *ad hoc* hypothesis for this may eventually be available from the uniformitarian standpoint, *but the data are definitely not discordant with the interpretation of catastrophic events ending around 687 B.C.*

CALIBRATING TO THE BRISTLECONE PINE

The bristlecone pine calibration curve extends to beyond 7000 B.P. Since trees this old are not still growing, the question naturally arises about how the calibration was extended to that time. Investigating this gives some insight into the application of the "scientific" method and reveals that the calibration of the radiocarbon dating technique depends on radiocarbon dating.

Information concerning the bristlecone pine was recently reviewed by H. C. Sorensen. [2] Dr. Sorensen is both a chemist and scientific advisor to the president of United Medical Laboratories in Portland, Oregon. The following notes about the bristlecone pine calibration are taken from Sorensen's article.

A typical growth cycle for a tree ring begins in the spring when large well-developed cells are produced. In the summer, as growing conditions become less favorable, the cells are formed smaller and more dense, and have a dark appearance. In the fall and winter, growth almost ceases. This cycle gives the appearance of "rings" for each growing season.

This straight-forward situation is sometimes complicated by two processes. First is the "multiple ring" year. After the production of small cells begins, non-seasonal rains may stimulate growth of large cells again. A trained observer can sometimes detect "false" rings produced by this process. The second problem is more difficult because it creates the mystery of the "missing" rings. In environmentally unfavorable years, no growth rings may be produced. Counting a "missing" ring is not possible directly, but its existence, or lack of existence, can sometimes be inferred.

There are two basic principles used in tree ring dating. The first is that one growth ring is equivalent to one year of growth, although this is not strictly true. The second is that two specimens of wood with similar distinctive growth patterns have grown at the same time and may be correlated ring for ring, year by year. This can be illustrated by the following: Suppose one finds a log cabin, and the cabin and its furniture were made from trees growing on the surrounding land. Outside the cabin, a growing tree is cut down and found to have eighty rings. The pattern of the inner twenty rings may be very unique and match the outer set of twenty rings found in one of the logs in the cabin's bed. The log from the bed has forty rings, so this then gives one hundred different year rings. Assume the inner ten rings of the bed log are also distinctive and match the outer ten rings of a log in the wall of the cabin. If this log has a total of seventy rings, the rings for sixty additional years are available. Rings can then be counted for one hundred and sixty separate years, although no tree that old was available. Correlating the distinctive patterns is called cross matching. Carbon dating wood from each ring should give a radiocarbon date for each counted year.

Theoretically, the method sounds quite reasonable. However, Sorensen points out that there are three practical difficulties in the implementation of the method. First, distinctive patterns are not as common as dendrochronologists might wish. In order to have a distinctive pattern, a tree must have grown during a time when distinctive climatic variations occurred, and it must have been sensitive to this variation. A tree at the bottom of a hill will undergo the same regional climatic changes as a tree at the top, but the one at the bottom may be near a stream or semipermanent water table and not show the distinctive pattern of the tree at the top.

Second, the rings tend to decrease in size as the tree becomes older. The closer together the rings, the harder they are to count. These problems, however, are usually considered minor.

The third problem is more serious. This problem has to do with the completeness of the data. Generally, the most distinctive patterns are the extremely thin rings formed during environmentally stressful situations. Sometimes as many as 10 rings per millimeter are found. Sorensen notes that "the location of a few missing rings in a large specimen may be inferred when attempting to cross match, but when as high as five percent of the rings are missing, cross matching is obviously questionable if not futile." Application of this method provides reasonable agreement when used on certain trees grown in the last few centuries. In fact, this technique was recently used to help establish the rights of Navajos to certain territories they occupied before 1848. Tree ring dating was applied to some of the well-preserved Navajo hogans (dwellings) and the dates were cross referenced with cultural records.

However, the application of cross matching to the bristlecone pine compounds the problems. Cross matching is required numerous times in samples difficult to cross match. In one specimen there are more than 1100 year rings in 12.7 cm (5 inches) and up to 10 percent of the rings may be missing. *The very thin rings most likely to form distinctive patterns are also the ones most likely to be missing.* This is because the thin distinctive rings are more likely formed in environmentally stressful times and these times are most likely to produce conditions when no ring is formed. This cuts down on the probability of obtaining a significant cross-match.

When attempting to match patterns which have "missing rings", the problem becomes so difficult that sometimes the distinctive patterns are not really distinctive. Some logs are used which would cross match regardless of their position in the chronology. What does one do in this stiuation? The problem was partially solved by carbon dating the two samples to find where they should match. Even with this additional aid, Ferguson, the scientist who arranged most of the samples for the chronology, said: "I often am unable to date specimens with one or two thousand rings against a 7500-year master chronology, even with the 'ball-park' placement provided by a radiocarbon date."

Thus, the calibration curve for carbon dating, which is supposedly independent of carbon dating, now depends on carbon dating.

In addition to some questionable procedures with respect to experimentation, Sorensen points out that Ferguson has followed some unusual procedures with respect to reporting a significant scientific advancement which has far reaching implications for many fields. Where one would expect abundant documentation, very little exists. Apart from a set of data containing a number of "missing" rings, no ring width data have been published for the components of the chronology. Only a "filtered" master chronology was published. Therefore, there is no real basis for independent determination of how well one sample correlates to another. When Sorensen asked for data, Ferguson said that he had strong reasons for publishing only adjusted data and he could not release original data.

Sorensen summarizes by first stating that the basic concept of dendrochronology has been shown to be useful for the recent past. He then briefly restates the highly questionable methods employed in the procedure as applied to the bristlecone pine and the refusal to allow independent unbiased analysis of some of the basic data. Sorensen concludes "that at this time there are no compelling reasons to accept the bristlecone pine chronology as valid." So although the trend of the calibration curve is consistent with catastrophic theories, there is no reason to force Egyptian history to fit a chronology based on the bristlecone pine calibration.

ASH

The need to make carbon dating correspond to the accepted dates for Egyptian history is part of what originally created a desire for a calibration curve. In its present form, carbon dating cannot easily be used *conclusively* to support the revised or conventional chronology. However, it can be instructive to review some of the carbon dating results and methods relating to these chronologies.

Soon after Libby's publication of information about the carbon dating method, Velikovsky began his attempt to have radiocarbon analysis performed on material from especially the 18th, 19th, and 20th Dynasties of Egypt. Parts of this correspondence were published in *Pensee* VI, 1974, and is fascinating reading for historians and sociologists of science as well as people interested in the "scientific" method. Velikovsky calls this the "ASH" correspondence, after the end product of the carbon dating process.

While reading the series of letters, one sometimes feels as though one is caught in a circle or merry-go-around. The circle that is repeated is as follows: Velikovsky requests dating of objects from particular Dynasties. He is informed that the dates for those are so well known they do not need to be reconfirmed by radiocarbon tests. Velikovsky then responds that Libby mentioned the need for known samples to help determine the usefulness of carbon dating for if the particular dynasties are so well known, why not test them for comparative purposes. The reply is usually vague. Additionally, it is claimed that no samples are available. When samples become available, they again do not need to be tested because the dates for these dynasties are so well known. The circle is then repeated. The stalling, contradiction and inaction would make any bureaucrat proud. Here now are some of the major points and quotes from this series of letters.

The first circle started in 1953 with a letter from Velikovsky to Libby. Velikovsky listed several dates he expected for certain Egyptian Dynasties and the Hittite Empire. He also noted that one of the dates already published by Libby was lower by some 800 years from conventional chronology, but the date matched the revised chronology more closely.

Velikovsky also noted that well-known experts in the field had investigated *Ages in Chaos* and felt that the theory was worth investigating. For example, Prof. Robert H. Pfeiffer of the Department of Ancient History at Harvard University, had been familiar with the first draft in 1942 and provided encouragement throughout its additional development. Also the renowned Egyptologist, Prof. E. Drioton, then Director of the Egyptological Department of the Louvre Museum, expressed the opinion that Egyptian and Middle Eastern history would need revision in light of the evidence presented in *Ages in Chaos*. Velikovsky also mailed a copy of the book to Libby. Libby quickly and cordially responded, but said that he was only the inventor and user of the radiocarbon dating and really knew little about Egyptian history. He also felt "constrained" to return the copy of *Ages in Chaos* because he would not understand it. Anyone who has perused the book knows that Libby either vastly underestimated his own capabilities or was trying to avoid a sticky issue. The logic in *Ages in Chaos* is straightforward and can easily be appreciated by someone without a vast background in ancient history.

MATERIAL FOR DATING

Samples from certain Egyptian dynasties were needed

for testing in case someone became interested in the test. Prof. Pfeiffer was willing to send some samples from the Harvard Semitic Museum to Libby for radiocarbon analysis. Unfortunately, the museum had none from the Dynasties in question, so the circular attempts at obtaining samples began. A friend of Velikovsky asked William C. Hayes, Curator of Egyptian Art of the Metropolitan Museum of Art, whether carbon dating had been done on objects from certain Dynasties of the New Kingdom. The reply was that "in the light of the very complete knowledge we have on this tightly dated and closely recorded period, it would serve no useful purpose to have this done..." We have already seen, however, that the chronology for the period under discussion is subject to question.

After discussions with Velikovsky, Hayes agreed to select three pieces, one each from the 18th, 19th, and 20th Dynasties, for radiocarbon analysis. He said, however, that the tests should be performed at the request of institutions instead of an individual, such as Velikovsky. Hayes agreed that the tests would be conducted only if he received a request from Pfeiffer.

Pfeiffer provided the letter to Hayes. Also Helen Dukas, who was secretary to Albert Einstein, wrote to Hayes mentioning a discussion in her presence in which Einstein stated he intended to write to Hayes requesting radiocarbon tests on behalf of Velikovsky. The sudden death of Einstein prevented him from writing the letter, but she assured Hayes of Einstein's intention.

Velikovsky also wrote a letter reiterating his conclusions and enclosing a section of galley proofs from the second volume of *Ages in Chaos*. He also suggested that the samples be numbered so that the testers would not feel obliged to find a particular date.

Hayes replied to Pfeiffer saying that the museum did not have material from all the requested Dynasties after all, but he did have possibly a small sample from the New Kingdom although not later than the Eighteenth Dynasty. Of course, this could only be relinquished to an institution and the request from Pfeiffer was no longer enough since it was not related to an officially blessed program of Harvard.

Attempts were made to obtain material from other museums, such as the Museum of Fine Arts in Boston and the British Museum. They responded that they did not have or could not spare the material or felt that there was no need to test material from such accurately known dynasties.

In early 1961, attempts were made to obtain, from the University of California, information about any carbon dating performed on material from the 18th, 19th, and 20th Dynasties of Egypt. The Department of Anthropology replied that they had no information about carbon dating of material from those Dynasties; however, they referred to the Department of Near Eastern Languages as having more updated information. From there came the following reply from Dr. Klaus Baer, then Assistant Professor of Egyptology: "As far as I know there are no radiocarbon datings of any objects from the New Kingdom. However, since the chronology of ancient Egypt is quite closely fixed by the astronomical evidence from the Eleventh Dynasty onward, in part, to the nearest year, radiocarbon, with its substantial margin of error, could hardly add anything to our knowledge of the chronology of the New Kingdom. Hayes, The *Sceptre of Egypt*, Vol. II, dates Rameses III to 1192-1160 B.C., and this date is not likely to contain a margin of error greater than about five years each way."[3] So the loop is complete. The date is accurate so there is no need to test. When asked about using it as a standard, there is no material. When material becomes available, there is no need to test. If the chronology of Egypt were really so accurately known, why not then use it, as Velikovsky suggested, to obtain an estimate of the usefulness of carbon dating?

The first session of letter writing ended with a letter in 1961 from Virginia Burton, Curatorial Assistant, Department of Egyptian Art at the Metropolitan Museum of Art in New York City. She explained that most of the material taken out of Egypt was contaminated so it would be useless to try to date it by radiocarbon.

PHASE II

Phase two of the ASH correspondence runs from 1959 to 1965 and focuses on the University of Pennsylvania Museum which has one of the world's finest radiocarbon dating laboratories.

The first letter is dated October 7, 1959 and was a reply to an acquaintance of Velikovsky's, Lynne O. Ramer, written by Froelich Rainey, who was director of the Museum. Rainey said he could not understand why Velikovsky would think that certain periods of Egyptian history were intentionally skipped for carbon dating. He said that there was a radiocarbon dating laboratory at the Museum and "we have a great many dates for all periods". Also, "by and large the hundreds of dates we now have from Carbon-14 confirm fairly closely the chronologies worked out by the archaeologists." In closing, he mentioned that the people at the Museum considered preparing an answer to Velikovsky's claims but decided it was not worthwhile. This letter was written nearly two years before letters from other museums which stressed three points: the work had not been done, the work did not need to be done, and all the material was contaminated.

Another acquaintance, Dr. David W. Baker, offered to help Velikovsky obtain radiocarbon analysis of objects from important time periods in Egyptian history. In January of 1961, Velikovsky wrote to Baker and referred to a paper published by Dr. Elizabeth K. Ralph, who performs carbon dating for the Museum at the University of Pennsylvania. Among the items she stressed were these: the period 2000 to 4000 B.P. gave very erratic results; the Middle Kingdom dates are 180-250 years younger than expected; and the only object dated from the New Kingdom (a beam of Seti I) was 200 years younger than expected. Some dates were discarded because of contamination. Velikovsky asked Baker if he could obtain more information about any other tests that may have been performed on New Kingdom material, and if he could find out how large a discrepancy in dates occurred before the sample was called *contaminated.*

Between the letter to Baker and Baker's chance to go to the University of Pensylvania Museum, Velikovsky had additional correspondence with Prof. Claude F. A. Schaeffer, one of the foremost authorities on archaeology of the Middle East. (Schaeffer held the Chaire d'Archelogies de l'Asie Occidentale at College de France.) One of the subjects was some Ras Shamra (Ugarit) material which Schaeffer had offered to Velikovsky for radiocarbon analysis. Schaeffer sent the sample to the University of Pennsylvania, Department of Physics. Schaeffer said he had been informed after an anomalous date was found, that contamination may have occurred.

In reference to the Museum having unpublished radiocarbon dates for the New Kingdom, Schaeffer said that he would publish, whatever the result, since he was "not concerned with opinions and chronological schemes, but only with the advance of knowledge." Also he noted that "the truth needs time to sink in. And so we must be in a position to wait."

Through mutual friends, Dr. Baker was introduced to Dr. Rainey, Director of the Museum. Dr. Baker found Rainey to be "a vigorous, enthusiastic, obviously very well informed, courteous gentleman..." This opinion was preserved possibly because at no time did Baker or anyone else mention Velikovsky's name. Baker's interest in the Exodus was given as being prompted by an interest in that area because of his position as Professor of Religion at Ursinus College.

Baker quoted Rainey as saying: "The dating of Egyptian history is one of the most controversial matters in the whole realm of Archaeology today. On the basis of radiocarbon dating we have come up with a very serious difference of 600 years between the old chronology and the radiocarbon evidence! We do not know how to account for it. It seems to extend throughout Egyptian history, but the earlier dates are off more than more recent ones. Fortunately we have an astronomical fix in the time of Seti I, so we are pretty sure of his date, but before him we are in real trouble. Right now our Museum, the British Museum, and the University of Leiden are working furiously to try to find out the cause of the discrepancy." We have seen how unfixed the time of Seti I actually is (Chapter III).

Baker asked Rainey–"Is it your opinion then that we may expect some very drastic changes in the dates of early Egyptian history in the next few years?" Rainey replied "Yes, and not only in Egypt, but in the dating of the entire Ancient World, especially the Near East." This is from the same person who said it was not worthwhile to answer Velikovsky's claims. Was it really not worthwhile or was it more difficult than they first imagined?

The same day, Baker talked to Dr. Elizabeth Ralph. He described her as a deeply serious dedicated scientist, and said she was quite willing to discuss her work. She confirmed Rainey's statements, except she did not know specifically of a 600 year discrepancy or of the work of the other museums. She did furnish Baker additional information. She showed him a curve displaying the trend of radiocarbon dates which were younger than expected, and she mentioned problems with contamination. She also mentioned the new half-life calculations for carbon-14. The old figure was 5568 years, and the revised one was 5800 years. She said she thought it was somewhere between these values, but the previously calculated dates would have to be changed. Both Rainey and Ralph mentioned the new work being done on the bristlecone pine. Dr. Ralph also said she had published all the tests she had made, but she said there was a problem obtaining samples. She said that "the present Egyptologist at the University is not much interested. In the future it may be different."

Thus Velikovsky resumed his attempt to obtain samples from the New Kingdom. He wrote to Mrs. Fuhr, in Munich, who was about to make a trip to Egypt. He requested that she pick up some samples in Cairo. He had made arrangements for them through Prof. Butrus Abd al Malik of Princeton University. The Professor was a friend of Dr. Zaki Iskander Hanna, the Chief Chemist of the Egyptian Museum in Cairo, and wrote to him that a friend in Princeton was interested in radiocarbon dating samples of the mummy of Ramses III.

In the meantime, Velikovsky met Dr. Ralph and described her as "a very pleasant person". She agreed to perform tests on the samples that Velikovsky hoped to acquire, and that no fee would be charged because she was interested in the results.

Dr. Malik's letter proved to be a valuable introduction and Mrs. Fuhr was cordially welcomed by Dr. Iskander. He told her that there was considerable doubt that what is called the mummy of Ramses III was actually the mummy of Ramses III. Various circumstances may have created confusion with regard to certain discoveries and there could be an error of 300 years not even considering the radiocarbon error. Dr. Iskander offered, instead, some material known to be from the tomb of Tutankhamen. This was quite agreeable and Mrs. Fuhr was given three pieces of wood to make enough for the analysis. Dr. Iskander thought the wood was probably not more than about 30 years old when it was used.

Velikovsky had Mrs. Fuhr mail the samples directly to the Museum. He said that "in no case would I like to have the wood sent to me. Since I am an interested party, I must be left out of contact with the sample." He also expressed reservations about the age of the wood when used, since wood was scarce in Egypt and was often reused. He preferred short-lived items, but was willing to go with what was available.

Velikovsky again asked the Metropolitan Museum of Art for additional material to be dated. H. G. Fischer, Associate Curator in Charge of the Department of Egyptian Art at the Museum, told him that they had disposed of an enormous amount of material during the previous 10 years and no longer could supply adequate samples of well-dated material. This was in 1963. The previous ten years were a time when the Museum supposedly had no material which could be disposed of in any amounts.

On February 25, 1964, Dr. Ralph wrote to Velikovsky and gave him the results of the test of the wood sent by Fuhr. (In the series of letters published under the title ASH in *Pensee*, this letter was not included because of the objection of Dr. Ralph.) She stated that they preferred not to release one date at a time so a list of previous results was also included. The wood from the coffin of Tutankhamen of the 18th Dynasty was labeled P-726. The age using the 5568 year half-life was 1030±50 B.C. and using a 5730 year half-life was 1120±52 B.C. Conventional chronology gives it a date of 1343 B.C. The revised chronology would put it about 840 B.C.

Obviously there is a problem, because King Tut could not have an object carved out of wood that was still growing 200 years after his death. There is no problem for the revised chronology, however, since it is possible that he had an object made from wood that had been around for awhile. As we shall see, wood easily gives carbon dates too old anyway, and this is why Velikovsky preferred short-lived items. In any case, the results were explainable by the revised chronology, but not by accepted chronology.

In a later letter to Dr. Ralph, Velikovsky mentioned two articles in *Antiquity* and one in *Science* which indicated that there was agreement between the radiocarbon dates of objects from Egyptian history and the conventional chronology. Both were published more than a year after Rainey and Ralph told Dr. Baker about the discrepancies.

Two articles were by Libby. (He is the one who felt incapable of understanding works on Egyptian history.) He claimed historical and carbon dating agreement in a 1200-year period on the basis of one analysis, that of wood from the time of Seti. Ralph had even discussed the possibility that the wood was reused. The other article was by H. S. Smith. He stressed that there is agreement between radiocarbon and conventional dates back to 2000 B.C.

This definitely *but incorrectly* implied that Velikovsky's revised chronology had been proven incorrect. Because of this, Velikovsky asked Dr. Ralph when the results of the Tutankhamen dating would be published so people could see that the question was still unresolved.

On May 6, 1964, Ralph replied that Rainey was strongly opposed to publishing single carbon-14 dates. They preferred to publish groups of dates and planned to publish the King Tut results only when it could be included with other Egyptian dates. Ralph did say that they planned to publish these results in early 1965 and even offered to date, "in the course of our present series", additional Egyptian material that Velikovsky might obtain.

PHASE III

Phase II ended with apparently no one willing to correct the totally false impression that carbon dating completely supported the conventional Egyptian chronology. Phase III is short but revealing. It starts with a letter of April 6, 1971 to Dr. H. N. Michael. The letter was written by Prof. I. E. S. Edwards, Keeper of the Department of Egyptian Antiquites of the British Museum, who reported the results of carbon dating of some reed and palm nut kernels. On March 2, 1964, Velikovsky, in a letter to Dr. Ralph, stated his expectation that short-lived items from Tut's tomb would give radiocarbon dates of around 840 B.C. as opposed to the conventional 1350 B.C. The letter from the British Museum designated the reed as BM 642A and the palm as BM 642B. The radiocarbon dates obtained were ca. 846 B.C. and ca. 899 B.C. respectively. Despite the assurance that these dates would be published "shortly", this never occurred. The dates were discussed in the May, 1972, issue of *Pensee* and this discussion precipitated the short series of letters described below.

Dr. G. W. Van Oosterhout of the Department of Chemistry and Chemical Engineering, Delft University of Technology (The Netherlands) wrote to *Pensee* in 1973 stating that he checked the published radiocarbon data from the British Museum but could not find any reference to the dating of reed and palm nut from the tomb of Tutankhamen. He asked for additional information.

Van Oosterhout's letter was referred to Bruce Mainwaring who received a copy of the original letter from the British Museum. He sent a copy to Van Oosterhout and described a conversation between himself and Mr. Burleigh, who was directing the laboratory at the British Museum. Although Burleigh said he expected the results to be published "shortly", "upon further questioning, he admitted that results which deviate substantially from what is expected are often discarded and never published". Mainwaring expressed the opinion that this had probably happened to the Tut results.

In April, 1973, Van Oosterhout thanked Mainwaring for the information and said that he had also received a letter from the British Museum stating: "With reference to your inquiry of 3rd January this laboratory has made no measurements on material from the tomb of Tutankhamen." It was signed by H. Barker. Van Oosterhout closed with the statement that "apparently Mr. Barker does not know what's going on in his laboratory, to say it kindly. This is much worse than what you said. Deviating results are not only not published, it is even denied that they have been found..."

CARBON CHEATING

In the discussion of the bristlecone pine, it was described how wood can give various carbon dates depending
on which part of the tree is used in the analysis. Israel M.
Isaacson demonstrated how selective use of this information
has been used to "prove" that conventional chronology is
correct for two different cities.

One of the cities, Pylos, was dated by relating it to Egyptian history and one, Gordion, was dated by other methods. The date for Gordion is about the same in both the
revised and conventional chronologies. The date of Pylos
should be lower by the revised chronology. Conditions for
carbon dating as discussed below were the same at both
locations, but "corrections" were applied at only one site.
The following material reviews the information presented
by Isaacson.

A palace and town were uncovered near the present day
Pylos in Greece. The remains are thought to be those of the
ancient Pylos mentioned by Homer. A particular burned
layer was given an absolute date by relating Mycenaean
pottery to the Egyptian chronology. If the Egyptian date
must be reduced by several hundred years, then so must
the date for Pylos. The same person (Blegen) excavated
Troy and used the same dating method. Isaacson points
out that abundant archaeological evidence indicates that
both Pylos and Troy could be centuries younger than the
ages decreed by Egyptian history. For now, however, we
will restrict ourselves solely to the carbon dating evidence.

Internal evidence at Pylos indicates that the burned
layer should have a date around 600 B.C. Pottery from
this time was plentiful, and in some cases was in the palace
rooms, adjacent to earlier pottery. Antiques can be collected, but items from the future are more difficult to explain. The situation would be similar to people today collecting pottery from the year 2600 A.D. Handwaving argu-

ments about "percolating" pottery from below and "intrusive" pottery from above are used to explain this exceedingly awkward situation. By the revised chronology there is no problem, since the pottery styles are contemporaneous.

The site of the city of Gordion, capital of the ancient Phrygian empire, is located in Asia Minor. Homer referred to this region as an ally of Troy. The Trojan War was thought to have been fought around the 13th century B.C., based again on pottery related to Egyptian chronology. However, archaeological evidence, unrelated to Egyptian history, indicates that Gordion's history extends only as far back as the 8th century B.C.; and there is no way to push its history to earlier times, since the accepted date for artifacts from Gordion is the 8th century B.C.

So the two cities, Pylos and Gordion, have conventional dates of about 1230 B.C. and 725 B.C. respectively. The Gordion date is about the same in the revised chronology, but the date for Pylos is reduced several hundred years in the revised chronology. Carbon dating, even with possible errors, may be revealing in regard to which chronology is most accurate. Published results claim agreement with the conventional chronology, but to make the date agree, some *corrections* in the data were necessary. In some samples from Gordion it was possible to date short-lived items instead of the outer layer of semi-unfinished logs. The short lived items should give a date near when they lived, and the outer part of a tree should give a date near that of when the tree was cut down. If Gordion was destroyed soon after the cutting of the log, the carbon date of the log and short-lived samples would be similar, and the date should be reasonably close to the time Gordion burned. Samples were tested, and the carbon dates of the short-lived material and the outer part of the log were in reasonable agreement with the date expected by both chronologies. However, samples from the inner part of finished logs gave dates several hundred years older. This can be reasonably explained.

A particular ring of a tree should give a carbon-date for the year the ring grew, since that is the only time that it is taking in radioactive carbon. Therefore, a tree that is 300 years old when it is cut should give one date for the outer layer and a date nearing 300 years earlier for the inner part. Material from a burned site may have been in use for many years, so the carbon date of a log may be off by an unknown amount of time because of this. Also, the logs generally would be finished by squaring or other methods which would affect the outer layers. If the logs were burned during the destruction of the site, this would expose more rings toward the center and make the carbon-date even older.

For the burned logs at Gordion, all this was taken into account. Some burned logs gave radiocarbon dates several hundred years older than expected, but burned, finished logs *should* give carbon dates older than the real dates; therefore, adjustments were made. [4]

At Pylos, the beams were also charred and some were known to be finished, but *no* correction was applied because the carbon date fit the expected conventional chronology without adjustments. If the same correction for the same conditions had been employed as at Gordion, the radiocarbon date would have been closer to the revised chronology. The conditions in both locations were identical; however, the correction could not be applied at Pylos because then the date would not have fit conventional chronology. In fact, the date would make it appear that the logs were grown *after* Pylos was burned. Under the revised chronology, there is no problem with applying the same correction to identical conditions.

The failure to apply the correction in both cases was not an oversight caused by two labs doing independent tests. These results came from the same lab and were published in the same paper. The results were *made* to conform to conventional chronology.

It is not uncommon to publish only dates that conform or can be made to conform to accepted views. Isaacson quotes Prof. Brew as saying that "if a C14 date supports our theories (conventional chronology) we put it in the main text. If it does not entirely contradict them, we put it in a foot-note. And if it is completely 'out-of-date', we just drop it." That this attitude exists was reaffirmed by David Wilson in *The New Archaeology*. Therefore, do not be surprised when someone informs you that carbon dating supports the conventional chronology. It should, because it has been adjusted to do exactly that.

AN "IDEAL" SAMPLE AND THE GREEK "DARK AGE"

It has been noted that Velikovsky mentioned the problems associated with carbon dating debris from logs, and suggested that short-lived items would give more accurate results. This has also been discussed in the literature by Dr. Ralph and others.

In the area of Pylos is a sample of the type considered "ideal" for carbon dating. This is pollen from olive trees. Yearly, new pollen is blown into the water at Osmanaga Lagoon, at the head of Navarino Bay, on Messenia's west coast. This has occurred for thousands of years and stratified layers of pollen are observable in core samples from the lake.

H. E. Wright, Jr. investigated these core samples and described his work in an article titled *Vegetation History*.[5] This work was also reviewed by Isaacson. He notes that it is generally agreed that intensive olive cultivation was practiced by Late Helladic Greeks. There is considerable archaeological and written evidence that the liquid gold of Mycenaean times was olive oil, and the creation, storage, transportation, and exportation of olive oil was a major economic activity.

The evidence indicates that there was a population explosion, and the area was the most densely populated part of Greece during Mycenaean times. There was a large labor force to care for the trees, produce the oil and arrange for transportation. Because of the conventional chronology, this time span was thought to be about 1550 to 1200 B. C. with the peak activity being in the 13th century B.C. Therefore one would expect the pollen to peak at this time. However, the radiocarbon analysis of the pollen indicates the peak took place during the 1100 to 700 B.C. period which is a part of the so called "dark age" of Greece when nothing was supposedly occurring.

Wright was rather perplexed by these results. The time of great population, facilities for manufacturing and exporting olive oil, and numerous olive oil lamps displays very little pollen, whereas the "dark age" of few people, where one would expect no activity and no olive oil lamps, shows a *peak* in pollen activity. Evidence from another lake, Lake Voulkaria, indicates the same trend: a rise in pollen production *after* the Mycenaean period. Thus, the oil lamp was in wide use before and after the time of peak olive production, but totally unknown during the time of maximum production.

The problem of the Greek "dark age" has often been discussed, and Carpenter (*Discontinuity in Greek Civilization*) advanced the theory that a drought caused the problem. Wright feels that the pollen count disproves this theory. Also a drought would not necessarily explain the disappearance of oil lamps during peak oil production. The situation would be similar to a future archaeologist dating peak oil production in the United States as being in the 20th century and someone else placing the peak auto production from Detroit as occurring sometime before Columbus left Spain.

With the revised chronology, this problem does not exist. Since Greek history is sometimes dated by association with erroneous Egyptian history, this causes errors in Greek history. The "dark age" problem is caused by the extraneous years of Egyptian history. Historians were faced with the problem of creating non-existent history for Greece or merely calling the gap a "dark age". They chose the latter course. In the revised chronology, the excess years of Egyptian history are deleted and there is then no gap in Greek history. Hence, peak pollen production coincides with peak lamp use as well as the peak in facilities for production and transport of olive oil.

SIGNIFICANT CARBON DATES

Carbon dating impacts Velikovsky's work in two separate areas. Information obtained from carbon dating can be related to natural events, such as those described in *Worlds in Collision*, and to historical events involving the chronology of Egypt as partially presented in *Ages in Chaos*, Vol. I. Since the limitations of carbon dating have been delineated, the significance of some particular carbon dates related to events in *Worlds in Collision* can be better understood. One that has already been presented is the carbon date of petroleum. We see that this carbon date is still significant even with carbon dating errors.

Another date relates to the last ice age. In 1950, the end of the last ice age was thought to have been on the order of 35,000 years ago, but Velikovsky suggested that it should be much closer to the present. Later, radiocarbon dating indicated that this date should be closer to 11,000 years ago and possibly even later. The dating method could even be a few thousand years in error and still support Velikovsky's idea that 35,000 years was more than a factor of two larger than it should be.

The third item associated with *Worlds in Collision* has historical significance but does not require the precise dating needed for certain conclusions related to the reconstruction of Egyptian history. Velikovsky noted that the Mesoamerican literature depicted the same events as the literature of other cultures. The stories did not appear to be acquired merely by diffusion but were descriptions of events which the cultures actually experienced independently. Velikovsky therefore reasoned that the Mesoamerican cultures were generally older than was recognized in 1950. He met strong opposition on this point by experts in Mesoamerican history who insisted that these cultures were formed in the 4th to 8th century A.D. To be specific, the Mexicologist George Kubler wrote in 1950: "The Mesoamerican Cosmology to which Velikovsky repeatedly appeals for proof did not originate until about the beginning of our era."[6] However, by 1956, the *National Geographic Society* announced that carbon dating had demonstrated the ancient cultures of Mexico were some one thousand years older than had been believed. By 1967 it was not only accepted that these cultures existed before the present era, but in some cases the major time periods of the culture were given in dates which tend to remind one of the times of catastrophes. For example, in an article about a specific Mesoamerican culture, Flannery, *et.al.*, gave the beginning of the major periods as 8000, 1500, and 600 B.C.[7]

The timing may not be exact, but largely because of carbon dating it is now apparent that the general time periods suggested by Velikovsky are reasonable, and the legends generated during these periods correlate to those of other countries. Frank Waters is well known for his writings about the history and myths of the Native Americans and Mesoamericans. In 1975 he published *Mexico Mystique* which is divided into two parts and describes the history and then the myths of the Aztecs, Olmecs, Mayas, Toltecs and other groups in Mexico. In his analysis of the mythologies of these cultures, Waters reviewed the work of Velikovsky which is relevant to these areas. He concluded that although the timing of some events still creates some problems, "....Velikovsky's theory runs parallel to Mesoamerican myth in general outline."[8]

THE NON-CONSTANT CONSTANT

The so called radioactive decay "constant" has recently been shown to be variable. For carbon-dating, this may cause a negligible error for the cases under discussion, but this is still being investigated. An interesting point about this problem is that here is another area of science that was considered settled, but actually it is a field which has exciting possibilities for new investigations.

The decay constant is thought to be unchanged by time or environment; hence, the designation "constant". Atoms can supposedly be in a material which is melted, shocked, immersed in electromagnetic and gravitational fields of varying magnitude for billions of years and not have change in the constant. Although this originated as an assumption, some experimental evidence was thought to have supported the assumption. However, there is also some experimental evidence which indicates that the constant may be variable. If this is true, it could affect nuclear dating anywhere from a negligible amount to an amount which might make certain methods useless for the extended periods they are now thought to cover. In either case, investigating the evidence, instead of ignoring it, could lead to new understanding of physical concepts.

Anderson and Spangler have recently reviewed the problem. [9] Dr. Anderson is President of ERA Systems, Inc., which manufactures technical products based on a number of patents he holds. Dr. Spangler is an Associate Professor of Physics at the University of Tennessee, and Consulting Physicist at Baroness Eslanger Hospital in Chattanooga. They have, independently and jointly, been interested in non-random radioactive emissions since 1969, and have presented evidence which, they claim, shows "that the generality of the thesis of independence of nuclear decay events is presumably invalid (at least if our evidence is confirmed) and that the nuclear effects which apparently cause the deviations from the random expectation appear to be environmentally related."

Although much of the related literature supports or accepts the view that the decay constant is constant, some exceptions have been published. This evidence is usually discarded as bad data, and other evidence is probably never published. However, Anderson and Spangler feel the work deserves more attention. They give some of the reasoning behind the assumption that the decay constant is constant and note that it is circumstantial and not conclusive.

Much of the original experimental evidence was published in the early part of the 20th century. One of the most noteworthy "exceptions" was published by Kurzner in the 1920's. His work was reported and confirmed by Curtiss in 1930, but these papers were forgotten or ignored, and trivial explanations are usually provided for what might be variations in decay rate. However, Berkson recently (1966) analyzed some of the earlier work and concluded that the evidence for a constant "constant" is not as convincing as previously thought. He felt that "a quite extreme departure from randomness" might occur and not be detectable by the tests performed. Also, most of the early work involved alpha emitters. It was then directly or indirectly assumed that if alpha decay is random, then all decay is random.

Because of their work with beta decay, Anderson and Spangler are convinced that the assumption of the "constant" decay constant needs re-examination. They note that additional work must be done, but their results "rather strongly suggest that, at a minimum, an unreliability factor must be incorporated into age dating calculations."

Ralph E. Juergens has recently reviewed the literature pertaining to assumptions used in radioactive dating. Portions of this work will appear later in the journal KRONOS, but the following is taken from a pre-publication print affably provided to me by Juergens. Juergens notes that in addition to the assumption of a radioactive decay "constant", an equally basic assumption is that nucleosynthesis does not occur on Earth. Nucleosynthesis is the creation of heavier elements from lighter elements, and this must have all occurred in primordial times for the nuclear decay equations to be solved.   If an unknown a-mount were primoridal radioactive material and another unknown amount were created later in place, there would be too many unknowns to solve the equation for the "age" of the material. Juergens refers to the work of Anderson and Spangler, and suggests that "perhaps even stronger doubt about both these assumptions has been raised by recent research on *pleochroic halos*".

Minute zones of discoloration observed when thin sections of certain materials are examined under polarized light are called pleochroic halos. The rainbow-like effect is similar to what is seen when two thin sheets of cellophane wrap are placed together and moved about. The pleochroic halos result from radioactivity in the small inclusions at the center of certain crystaline material. Only alpha emission results in the production of radiohalos.

These halos helped establish the art of radiometric dating as a reputable occupation. Recent evidence, however, suggests that too much faith was placed in the implications of the early work, and the evidence refuting these implications was ignored.

Joly, one of the two physicists who in 1907 independently arrived at the conclusion about the origin of radiohalos, suggested examining what are thought to be ancient samples to determine whether or not their radiohalos exhibited dimensions expected on the basis of modern decay rates. Early investigations appeared to confirm that the halo sizes were the proper sequence and magnitude for all geological ages. Thus, it was considered proven that the decay constant has been, is, and will always be constant.

However, one scientist of little faith started, in the early 1960's, to review this work. Also, with modern equipment, he examined thousands of radiohalos in rocks from all parts of the world. Almost immediately, he discovered that too much faith and not enough science had gone into the early work, and all was *not* well-established in this long-neglected field. The new work was performed by Robert V. Gentry, who is with the Division of Chemistry at Oak Ridge National Laboratory. In one of his earliest reports Gentry emphasized that "little or no justification is found for the usual arguments proving the stability of the decay constant over geological time from pleochroic halos data." [10] His later work additionally supports the result that no conclusion can be drawn about the constancy of the decay constant.

So we see that not only does carbon dating have problems, but the entire field of nuclear dating is being re-examined. The error in carbon dating may be small enough so that basic trends of time scales can be determined from this method, but basic trends of nuclear dating over long geological time periods may be quite uncertain.

It should be kept in mind that any problems with carbon dating exist whether the carbon date fits conventional views or fits Velikovsky's. A carbon date supporting Velikovsky cannot blindly be accepted as valid; however, defenders of conventional views should not summarily reject a carbon date merely because it supports Velikovsky's work.

Chapter VII

THE EARTH

Terrestrial geologic data are more easily obtainable than data from other planets, but they are also subject to interpretation. Some of the geologic data and some of the interpretations that are related to the ideas of Velikovsky are described in this chapter. The opinions of authorities will be given.

Some of them did not conduct their investigations with Velikovsky's ideas in mind, but their results do not conflict with his suggestions. Others have specifically investigated Velikovsky's ideas with respect to their own particular specialties and found his suggestions to be quite reasonable. Of course, these people are only expressing opinions, but those who offer interpretations unfavorable to Velikovsky's work are also only expressing opinions.

The comments in this chapter are not intended to settle the issue; they demonstrate, however, that there is geologic evidence which can be interpreted in terms of catastrophism, and that some reputable workers actually interpret the data in this manner.

It should be remembered that Velikovsky does not claim that the earth lived in peaceful co-existence with the other planets for billions of years, and that then, suddenly, the Dragon Planet Venus and the Red Planet Mars ended this primordial detente a few thousand years ago. Velikovsky does not speculate about the exact age of the earth. He does suggest however, that geologic evidence indicates that there have been catastrophes throughout its existence. The agents causing the most recent destructions can be identified because people were present to observe, remember, and report the events. The only evidence we have of catastrophes that occurred before the arrival of man is from the geologic record.

PROBLEMS IN INTERPRETATION

Locally, catastrophic events obviously occur today and have often occurred in the past. Earthquakes, tornadoes, volcanic eruptions, and tidal waves seem like major catastrophes to those of us who are personally involved, but to much of the rest of the world, they are just stories to sleep through during the evening news. The only reason so many people are made aware of them is that we now have excellent communications systems. Such catastrophes, localized and relatively unimportant on a global scale, are soon forgotten by those who are not affected by them. The few special cases that are not forgotten are never exaggerated in memory as global events.

A truly global catastrophe might be composed of numerous local catastrophes. It is important, then, to determine how widespread an historical event might have been, whether it actually was composed of numerous minor events. If many local events occurred, it is of great importance to pinpoint their times of occurrence. Characteristics of time and place are interrelated and complicate the problem.

If the close approach to Earth of a massive body were to cause one hundred earthquakes and fifty volcanic explosions, the event would be considered catastrophic. If the approaching body were widely observed, it would be easy to convince survivors that a global catastrophe had taken place. However, if the body were not observed, or for some reason the observations were discounted, the evidence would become open to interpretation. Then, an ability to date events accurately would become of major importance.

Unfortunately, as we have seen, accepted dating methods are very questionable. Even if they could be assumed correct, events a few thousand years old could be dated only to the nearest hundred or so years, and many older events only to within millions of years. Therefore, it would not be possible to tell if the one hundred earthquakes and fifty eruptions occurred all in one day or if they occurred one each year for one hundred fifty years. The latter could easily be interpreted as a normal sequence, quite in line with modern experience.

Another important point to consider would be the extent of the damage caused by the hypothetical body. Some people infer that a global catastrophe would leave evidence on every square inch of the earth. Then, since such evidence cannot be drawn from every inch of the earth and correlated to a single catastrophe, they conclude that no global catastrophe occurred. However, more than half of the surface of the earth might bear no evidence of the encounter just postulated. Finding an undamaged area in an earthquake-stricken town does not prove that the earthquake was imaginary. Similarly, it is unreasonable to expect the results of past global catastrophes to be evident in all geologic data.

A report was issued in 1975 from the Institute of Geology in Uppsala, Sweden. It stated, "Analytical methods of experimental psychology applied to observations of geological data reveal that what geologists perceive in, and remember of, rocks is not necessarily the same as what is actually there." [1] The next year the same writer discussed certain illusions in geological context and stated that "the illusory perceptual data are more likely to mislead when they favour an investigator's geological hypothesis than when they did not." [2] The writer was discussing specific cases, but the results are probably true in the general case. It is true that people for both sides of two different theories will have this problem, but the proponents of the accepted theory accuse the opposition of misinterpretation merely because their views do not fit the conventional interpretation.

An example of interpretation relating specifically to this discussion can be found in an article by H. E. Wright. [3] He analyzed pollen from cores of certain lakes in Iran. In the text of his article he stated that pollen production reached a peak about 5500 years ago and that these levels "have since been maintained". However, the graph of his

data revealed a large gap in the time region of catastrophes Velikovsky proposed and this gap was labeled
"poor in pollen". Certainly the straight line assumed for the
gap is an interpretation and not necessarily one consistent
with what actually occurred.

UNIFORMITY

Uniformitarianism is a philosophy based on the assumption that all geologic processes affecting the Earth
in the past were those, and only those apparent today,
and that they always operated at the intensities and rates
that they do now. Geologic features are clearly influenced
by the cumulative effects of gradual changes caused by
now-active, small-scale agents, such as wind and rain.
Geologists *must* recognize this as a starting point for most
of their investigations. Unfortunately, as a corollary to
this it has been assumed that geologists *may not* consider
alternative agencies.

One geologist, J. B. Kloosterman, recently said that
when many geologists consider uniformity thoughtfully,
they realize that they cannot really accept it. He notes
that too much evidence pertinent to the Earth's history
simply does not fit into a uniformitarian framework.
Also, he states that final explanations for such evidence
will come from inspired searches for clues and not through
the application of methods acceptable only to medieval
scholastics or nineteenth century rationalists.

Despite claimed allegiance by geologists to uniformitarian principles, catastrophic hypotheses abound in the
scientific literature. Several of these cases, to be discussed
here, support Kloosterman's statement that, "When proposed by geologists of non-catastrophic persuasion, such
hypotheses are taken seriously, but when similar ideas
are forwarded by less conditioned outsiders, they are regarded as evidence of lunacy simply because they violate

uniformitarian dogma". [4]

When hypotheses of this nature are presented, they lean heavily on opinions and on interpretations and appraisals of field data. However, the evidence must be very compelling; otherwise, catastrophic events would never be proposed. Many features of the Earth could be results of catastrophes, but whenever evidence can be forced into the uniformitarian scheme, uniformitarian explanations are proposed and generally accepted.

COAL

We shall start with a discussion of coal, since it is familiar to most people and is of great recent interest especially due to a decrease of availability of black liquid gold (oil) and an increase in price of solid gold. Also, coal geology is a field where at least one specialist investigated various ideas about the origin of coal and concluded that Velikovsky's and a similar view by Nilsson were the most reasonable.

Velikovsky described some properties of coal in his book *Earth in Upheaval,* [5] a partial reply to those who said that no evidence for catastrophes existed other than in legends written by ill-informed ancients. In this work, Velikovsky presented evidence mostly written by the geologists who had made their own field observations; he made no reference to literary works of the ancients. Even if only half of this material was interpreted correctly by geologists, there is still an impressive amount of data indicating that unusual events must have happened many times in the past. Velikovsky's explanation for the formation of coal was impressive to at least one world authority on coal.

There are four commonly recognized types of coal: Brown coal, lignite, bituminous coal, and anthracite (hard coal). The first consists largely of compacted plant remains, and lignite is largely wood only partially converted to coal. Bituminous coal, or soft coal, is brittle, has a bright luster, and contains a large amount of sulfur which has recently taken much of the blame for pollution of the atmosphere. Anthracite is nearly pure carbon and is metamorphosed bituminous coal.

The organic origin of most coal is obvious, and plant remains are quite abundant. Many of the plants and tree remains found in coal are types that are common today.

The theory about the origin of coal most likely to be encountered in schools is the peat bog theory. According to this theory, plants died, accumulated in marshy areas, and then were slowly covered by sand, so that another layer of plants could grow. The process was supposedly repeated for thousands of years until thick seams of coal were formed.

There is no doubt that peat bogs exist. P. V. Glob has described them and their preservative properties in his fascinating book, *The Bog People*. However, the existence of bogs does not mean their origin is properly understood or that they can be used to explain coal.

It has been thought that the peat bogs in England resulted from a deteriorating climate, but one investigator, Tallis, recently tried to blame humans. [6] Evidence indicates that some peat started forming about 7000 years ago, and there is also evidence of widespread burning. This could have prevented trees from growing in the area and enhanced the growth of peat. The fires could have been natural, catastrophic or otherwise, but Tallis claimed that people could have caused them.

Several properties of coal make the peat-bog theory questionable. Some coal seams are over fifty feet thick. A one-foot layer of coal has been estimated to require a twelve-foot deposit of peat. This, in turn, would require an estimated one hundred twenty-feet of plant remains. Some seams of coal must then have been formed from six thousand feet of debris.

There are other qualities of coal which do not neatly fit the swampy-area, peat-formation theory. Much of the plant material found in coal does not grow in swampy areas. When these plants die, they fall to the ground and decay. Their remains would not be around long enough to be included in coal production. Also, single, thick coal formations sometimes divide into many thin coal layers with limestone or other rock formations between.

Ager mentioned that a fossil tree 38 feet high, still standing in its living position, was found in the late carboniferous coal measures of Lancashire. He concluded that sedimentation must have occurred rapidly enough to bury the tree and petrify it before it had time to rot.[7]

In addition to mixed plant debris from different botanical zones, some coal contains fossils of marine organisms which, when living, required vastly different environments. Erratic boulders and chunks of iron are also found in coal seams. These characteristics encouraged the suggestion that some materials washed down rivers and stacked up in bends to form coal. This overcomes many of the peat-bog problems, but does not explain the presence of ocean-dwelling species and the fact that deep-sea crinoids and clear-water ocean corals often alternate with coal seams in thick beds.

The suggestion of Velikovsky was as follows:

"Forests burned, a hurricane uprooted them, and a tidal wave or succession of tidal waves coming from the sea fell upon the charred and splintered trees and swept them into great heaps, tossed by billows, and covered them with marine sand, pebbles and shells, and weeds and fishes; another tide deposited on top of the sand more carbonized logs, threw them in other heaps, and again covered them with marine sediment. The heated ground metamorphosed the charred wood into coal, and if the wood or the ground where it was buried was drenched in a bituminous outpouring, bituminous coal was formed. Wet leaves sometimes survived the forest fires and, swept into the same heaps of logs and sand, left their design on the coal. Thus it is that seams

of coal are covered with marine sediment; for that
reason also a seam may bifurcate and have marine
deposits between its branches."[8]

Just before the publication of *Earth in Upheaval* in
1955, Velikovsky found an extensive work by Nilsson
published a short time earlier. Nilsson was a professor
of botany at Lund University when he published the two-
volume work entitled *Synthetische Artbildung*. He discussed results of various botanical studies of certain coal
from Germany. The dominant species were tropical plants
that do not even grow in the subtropics. Less abundant
species were from almost every other section of the earth.
Exceptionally well preserved insects were found; some of
these species still survive in Africa, East Asia, and America. The coal was also a grave-yard for reptiles, birds,
and mammals from diverse climates. Apes, crocodiles,
marsupials, an Indo-Australian bird, an American condor
tropical giant snakes, and East Asian salamanders were
among the creatures who donated their remains to the
German coal deposit.

The state of preservation of the various remains indicated that unusual conditions caused their burial, if not
their demise. In some cases chlorophyll is preserved in
the leaves. Billions of leaves from different parts of the
world form one stratum. Some of their fine structure is
preserved, although the leaves are torn to shreds. The
fine structure of soft animal tissues is also preserved.
Membranes and even colors of insects are preserved,
although complete insects are rare. Most of the insects,
like the plants and the higher-order animals buried with
them, were torn apart at the moment of death.

In Nilsson's opinion, the debris trapped in the coal
was deposited by onrushing water from all parts of the
world, but mostly from the coasts of the equatorial belt
of the Pacific and Indian Oceans.

Velikovsky noted: "One thing is, however, evident:
coal originated in cataclysmic circumstances".

This view was defended by Wilfrid Francis, author of *Coal, Its Formation and Composition.* [9] In the second edition of his book (the first edition was printed in 1954) he reviewed the ideas of Velikovsky and Nilsson along with other ideas about the origin of coal. After a discussion of the theories of catastrophic origin of coal, Francis mentions evidence of volcanic activity at the time when coal was being deposited in marine strata and of high sulphur concentrations and petroleum associated with coal deposits. He notes that "These facts are highly significant and lend support to ...the views of Fox, Nilsson and Velikovsky". [10]

In later chapters Francis analyzes the properties of coal and other theories, mainly uniformitarian in nature, about the origin of coal. Then in review of some of the material he says "The evidence strongly supports a process of carbonization in forest fires, which were extensive, but were checked by flooding before destruction of the forests was complete. This evidence accords well with the views on the formation of coal expressed by Velikovsky and summarized in Chapter I'. [11]

In the preface to the second edition, Francis mentions several books: *The Natural History of Indian Coals*, by C. S. Fox; *Synthetische Artbildung*, by H. Nilsson; and *Earth in Upheaval*, by Velikovsky. Francis said "These books contain much well authenticated evidence that relates to the above problems of coal formation and a summary of this evidence, which cannot be ignored in a systematic study of the formation and composition of coal, has been included in the first chapter of this new edition". [12]

It is also of interest to note that on the same page of his preface Francis writes: "The review of this literature has been made retrospective and extensive in an endeavor to ascertain how far modern work takes into consideration past experience and, particularly, to ascertain whether the modern trend follows a set pattern based upon the orthodox teaching of geology, biology and chemistry, which sometimes ignores evidence that cannot easily be reconciled with theory, or whether the modern outlook is efficiently flexible to amend classical doctrines when these are not in accord with facts". That is common knowledge, but it is not often stated so openly.

PLATE TECTONICS

The locations of some coal deposits would be difficult to explain by uniformity were it not for a theory such as plate tectonics. This theory is the recent formulation of the ideas associated with continental drift. Since the east coast of North, Central and South America appear to fit the west coasts of Europe and Africa as pieces of a jigsaw puzzle might fit, it has been postulated that all these land masses were once joined, but later split and drifted slowly apart. Coal is found in Antarctic regions where one would be hard pressed to encounter a forest today. According to plate tectonics, however, coal is supposedly transported to unusual places, by a slow, uniformitarian process.

Juergens noted that the reasoning behind plate tectonics is an inversion of uniformitarian thinking. Traditionally, geologists have inferred long-term effects from observable, presently operating causes. Plate tectonics, however, seeks to explain presumedly observable long-term effects by inferring the present existence of unobservable processes.

Plate theory is related to the Velikovsky discussion in two ways. First, some people claim that plate theory can explain all geological evidence that appears to have had catastrophic origins. Second, this theory is taught as fact, yet it has more problems than Velikovsky's theory. Whether or not the theory actually is true does not matter as far as the concepts presented by Velikovsky are concerned.

Coal had catastrophic origins. Plate theory may be able to explain otherwise odd locations of coal, but the origins of the coal must still have been catastrophic. This is one of numerous items overlooked by Sullivan, science editor for the New York *Times*. He appears to feel that the shifting-continent idea is a cure-all for any theory involving catastrophes. Many experts in geology do not share this myopic attitude.

During a discussion of Velikovsky's work, Sullivan told me that there is no geologic evidence for catastrophes. [13] At the time, Sullivan's book, *Continents in Motion*, had just been released, and whenever I mentioned specific topics I was assured that if I read his book I would see that there was no evidence for anything unusual in light of the drift theories. From a reading of the book, it is obvious he *thinks* there is no evidence for catastrophes, but his presentation does little toward explaining the events of the past.

Our discussion lasted only a few minutes and was not necessarily informative to either of us. When the subject of orbital changes arose, I asked him if he had read the articles by Bass in *Pensee*. Sullivan said that he had been given the *Pensee* series but did not read them because there might be errors in the articles. With such an excuse for not reading *Pensee*, he would also have to avoid reading *Science, Nature*, and every other existing publication. All journals contain some fact and some opinion, and none is 100% correct about either. Sullivan again assured me that everything is explained in his book, so there is no need for orbital changes. Sullivan may believe that anyone can satisfy himself about all past events by reading his book, but a review of more objective scientific literature demonstrates that all odd geologic formations cannot be explained by invoking plate tectonics. (In our conversation and in his book, Sullivan also claimed that there was absolutely nothing unusual about the demise of any mammoth. Although catastrophists as well as uniformitarians entertain certain common misconceptions about the mammoths, not all of the evidence is explainable by uniformity. For those interested in investigating both sides of this issue, Cardona has written an excellent review article.) [14]

For a number of years, Ager has taught geology, mainly uniformitarian style, at the University College of Swansea in England. In 1973 he published a book on *The Nature of the Stratigraphical Record*. He discusses plate tectonics and other drift ideas, but he also gives some anti-drift arguments. He seems to indicate that some, although not all, formations might be explained by drift. However, he believes that the standard uniformitarian ideas about deposits are not totally adequate and that some catastrophic ideas *must* be considered.

Ager prefers to rely on earth-generated catastrophes, but for one of the great ancient anomalies in the stratigraphic record he says that there "is no evident explanation" available in the drift concepts, and he expresses the opinion that at least in this case, "we must appeal to an extra-terrestrial cause".

So, although drift ideas may be interesting and useful, they do not explain everything, and they leave a number of problems still to be addressed.

Continental-drift theories have been discussed since the nineteen twenties, although similar ideas probably occurred to many people before then. In 1950 the British Association for the Advancement of Science debated the subject and then *voted* on the truth of the concept. The vote was tied. As C. R. Deyo said, "The tie goes to the winner", and in this case the winner was the one enjoying the better publicity; drift theories lost favor. For a while, geology professors cited people who wished to discuss drift as examples of how unscientific people could be. But about ten years later, geology professors (the same ones, in some cases) were pointing to anti-drift holdouts as examples of unscientific thinkers.

Although there is widespread belief in the theory of plate tectonics, there are many questionable aspects of the theory. These problems may eventually be solved, or it may be determined that some of them do not really contradict the theory in view of new evidence. Also, adjustments may be made in the theory to accommodate these problems.

Whether or not these questions are satisfactorily answered is irrelevant to our discussion. The important point is that there remain *major* unanswered questions, yet the theory is widely believed and in some cases assumed to be proven.

At a NATO advanced-study institute, participants were asked to assume drift as proven in principle and to examine how the concept might have bearing on their fields.[15] If this reasonable approach can be taken for one controversial subject it can be taken for others. In reality, however, this approach has been adopted in a one-sided manner for years. It is always assumed that uniformity is correct, and alternatives are ignored.

Plate tectonics, like uniformity, is now so well accepted that many people do not realize that there are still many unanswered questions. Therefore, a few papers concerning plate tectonics will be discussed. These were written by geologists who happen to oppose the theory. Agreement with their questions or conclusions is not intended. Reference to these papers is simply a demonstration that doubts remain.

The field is changing so quickly that some of the questions raised may have been answered by now. However, from personal correspondence with one of the authors, and from perusal of the literature, I would judge that new questions arise about as quickly as old ones are answered.

In an article on "Objections to Continental Drift and Plate Tectonics", published in the *Journal of Geology*, Paul S. Wesson of Cambridge University lists 74 shortcomings of the drift theories.[16]   He cites the work of numerous other authors and reaches the following four conclusions, which he lists in what he considers the order of their probability: (1) The continents have almost certainly not moved with respect to each other; (2) convection cannot take place throughout the earth's mantle; (3) even if convection is active in the upper mantle, it cannot account for drift; and (4) pole positions derived from paleomagnetism, and results of paleomagnetic investigations on a global scale, generally are afflicted with unknown causes of error and are in any case too inexact for drift reconstructions.

Whether or not his conclusions are valid, Wesson makes some interesting points. He notes that *all* coastlines generally fit together, and congruence of coastlines that can never have been joined has been demonstrated. Australia in contact with the east coast of America and other unlikely fits have been made. To make the fits which allegedly support the theory, existing pieces are left out and non-existing parts are added to make the fits better. This may actually be a valid procedure in some cases, but can people who pick and choose their evidence in this way reasonably insist that Velikovsky have perfect data to support all his theses before publishing his general conclusions?

In addition to numerous other problems, Wesson discusses paleomagnetism. Paleomagnetism involves analysis of remanent magnetic fields in rocks, as previously discussed with respect to the moon. Wesson believes that, because of the numerous other objections to drift that he mentions, drift theories probably would not have survived without the impetus given by paleomagnetic studies. Yet many questions have been raised about the paleomagnetic data, also.

Wesson cites one author who complains that paleomagnetic results which do not fit accepted schemes are "conveniently left out of account". Even if the paleomagnetic postulates are assumed to be correct, the scatter of the data in some cases precludes reasonable interpretation. One researcher showed that, even if one accepts only the most reliable data, several parts of the earth's surface appear to have occupied the same location simultaneously. In addition, one section of Siberia seems to have traveled (drifted) independently of the rest of the continent.

Wesson admits that plate-tectonics concepts are considerably better than classical drift concepts, but insists that most of the objections raised against the classical theories also apply to plate tectonics.

There are additional objections to be brought against plate tectonics alone. His objections 52 through 74 pertain specifically to this area. Most objections involve mechanical problems of plate tectonics, but faunal-distribution problems are also mentioned. All, however, should be of interest to anyone desiring to investigate continental-drift theories.

Mantura has also taken the approach of listing difficulties encountered by drift theories.[17]   In one article he lists 20 problems related to global tectonics, and later he outlines many additional problems. He notes that, upon examining rocks of paleozoic age, one finds perfect matches between various locations in Africa and Europe. This occurs on both sides of the Strait of Gibraltar as well as at other locations. He then describes some of the later movements ascribed to these two continents and claims that a near-miraculous pin-point docking maneuver was required to bring the continents together again precisely at their original contact points. In another case, part of Greece supposedly was torn off and rafted here and there, only to be later reunited perfectly with the rest of Greece. (The docking skill of these land masses is unequaled, even by the crews of Apollo and Soyuz.)

It may be debatable whether or not drift concepts are basically correct, but there is no doubt that there remain many unsolved problems. Some people believe that these theories are required to preserve uniformity. Oddly, however, the solutions to the problems that vex these theories may lie in the very catastrophes that some plate-tectonics proponents so vehemently deny.

STRATIGRAPHIC RECORD

Ager's book, *The Nature of the Stratigraphical Record* is not devoted only to plate tectonics. He describes a number of instances in which geologic structures are not best explained by uniformity. Apparently he feels that uniformity is involved and may persist over long periods of time, but that the geologic record consists mainly of the effects of brief catastrophes. Ager argues convincingly that geologic formations primarily record short periods of high activity, and that the gaps, or "missing" layers, represent time spans considerably longer than do the layers themselves.

As does Velikovsky, Ager takes the approach of the interdisciplinarian. Ager believes that if one has an overview of geology and does not immerse oneself in the minute study of one or two strata, then the conclusions one reaches are "inescapable" and identical to his own. He concedes that sometimes he may be too general; he might have had other thoughts had he been more of a specialist. But then he might have not noticed certain things, since "experts always tend to obscure the obvious".[18]

As a generalist, Ager concludes that frequently too much reliance is placed on uniformitarianism in the interpretation of the fossil record. His discussion of this subject leads to what he calls the second proposition of his book: "PALAEONTOLOGISTS CANNOT LIVE BY UNIFOR-MITARIANISM ALONE".[19]   He also calls this the "Phenomeon of the Fallibility of the Fossil Record".

Several examples serve to illustrate Ager's contention that a portion of the record is missing. He also offers some calculations based on observed sedimentation rates and notes that in some cases it would take over 200 years, at present rate, to bury a small fossil. Of course, rates vary with location, but even such variation is consistent with Ager's suggestion of gaps in the record, and he maintains that the most accurate suggestions concerning the stratigraphic record would be ones encompassing long gaps accompanied by only occasional sedimentation.

In discussing modern rates of sedimentation, Ager mentions that not all materials really stay where they are first deposited. He thinks that too much effort is devoted to determining how sediments are laid down, and not enough to determining the probabilities of their remaining in place.[20] He notes that many cases are known where there is a nice textbook buildup of sediments, but these same sediments are subsequently eroded away and deposited elsewhere. On the basis of calculations concerning deposition rates, Ager concludes that it is more likely the odd event rather than the gradual common process which creates thick sediments. Ager naturally believes that most of these events have natural earth-based causes; however, it can also be noted that he does not dogmatically exclude the possibility of an occasional external influence. He said, "It seems to me, from a number of recent papers (and from common sense) that the rare event is becoming more and more recognized as an important agent of recent sedimentation".[21] He also said that given enough time, which is available, the probability of the rare event approaches the value 1.0 (or certainty).

In his discussion of rapid erosion and sedimentation, Ager draws an anology between geologic and archaeologic evidence. He points out that the normal, uniformly repeated operations of daily life are the ones which consume the most time; however, they leave little in the way of archaeologic records. It is floods, earthquakes, tidal waves, and other events which make great movies, that have preserved much of the history of man. He feels that the same can be said for the geologic record. The everyday processes used up most of the history of the earth, but the stratigraphic record is more representative of catastrophic (although not always global) events.

Whether it was constructed by a series of small events, a number of simultaneous "local" events, a series of events triggered by an external body, or any combination of the above, the geologic record does not portray quiescent times of the past. Ager writes: "Traditional concepts such as gentle, continuous sedimentation (and perhaps similarly continuous evolution) are not adequate to explain what we see". [22]

CATASTROPHIC EVOLUTION

Ager's view is similar to that expressed by Velikovsky in *Earth in Upheaval*, wherein he describes many not-easily explained geologic formations and discusses what he terms "cataclysmic evolution". Velikovsky expresses the idea that some of the problems of the theory of evolution could be solved by consideration of catastrophes. He says: "The theory of evolution is vindicated by catastrophic events in the earth's part; the proclaimed enemy of this theory proved to be its only ally. The real enemy of the theory of evolution is the teaching of uniformity, or the non-occurrence of any extra-ordinary events in the past. This teaching, called by Darwin the mainstay of the theory of evolution, almost set the theory apart from reality". [23]

The mass extinctions of well-adapted species about the end of the last ice age can be reasonably accounted for by catastrophism. Catastrophic events also provide an explanation for the ice ages themselves. And during the same events that caused the extinction of species, it is readily conceivable that conditions were right for the generation of new species.

Professor Lewis M. Greenberg has collated recent material concerning evolution. He notes that "it is now becoming glaringly obvious that scholarly research and thinking of the sixties and seventies both echoes and supports Velikovsky's contention that evolution is a *cataclysmic* process". [24]

MAGNETIC FIELD REVERSALS

Evolutionary changes have recently been correlated with time periods when the earth's magnetic field became reversed. Such reversals have been hypothetically associated with Earth-Comet encounters. These matters will be discussed, but first some background about magnetic field reversals of the earth will be presented.

Like lunar rocks, materials on the earth may acquire remanent magnetism under proper conditions. Analysis of this effect in rocks can give an indication of the direction of the earth's magnetic field in the past.

In *Earth in Upheaval*, Velikovsky cites work performed by Giuseppe Folgheraiter, who investigated Attic (Greek) and Etruscan vases of various centuries. [25] He attempted to determine the orientation of the earth's magnetic field by studying remanent magnetism in clay vases. The vases were found in the positions in which they were originally baked. The conditions then were similar to situations where magnetic field directions are studied in lava flows. After studying the direction of the iron particles in the clays, Folgheraiter concluded that the earth's magnetic field was reversed in the eighth century B.C., at least in Italy and Greece. If these results are correct, a reversed magnetic field during that time period would not be surprising in view of the events Velikovsky describes.

Until recently, however, the last reversal was considered to have occurred about 700,000 years ago. In the early 1970's *Science News* contained a review of the magnetic field-reversal information in which they listed this date as the last reversal. A reader wrote to the editor and mentioned the reference given by Velikovsky and asked if the work of Folgheraiter had been refuted. The editor ignored the question but used the letter as an opening to perpetuate the false impression that no geologist took any of Velikovsky's ideas seriously. Folgheraiter's work was recently mentioned in an article in *Nature* (by me, with a reference to Velikovsky) and no one informed me that the work has been refuted. [26] This does not, of course, mean that refutation is lacking; it means only that neither the editor of *Science News*, nor certain referees for *Nature*, nor I have yet run across it. Therefore, it is reasonable to keep this open as a possibility.

Not long after the official pronouncement that 700,000 years was the span of time since the earth's last magnetic-field reversal, new evidence was discovered which indicated that the last reversal may not have been so long ago after all. A section of sediment dated at about 12,500 years was found to be reversely magnetized. [27] Whether or not this section can be proven to represent a global field reversal, it is now becoming widely accepted that a number of short-lived reversals may yet be discovered. Unfortunately, it is also obvious that these brief events will be difficult to detect.

Berbetti and McElhinny recently discussed the possibility that a reversal occurred about 30,000 years ago. [28] They conducted experiments similar to those of Folgheraiter; however, their investigations were of aboriginal fireplaces in Australia around Lake Mungo. They noticed that consistent directions were almost always obtained when several stones from the same oven were analyzed. Thus they felt that if a reversal had occurred during the time the site was occupied, they might be able to detect it by analysis of a number of fireplaces in the immediate area. They concluded that an event did occur about 30,000 years ago. They call it a "geomagnetic excursion" since it was not a complete 180° reversal. They also noted that work performed in Czechoslovakia indicated an "excursion" which occurred about the same time and lasted for the same length of time. They do not know the cause of these events, but they speculate, without quantitative analysis, that these events may be "a manifestation of some fundamental property of the geomagnetic dynamo". They add that whatever the cause, at least two major "excursions" have occurred during the last 35,000 years.

CORRELATIONS TO MAGNETIC FIELD REVERSALS

A number of scientists are now beginning to note correlations between large-scale, unusual activities in the geologic record and changes in various life patterns. Some even mention encounters between the earth and external objects as possible triggering mechanisms for such events. Concerning this type of encounter, Ager remarks: "Such hypotheses have been postulated by highly reputable geologists when no other possible cause can be found to explain certain phenomena. I make no apology for joining a distinguished band of predecessors".[29]

As oceanographic studies became more popular, and more data became available, important correlations began to come to light. In 1966 Opdyke and others made a paleomagnetic study of deep sea cores from the Antarctic. One of their conclusions was that a coincidence or near-coincidence of faunal changes with reversals of the earth's magnetic field suggested a cause-and-effect relationship.[30]

The next year Watkins and Goddell reported results of their investigation of geomagnetic polarity changes and faunal extinctions. They referred specifically to radiolarian changes at the time of a field reversal 700,000 years ago. They stated that "we must consider the possibility of a direct connection between geomagnetic polarity and faunal changes".[31]

The same year Waddington mentioned the cosmic-radiation increase which would result from a zero magnetic field during a reversal and expressed the opinion that this alone might be enough to produce the observed faunal changes.[32]

Hays and Opdyke presented additional evidence of faunal boundaries coinciding with magnetic field reversals.[33] Evidence became impressive for these correlations, although not all investigators agreed that the evidence was conclusive.[34]

FIELD REVERSALS, TEKTITES AND EARTH-COMET COLLISIONS

Tektites are small glassy objects, some of which have shapes characteristic of raindrops. They have long been a puzzle to geologists. In 1957, Harold Urey suggested that tektites were produced by comets colliding with the earth.[35] He continued to pursue this approach and in 1963 co-authored another article discussing the origin of tektites in cometary collisions. [36]

The same year Lyttleton suggested that cometary material, falling to earth, formed tektites. [37]

In 1966, Lin argued for a terrestrial origin for tektites, but he noted that their formation might be connected with an Earth-comet collision. [38]

Later, Lyttleton wrote another article on the origin of tektites and noted that the comparative rarity of tektite fields would be consistent with rare catastrophic events, such as cometary encounters or large meteorite impacts. [39]

In 1971, Durrani and Khan published a paper on microtektites and magnetic-field reversals. [40] They correlate various tektite deposits with known geomagnetic-field reversals. They also cited studies indicating that certain marine microorganisms became extinct, while others suddenly appeared, in sediments associated with the magnetic-field reversals. After noting Urey's suggestion of tektites being produced by earth-comet encounters, they discuss possible effects that ammonia and methane introduced into the atmosphere would have on different life forms. They also mention the possibility of large explosions in the atmosphere due to lightning discharges in the gaseous mixtures then available. Durrani and Khan conclude that the last two geomagnetic-field reversals seem to correlate with microtektite and tektite deposits and that a causal relationship is possible.

Kennet and Watkins have also drawn attention to correlations between field reversals, widespread faunal extinctions, climatic changes, and maxima of volcanic activity. [41]

All these activities could reasonably correlate with collisions or near-encounters between the earth and external bodies.

Tarling notes that polarity reversals sometimes last only for short times, and as a result their detection and analysis are difficult. [42] He claims that these events result from short-lived geophysical processes, but he also claims that the processes must occur at the core-mantle interface of the Earth. He does not consider the possibility of external influences.

However, Glass and Heezen have suggested that an encounter between the earth and an external body could have mechanical or electromagnetic consequences on the magnetohydrodynamic motions of the earth's core.[43] They speculate that encounters of this nature may have caused some of the geomagnetic reversals on the earth.

Velikovsky made this suggestion in *Earth in Upheaval.*[44]

In line with the discussion of drastic changes caused by Earth-comet encounters is a surprising paper by Harold Urey. He is vehement in his opposition to all Velikovsky's works (although he also claims not to have read those works). Perhaps he did not realize the similarity between his and Velikovsky's suggestions when he suggested in 1973 that the geological ages were ended by catastrophes. He even suggests that these catastrophes were caused by collisions between the earth and comets.[45]

Earlier, Urey proposed that a collision between the earth and a comet produced events so violent that rocky materials and water escaped the earth and were captured by the moon.[46]

THE TRIGGERING MECHANISM

The comets in the collisions hypothesized by the previously mentioned scholars could be considered as global triggering mechanisms for exceptional numbers of natural local events, such as earthquakes and volcanic explosions. Some of these local events could have been of an unusually large magnitude, with normally slow processes simply having been accelerated. But pointing to the geologic results of these local events and saying that these features are caused by oversized natural causes does not fully explain the data. Although it is true that earthquakes and volcanic eruptions are local "natural" events, the exceptional magnitude and unusual number may have been precipitated by another natural cause on a global scale, such as the close approach of an external body.

There is abundant evidence in the geologic record to indicate that certain events of the past occurred on a scale totally unlike that of today. Ager naturally prefers to attribute as much evidence for catastrophes as possible to presently seen processes, such as earthquakes or hurricanes, but he admits that some of the evidence indicates that catastrophes occurred in the past of magnitudes unheard of in our time.

In *Earth in Upheaval*, Velikovsky cites evidence for events of this type. Ager has presented additional examples. As we have seen, many scientists are now considering the possibility that some of these events were triggered by external influences. (Another example from the geologic record suggests that a world-wide cataclysm occurred about 1,300 million years ago, and one suggested cause is the capture of the moon by the earth.)[47]

ERRATIC BOULDERS

A triggering mechanism outside the earth could also explain some odd effects of a less extensive nature. In *Earth in Upheaval*, Velikovsky included a section about erratic boulders, which are boulders that were apparently formed some distance from their present location and are distinctly unlike the deposits around them. He listed many locations where erratic boulders are now located and their suspected points of origin. On impressive example was an erratic mass of chalk stone about three miles long, a thousand feet wide and over one hundred feet thick near Malmo, Sweden. England posesses a similar erratic chalk slab which has a village built on it.[48]

Ager noted that there are a number of "smashed-up-looking" deposits around the world, and in many of them

are found erratic boulders. He considers the most remarkable among those of which he has knowledge to be
that on the island of Timor. This island exposes an out-
croping about 60 miles wide, 1.5 miles thick, and some
600 miles long, known as Bobonard Sealy Clay, which
may extend for thousands of miles. Imbedded in this layer
on Timor is a large, rounded, igneous rock. The rock is
about 100 feet in diameter, although it is more pear-
shaped than spherical. Ager says that, not even considering the problem of how the rock happened to become
rounded, "it is difficult to use a term other than 'catastrophic' for the arrival of such a pebble."[49]

THE BLACK SEA

Evidence for sudden changes, which may have been
triggered by an agent external to the earth, closely correlates to the times of the recent events described by Velikovsky.

In 1970 an article was published about the recent
sedimentary history of the Black Sea. A number of core
samples, taken at intervals for a distance of over 600
miles, showed that three distinct sedimentary units were
correlated throughout that entire distance on the sea
bottom. In most cores, three "abrupt stratigraphic changes"
could be observed.[50]   The dates of these events were
approximately 5000, 3400, and 900 B.C. The investigators claim that the horizons between units are obviously
related to environmental changes.

These changes may have been triggered by the same
processes which caused environmental changes about the
same time throughout the world.

Chapter VIII

THE MODERN AFFAIR

For several years after *Worlds in Collision* was published, many members of the scholarly community reacted to the book in a totally irrational manner. This is even admitted by people who oppose Velikovsky's ideas. They further claim that the irrationality has stopped, but unfortunately this is not so. In this chapter, some recent events in the Velikovsky affair will be discussed, and several possible causes of the attitudes behind them will be considered.

THE AAAS MEETING

The 1974 meeting of the American Association for the Advancement of Science (AAAS) has been mentioned several times in connection with specific scientific topics; however, it deserves mention here because, although it was billed as a scientific meeting, it fell considerably short of this status. In June of 1973 an announcement appeared in *Science* requesting suggestions for topics to be discussed during the February 1974 AAAS meeting. The year before, Walter Orr Roberts, an astronomer, atmospheric scientist and a past-president of the AAAS, had publicly suggested that a symposium on Velikovsky's works be held, and he wrote to an AAAS official about this possibility. Therefore, it seemed reasonable for people interested in Velikovsky's work to submit a proposal in response to the announcement in *Science*, and this was done.

The AAAS was "unable to accept" this proposal, but they did accept a similar one submitted by the AAAS Astronomy Committee. Ivan King, who teaches astronomy at The University of California, Berkeley, visited Velikovsky and discussed the proposal. Later, Donald Goldsmith, an assistant professor of astronomy at the State University of New York, Stony Brook, wrote to Velikovsky to confirm King's invitation to participate and to discuss an outline for the symposium. Goldsmith said that because of time limitations the symposium should be centered on the nature and motions of the planets, particularly Venus and Jupiter. Although the schedule was tight and specific areas of astronomy were to be discussed, Goldsmith did mention that the committee hoped to "work in" a sociologist to "examine the reception of unpopular scientific ideas".

Frederic B. Jueneman is Director of Research for Innovative Concepts Associates of San Jose, author of *Limits of Uncertainty*, and the writer of an intriguing regular feature, "Innovative Notebook: Scientific Speculation by Jueneman", in *Industrial Research* magazine. Jueneman called King to inquire about the symposium and the events which led to it. According to Jueneman, King stated that the intent was to take another look at Velikovsky's work, since there was a renewed interest in it. He also said that the participants would be from the "hard" sciences, which do not include sociology.

Jueneman asked if this might be a move to stem criticism of the AAAS for the actions of its members in the Velikovsky affair. King replied that to some extent it was, but that only individual members of the AAAS were involved in the excesses against Velikovsky, not the AAAS itself. (This is the updated version of the "nothing really happened, and, besides, it was them and not us that did it" game.)

Soon it became apparent that the organizers of the symposium had no intention of pursuing a scientific discussion. King later said, "None of us in the scientific establishment believes that a debate about Velikovsky's views of the Solar System would be remotely justified at a serious scientific meeting". Either this was intentionally misleading and malicious propaganda, or King was unaware of recent work in his own field. It is clear, however, that the meeting was arranged, as Jueneman said, to be a contemporary court of inquisition, and that the discussion was designed to convince the public that they should ignore the increasing number of scientists who were taking the time to analyze Velikovsky's work. Since the organizers admitted that they did not consider the meeting a scientific one, perhaps this is how they justified, to themselves, the misleading and sometimes false statements used to support their positions.

STORER

The first speaker at this meeting which the AAAS so carefully and accurately described as non-scientific, was Norman Storer, Professor of Sociology, Baruch College, City University of New York. The first two–thirds of his talk was devoted to sociologically accepted platitudes about the way science and scientists act. Not that they are this way, but this is what sociologists like to believe. The rest of his talk concerned the Velikovsky controversy, but exuded the impression that, although the actions against Velikovsky were sometimes a bit uncouth, overall they must have been in some way justifiable. As it was phrased in *Pensee*, "the peculiar ways of science in the Velikovsky affair were obscured in a fog of sociological 'explanation'".

During the question-and-answer session after Storer's talk the resistance of scientists to new ideas was mentioned. Dr. Mulholland, another symposium participant, responded with two examples which he claimed demonstrated that scientists readily accept unexpected new concepts: Mass concentrations on the Moon; and the internal heat of the Moon. Velikovsky then asked Mulholland if he knew who happened to have been the first to claim that the Moon had internal heat, and if there is an explanation for the mass concentrations other than encounters of the Moon and other celestial bodies. Velikovsky also asked Mulholland if he considered these two observations to be fundamental theories.

Mulholland replied that he did not know who was the first to suggest the internal heat of the Moon, and appeared not to realize that it was Velikovsky. Mulholland admitted, however, that Velikovsky "put his finger on a weak point in my statement, because what I gave as a response a moment ago were observations and determinations rather than theoretical suggestions."

HUBER

One of Storer's justifications for the unethical treatment of Velikovsky by many scientists was that he wrote about areas which were not in his original field of formal training. Oddly enough, the second speaker discussed a subject not in his original field. This was acceptable, however, since he was speaking in favor of the standard opinion. The speaker was Peter Huber, Professor of Mathematical Statistics at the Swiss Federal Institute of Technology, who spoke about early cuneiform inscriptions.

One of Huber's arguments was that Venus was known soon after 3000 B. C. He presented some documentary slides supporting this. This was not surprising, since Velikovsky had presented evidence in *Worlds in Collision* that Venus was known before the first Venus-Earth encounter. At the meeting Velikovsky stressed, as he has done often before, that he does not know how long Venus existed before its first encounter with the earth. Huber claimed that, before

1500 B.C., Venus was referred to as having a morning
and evening-star appearance; hence, it must have had an
orbit lying totally inside that of the Earth, as it does today.
Evidently Huber was not familiar with modern astronomy's most recent spectacular triumph, Comet Kohoutek.
This object made much of the public aware that a body
need not have an orbit totally inside that of the Earth in
order to be seen both in morning and evening appearances.

A member of the audience pointed out that some of the
early drawings of what Huber claimed was Venus definitely resembled a comet. Huber admitted that this was
true, but said that more elaborate representations did not,
as if this explained the ones that did.

During the discussion of ancient descriptions of Venus,
Velikovsky mentioned a portion of text which described
Venus as being at one time as "bright" as the Sun. Huber
claimed that the passage should properly be translated,
"sends out light like the sun". The subsequent discussion
by Huber emphasized the possibility that Velikovsky's
translation was not exact and ignored the idea that comparing Venus to the Sun, as many ancient cultures did,
is not reasonable under conditions prevailing today.

Huber's second major point related to the so-called
"Venus Tablets of Ammizaduga". Although the dates of
observations recorded in these tablets are open to question,
there is agreement that they date to before the last catastrophe described by Velikovsky. Huber ignored the extensive discussion of these tablets in *Worlds in Collision*;
he also ignored the astute analysis of the tablets by Rose
and Vaughan (which had already been presented in a
paper by Rose[1], and afterwards was developed further in
an article co-authored by Rose and Vaughan[2]). This left
the false impression that the tablets were unknown to or suppressed by those interested in Velikovsky's work. If Huber
merely was unaware of the discussions by Velikovsky and

Rose, that might support his image as an ethical man, but it would hardly enhance his image as a researcher. One scholar cannot be expected to locate every last paper related to a given subject, but since one very pertinent document was in the book being discussed and another was in the then only journal discussing the ideas of Velikovsky, an appropriate analysis of the "Venus Tablets" should have included a discussion of the writings of Velikovsky and Rose.

Since it did not, all three will be mentioned here.

Huber basically claims that if you leave out about 30 percent of the observations given in the tablets you can make them agree with what would be expected if no change had occurred in the solar system. No doubt some of the data in the tablets are erroneous; however, deleting data not fitting the accepted theory is not always justified, and as Rose and Vaughan have skillfully shown, it is definitely not justified in this case.

In *Worlds in Collision,* Velikovsky cautiously does not claim to know when the observations were made or the precise planetary motions which would produce such observations; he only comments that the observations are not understandable in terms of the present order of the Solar System. Although some of the data may be explained away as scribal errors or other mistakes, he notes that such inaccuracies may account for a few days, but not for differences of months. Also, since "each item in the record is stated in dates as well as in the number of days between the dates", this reduces the probability that all questionable entries are errors. These tablets are not poetical works which require interpretation, but dry, observational records.

What is similarly striking is the fact that Hindu records present the same problem. These writings are thought to be corrupted, since the details referring to Venus do not conform to modern, retrospective calculations.

Rose presents a more detailed analysis of the "Venus Tablets of Ammizaduga". One of the conclusions he and Vaughan reached was that the tablets may be misnamed and have nothing to do with Ammizaduga or his time.

Rose's report stresses that the data given in the Babylonian tablets is divided into three groups. The "idealized regularity" of Venus' apparitions in the second group, he says, makes them "very suspicious-looking". These data would definitely not support uniformitarian ideas, but the "idealized and somewhat numerological character of this group of data has led most readers, probably correctly, to suspect that this group of 'observations' is not directly based on observation at all..." As for the "observations" which appear to be actual observations, Rose notes that modern astronomers feel justified in changing them to reflect what they think they should say, as opposed to what they actually do say. This, through some unbelievable adjustment, led to totally unfounded statements which are now assumed to be true. Rose quotes Sarton as saying "As early as the close of the third millennium, Babylonian astronomers recorded heliacal risings and settings of the planet Venus." This is supported by a footnote in Sarton's book mentioning Kugler and Schiaparelli, but Schiaparelli dated the tablets around the seventh or eighth century B.C., which is in general agreement with the suggestion by Rose and Vaughan. Kugler dated them from 1977 to 1956 B.C. Assigning the latter dates to the third millennium is like calling the present time the twenty-first century. Rose comments: "if you think that's bad, consider what happened in 1950. In the rush to find evidence against Velikovsky, Sarton's sloppy use of 'the third millennium' as a substitute for '1977-1956' was resurrected from the libraries and rephrased as '3000 B.C.' by people like Kaempffert. This whole comedy of errors is traceable back to Kugler. Why Schiaparelli was implicated in it escapes me." Rose also aptly demonstrates that selecting one or two "good" observations and trying to place them properly in history does not really do justice to the uniformitarian cause. The "bad" data are bad no matter where they are placed. Rose points out that both sides in the controversy cite exactly the same evidence. "But when you examine the content of those tablets, they turn out to support Velikovsky and not his critics."

The third major point raised by Huber related to ancient eclipses. Huber claimed that eclipses mentioned in ancient records are in agreement with calculations based on the assumption that nothing has changed. Some of these accurately determined eclipses date from before the last catastrophe, he claimed; therefore, the catastrophe could not have occurred.

This was a revival of the old eclipse trick first instituted by astronomer J. Q. Stewart in 1951. Stewart cited three ancient eclipses which he claimed conformed to uniformity. In a reply to Stewart, Velikovsky demonstrated that in each case either the location, the date, or both were not known about the ancient eclipse; hence, any correspondence with retro-fit calculations was only an assumption. Huber apparently agreed that Velikovsky had been correct in refuting Stewart's argument.

Velikovsky then mentioned the most-often-cited recent reference which seems to fit an ancient eclipse to uniformitarian calculations.[3] This was supposedly an eclipse recorded in Ugarit on May 3, 1375 B.C. A tablet was found which had writing on both sides. On one side was "The Sun went down (in the daytime) with Rashap in attendance". Rashap is identified as Mars. The other said that the vassals attacked the overlords.

The translator appears to have considered the two sides unrelated. Treating the side about the Sun going down at an unusual hour, he assumed that this must refer to an eclipse. (The only other conceivable possibilities being catastrophic, one rules them out as "unthinkable" and thus "proves" it was an eclipse.)

The time the tablet was written was unknown, but a few assumptions were used to set some limits. It was assumed that conventional Egyptian chronology is correct, which would then put the time of destruction of the city where the tablet was found in the thirteenth or fourteenth century B.C. (In the revised chronology, the time would be the ninth century B.C.) If the event occurred not long before the destruction of the city, then the fourteenth century would be a reasonable place to look, assuming conventional chronology. Retro-calculations indicated that an eclipse should have occurred in the area on May 3, 1375 B.C. It was not really a total eclipse at the location where the tablet was found, so, Stephenson suggested, maybe someone up the coast saw the eclipse and ran down to Ugarit to write about it. If this is not satisfactory, one may assume that the partial eclipse was great enough to be noticeable or that advanced techniques for observing the Sun had been developed. The same uniformitarian calculations revealed that Mars should not have been visible, so the reference to Mars was assumed to have been a mistake.

So it appears that there are enough assumptions to make this particular eclipse questionable. The discussion was then reduced to analyzing the one total eclipse about which the audience was assured there was no doubt. Unfortunately, Huber pointed out that the proof for this eclipse had not yet been published, but he guaranteed it to be irrefutable.

In 1971, one of the later speakers, Mulholland, reviewed a book about ancient astronomical observations. In this review, Mulholland emphasized the same point that Velikovsky had so often made.[4] Concerning ancient eclipse records, Mulholland said: "nearly always the date and location of the observations are unknown....it seems clear that there is much room to suspect the classical results of serious bias". Mulholland, however, did not mention this when he could have supported Velikovsky. His inaction fit with moderator King's interpretation of what should be done, since King had made it clear that the meeting was not intended to be scientific.

VELIKOVSKY

The third speaker was Velikovsky. Much of the content of his talk is discussed elsewhere in this book; however, one item relates to the controversy in general and to the AAAS meeting in particular. While describing some of the reaction to his views, Velikovsky, as he has done many times, made it clear that he does not consider himself infallible. Toward the end of his talk he said, "Those who prefer name calling to argument, wit to deliberation, or those who point a triumphant finger at some detail that they misinterpret, yet claim that my entire work ought to collapse, and boast of their own exclusiveness as a caste of specialists--as if I claimed omniscience and infallibility and as if I wrote a sacred book that fails for some possible error--are not first in their art. I shall quote Giordano Bruno, and one of the organizers of this symposium, Professor Owen Gingerich, Harvard's historian of science, is well familiar with Bruno's description of how his contemporaries used to conduct a dispute:

"With a sneer, a smile, a certain discrete malice, that which they have not succeeded in proving by argument-- nor indeed can it be understood by themselves--nevertheless by these tricks of courteous disdain they pretend to have proven, endeavouring not only to conceal their own patently obvious ignorance but to cast it on to the back of their adversary. For they dispute not in order to find or even to seek Truth, but for victory, and to appear the more learned and strenuous upholders of a contrary opinion. Such persons should be avoided by all who have not a good breastplate of patience."

After quoting this, Velikovsky made a major point to which many of his opposition have been and are still oblivious. He said that it does not matter "what Velikovsky's role is in the scientific revolution that goes across all fields..." It is not just Velikovsky against the world, as some like to advertise. Velikovsky was instrumental in formulating certain concepts, but his work has gone beyond the reach of one man. Seeking a mistake in his writings so as to claim that his entire concept is therefore wrong is not unlike seeking a minor error in a paper about Bose-Einstein statistics and claiming, when you found an error, that all work by everyone in relativity should be ignored.

Velikovsky then expressed the unfulfilled hope that the meeting would be a "retarded recognition that by name-calling instead of testing, by jest instead of reading and meditating, nothing is achieved". Part of his next sentence was removed from its obvious connection to the rest of the paper and was used for jest and name-calling. Although Velikovsky had stressed that he was not infallible, he noted that misquoting his books and attacking the misquote was not a fair way to show that he was fallible. In concluding, he noted that no one can change the evidence that turned out in his favor, and "nobody can change a single sentence of my books". This obvious reference to the misquotation of his books was itself misused. Sagan gave reporters the impression that Velikovsky had claimed to be infallible, and this false impression was extensively publicized.

MULHOLLAND

The fourth speaker was J. Derral Mulholland, Professor of Astronomy at The University of Texas at Austin. Most of the major points by Mulholland have been discussed in the section in Chapter IV about celestial mechanics. It is of interest here to note that Bass wrote a concise reply to some of the points raised by Mulholland, and Bass asked to be allowed to mention them at the open evening session, where anyone was supposed to be allowed to speak. Bass was told that he would not be able to present his arguments, since the public might become confused if a noted authority disagreed with the expert chosen by the panel.

SAGAN

Sagan is a popular humorist who is with the laboratory for Planetary Studies at Cornell University. His paper contained nothing which furthered scientific debate. However, his paper was presented exceptionally well, and his charisma added to the effectiveness of the presentation. Most of the audience did not know and, because of his captivating delivery, did not care that many of his points were irrelevant, incorrect, or misleading. His entrancingly arrogant delivery exuded the air of a great evangelist who had come to lead the people along the true uniformitarian path. Unfortunately, many in the audience were taken in. (The reaction of people in this manner is why many states have passed laws which give one three days to cancel a contract made with a silver-tongued door-to-door salesman.)

Some of the following information is from the most recently available revision of Sagan's paper. Some of his pre-AAAS meeting comments were drastically revised for the paper given at the meeting. After many fallicious points about his paper were revealed in *Pensee*, the paper was again corrected.

Although many of Sagan's statements contained fictional qualities, one statement in particular abounded with misinformation. *Pensee* said: "Only so fecund a source of error as Sagan, it seems, could offer the following statement, wrong in virtually every particular." Sagan, trying to prove that some scientists were wrong when they suggested Velikovsky be given credit for certain ideas, said:

"In the famous letter to *Science* by Bargmann and Motz (1962) and in some of the correspondence of the late Harry Hess, Velikovsky's prognostication that the clouds of Venus were made of carbohydrates was hailed as an example of a successful scientific prediction." The only part of this statement that is correct is that Bargmann and Motz did write a letter to *Science*. However, they made no mention of the clouds of Venus, or their composition; Hess never discussed the subject, and Velikovsky's claim involved hydrocarbons, not carbohydrates. This indiscriminate mixing of the terms hydrocarbons and carbohydrates by Sagan was in the very talk where he accused Velikovsky of confusing the same two terms.

Sagan claimed to have made a calculation showing that the odds against the events happening as described by Velikovsky were 10^{23} to one. These high odds were widely quoted as making any hypothesis "untenable".

Sagan referred to an appendix in which it was supposedly demonstrated how he arrived at these odds. Presumably he used a method other than contacting Jimmy the Greek, but the appendix to which Sagan referred was not given out with the paper, so his exact method was not then available. This, among other inconsistencies in Sagan's presentation, led Dr. Robert Bass to make some inquiries of Sagan after the talk.

Bass asked Sagan how he had made the probability calculations without using a particular mathematical process. Sagan gave three replys. One reply was to the effect that it was unfair for Bass to ask such complicated questions, since Bass knew more about the subject than did Sagan. Another reply was that Bass should talk to Mulholland since Mulholland also knew more about the subject than did Sagan. The third reply was that Sagan had assumed that the events were independent. Concerning this last point, Bass remarked: "This Sagan assumption is so disingenuous that I do not hesitate to label it as either a deliberate fraud on the public or else a manifestation of unbelievable incompetence or hastiness combined with desperation and wretchedly poor judgment."

Perhaps Sagan's most quoted statement from the symposium was this: "My conclusion will be that where Velikovsky is original, he is very likely wrong; and that where he is right, the idea has been pre-empted by earlier workers". Whether this lie was original with Sagan or was fabricated by an earlier worker, it is flatly untrue; yet it was quoted in almost every news account of the meeting. This was more of an attempt at creative writing than a "conclusion" reached after an investigation. His failure to attempt to document this statement was perhaps due to a realization that it was not possible. *Pensee* stated that "such an effort to discredit another scholar's work is highly unethical, and deserves investigation by the official AAAS committee on ethics."

Although Sagan's statement is catchy and quotable, it is much more accurately applied to Sagan's own work. When it is pointed out that Sagan has an extremely poor record, he defends this by saying that it is scientific to be open-minded and willing to change one's mind. He leaves the impression that it is better to be wrong so you can change and prove you are "scientific" than it is to be right and have people wonder about your status. If being wrong is scientific, then Sagan is certainly scientific.

MICHELSON

The last speaker was Dr. Irving Michelson, Professor of Mechanical and Aerospace Engineering at the Illinois Institute of Technology. Portions of his paper are discussed elsewhere in this book (Appendix I). *Science* claimed that he had been chosen to "say something good" about

Velikovsky's ideas. However, Michelson corrected this: "It was not my purpose to say something good about Velikovsky's ideas, any more than it was my purpose to say something bad. If there were others blindly committed as pro or con, my purpose was to perform not an act of faith but an act of objective scholarship--and I would still not venture to estimate to what degree my remarks, Mechanics Bears Witness, were either good or bad for his ideas."[5]

Following Michelson's presentation, Mulholland said that the energy of a solar flare would be reduced by 10^8 by the time it reached the Earth and therefore, Michelson's calculations were off by that factor. Since Michelson had clearly referred to the energy of a geomagnetic storm and not that of a solar flare, he preferred to continue to another question instead of pointing out how trivial and irrelevant Mulholland's remark was. The only mention that *Science* gave to Michelson's unique article was to say that he was off by a factor of 10^{18} on his calculation about the Earth's rotation change. The discussion, however, was about the tilt of the Earth's axis, and *Science* had increased Mulholland's number from 10^8 to 10^{18}, which they probably felt was justified since the number was meaningless anyway. When Michelson wrote to *Science* and mentioned their rather gross errors, they refused to publish his letter. This incident was related in another magazine, and a group of scientists from a scientific laboratory in Canada wrote to *Science* and asked them either to print Michelson's letter or to explain why it was not true. The exact reason is not known, but *Science* then printed the letter from Michelson.

CONTINUED AFFAIR

The problem encountered by Michelson in having his letter published reveals that the modern Velikovsky affair did not stop with the AAAS meeting. Other events have also taken place in this modern affair.

The AAAS wanted to publish a book about the proceedings of the Velikovsky symposium. As with the meeting, they wanted to proportion the alloted space in a manner best to support accepted opinion. After having presented question after question, they limited the space allotted to Velikovsky for replies to the questions. Had Velikovsky answered only those questions he could in the limited space, his opponents would have argued that he could not answer the others. If he answered none because there was not enough space to answer properly, they would say he capitulated. What was also a problem, and one that has occurred previously, was that he could send in his reply and then the writers of the other articles would correct the mistakes he pointed out about their articles. This makes it difficult for one to decide which way one's work will be misrepresented the least.

The AAAS was to provide a copy of Sagan's paper to Velikovsky so that he could reply. Sagan's revised paper (many of the original gross errors were corrected or dropped) was delivered to him in February of 1976, two years after the symposium. Obviously Velikovsky could not reply to an article he had not read (although scientists sometimes try this approach); however, over two months before he received Sagan's paper, Velikovsky was accused of delaying the publication of the AAAS proceedings.[6] After Velikovsky decided to answer in detail in KRONOS instead of partially in the AAAS book, the AAAS proceeded with plans to publish without contributions from Velikovsky. This made it obvious that Velikovsky was not the controlling factor.

Since the appendix was not provided with Sagan's original paper, reporters had to accept Sagan's opinion that he had supported his statements. Over two years later, the appendix appeared with the revised paper. After reading it, one readily sees why Sagan wanted his appendix removed. Its arguments might sound convincing to someone untrained in physics, but any physicist would easily notice that the appendix does not contain a rational physical analysis. While writing it, Sagan could only have hoped that no one informed about physics would ever read it.

First, Sagan attempted to calculate the probability that the events happened. He did not confirm his widely quoted probability of 10^{23} to 1, so the origin of that number remains a mystery. This is surprising since, with the freedom of assumptions he allowed himself, he could have produced just about any number he desired. He used one of several methods of calculating the probabilities of collisions, and depending on the assumptions, these give widely different probabilities. (See references [7] and [8] for recent methods.)

Sagan also cluttered the calculation with unnecessary details in order to make the odds against collisions higher. If enough specific restraints are placed on an idea, anything can be "proven" to be improbable. For example, it is known that a 10 pound meteorite fell through the roof of a house and hit a Mrs. Hewlett Hodges in her left side just below the ribs. Obviously a person being hit by a meteorite is a rare event. An estimate of about how rare the event is might be obtained by calculating a "probability" that the event would happen. This might be done by using estimates about the number of meteorites hitting populated portions of the earth per year, and the average number of people per unit area in populated areas. However, Sagan's technique would more closely resemble the following: He would calculate the probability that someone named Hewlett Hodges would be born and eventually get married. Then he would calculate the probability that a house would be hit by a meteorite and that Mrs. Hewlett Hodges would be home at the time. If it were a 10 room house, he would calculate the probability that she was in the room that was hit. He would then assume a certain size room and calculate the probability that she was in the part of the room that was hit. Included would be a fifty-fifty chance that she was facing the proper direction so that she would be hit on the left side. He would also add an estimate of the square inches on her body and the area just below the ribs to get a probability that this is where she was hit. Combining all of this, his final number would be used as "proof" that this did not happen because the odds are improbably high. Of course the event is rare, but you cannot "improbable" it out of existence. A calculation including all of the above factors would be totally meaningless. The same is true of Sagan's calculation about the events described by the ancients.

After his basic calculation, he assumed that all of the recent events were statistically independent. As Bass noted, this is not a realistic approach. The events were causally related, and not independent.

If the events happened, it does not matter how small the probability is, and if they did not happen, it does not matter how large the probability may be.

Sagan's second appendix related to the stopping of the rotation of the earth. He admits that people would not fly off the earth, but Sagan calculated that the heat generated would kill everything. His assumptions in doing so were no more realistic than those for the probability calculations. For example, he assumed that *all* the energy would be directly converted into evenly distributed heat.

The third appendix related to the temperature of Venus. At the AAAS meeting, Sagan said that if Venus were ejected from Jupiter, the heat generated would have been enough to vaporize Venus.

Evidently he then assumed that if Venus managed to get out of Jupiter, it did so without being heated at all, since he described its heating as being caused only by the encounters with the Earth, and Mars and its close approach to the Sun. Sagan then incorrectly attributed these statements to Velikovsky. [9] Sagan said, however, that Venus would have had time to cool since the time of these encounters, so its temperature could not be attributed to these encounters. Appendix three was an attempt to convince non-physicist that this was true. Sagan generously assumed that Venus could have been heated to 6000 K, but then he assumed that it received *no additional radiation for 3500 years*. He then calculated that Venus would be only 79 K now. This is near the freezing point of air. Since Venus is closer to 750 K, Sagan claims this proves that Velikovsky is wrong. However, Sagan's calculation is obviously completely detached from reality; he uses the implied assumption that there was no radiation from the Sun to Venus in the last 3500 years.

At the AAAS meeting, Sagan claimed that the heat of Venus was not only anticipated by scientists but was well explained long before the publication *Worlds in Collision*. He referred to the work of Rupert Wildt, who in 1940 was probably the first to suggest a greenhouse effect on Venus. (Before the AAAS meeting, Wildt's work was twice brought to the attention of scientists by Velikovsky-related publications.) Curiously enough, Wildt does not seem to be remembered when Sagan graciously accepts credit for being the originator of the greenhouse theory, and Wildt was not even referenced in one of two articles which Sagan claims as his announcement of the greenhouse effect. Could this be for either of the following reasons: First, Sagan may know Wildt's work has nothing to do with the subject; second, he may think it has something to do with the subject, but prefers credit for the idea unless his image can be enhanced by admitting that someone else first suggested the idea. Wildt died in 1976, and several science publications mentioned his major contributions to astronomy. Suggesting the greenhouse effect for Venus was not listed among them. (In his 1964 *Biographical Encyclopedia of Science*, Asimov did not even list this as a noteworthy item about Wildt, although Asimov did think Wildt's suggestion of formaldehyde in Venus' atmosphere was worth mentioning.) That the greenhouse theory is very questionable was previously discussed in Chapter V. Had Sagan revealed more facts about this problem, the audience would have noticed that the facts did not quite support his claim.[10]

Sagan's final appendix concerned the effects of electromagnetic radiation, and this subject is mentioned in Chapter IV and Appendix I. An assumption in Sagan's paper helped simplify his calculations. He assumed that the body external to the Earth had no fields. This is similar to assuming that a magnet acts on a piece of common rock in the same way the magnet acts on another magnet.

THE CAUSES

Although there are numerous other examples, pursuing this line extensively does not add to the understanding of why such behavior occurs. After investigating the behavior, one finds that there are a number of causes for it. Some of these causes are directly related to Velikovsky's views, and some are general causes which create irrational reactions toward any new concept whether it is right or wrong.

VESTED INTEREST

One of these latter considerations is vested interest. If a person has developed and taught a particular theory for years, he has a vested interest in keeping an opposing theory from becoming popular. Scientists like to leave the impression that they are willing to accept new concepts and that it is the man in the street who blocks progress. It has been my experience that the general public is quite open to new ideas, especially if their results do not drastically degrade their lives. Also industrial scientists, who are more closely related to reality than theory, appear eager to encourage the discussion of new ideas. It is the academic scientists, however, who historically have reacted to new ideas less scientifically and more violently than other people.

Arthur Koestler concisely described this and its basis when he said: "The inertia of the human mind and its resistance to innovation are most clearly demonstrated not, as one might suspect, by the ignorant mass--which is easily swayed once its imagination is caught--but by professionals with a vested interest in tradition and in the monopoly of learning. Innovation is a two-fold threat to academic mediocrities; it endangers their oracular authority, and it evokes the deeper fear that their whole laboriously constructed intellectual edifice may collapse."[11]

CONFUSION OF FACTS AND ASSUMPTIONS

It has been shown that there is not always the proper distinction made between data and interpretations of data. Often when a scientist says that people are not facing facts, what he actually means is that they are not interpreting the facts to fit the theory he prefers. Scientists may not always fool themselves because of this, but they often leave false impressions with others. Scientists do sometimes lose track of what is assumption and what is fact, and they defend the assumption in a manner that should be reserved for defense of facts. Later, this makes some of their actions appear totally irrational.

PROTECTION OF THE PUBLIC

During these irrational moments, some scientists feel that, *at any cost*, the public should be shielded from untruths. Sometimes protecting a person from something does more harm to everyone, and it is certainly more costly in time and money. Volumes could be written about this subject, so I will mention only that protection of the public by those who *assume* they know the truth has always been a dangerous practice.

MAJOR CHANGES

Scientists as a group do not have a good record for being open-minded. They give the appearance of being open-minded because they readily accept new facts. If a measurement is made and repeated by independent researchers, the results of the measurement are quickly accepted. In the world of advanced technology, there are many new measurements made daily, but few revolutionary theories are advanced daily. Therefore, when scientists calculate their open-mindedness by including acceptance of new facts with acceptance of new concepts, they have a high open-mindedness average. However, as history reveals, in their acceptance of new concepts they are probably no better than anyone else or even worse.

Some of the breakthroughs that are thought to be examples of scientists' willingness to embrace new concepts are the transistor and laser. However, these were hardware items, and it took very little imagination to accept them as real. Also the theoretical development was progressing simultaneously with the hardware development. This uniformity in the evolution of scientific development is easy for almost anyone to accept. It is when a scientist skips some steps that other scientists become upset. Major jumps are not appreciated. If a theory exists, or only a slight modification of a theory is needed to explain an observation, the observation is welcome. Unfortunately, if no theory exists, unexpected observations are treated as mental maladies. If the observation is not made by a person with proper credentials, the reaction is even worse.

INCORRECT THEORIES

Scientists can be justly accused of irrational reactions to some useful ideas, but often it is because they have been pushed into refusing to consider all non-standard theories. It is understandable why some scientists choose to disregard all inputs that appear the least unorthodox. They are constantly receiving requests to analyze perpetual motion machines and numerous incoherent theories. The originators of these theories often feel that any criticism stems from a desire of scientists to suppress ideas beneficial to the world. If the scientist is not blamed directly, the finger is pointed at business. Stories are common about the home inventor who developed a small tablet that can change ten gallons of water into gasoline, but the oil companies would not allow him to use it. Scientist are besieged by people with irrational claims that cannot be supported, and these people object when scientists provide facts (not merely opinions) refuting these claims.

It is discouraging to spend a great deal of effort developing a theory and then to discover it has a flaw, but this happens in science quite often. Sometimes people make new discoveries this way, and even working on a problem with a flaw increases your understanding of the situation. However, when a scientist finds a flaw in a work mailed to him from a non-scientist, the non-scientist is often not only ungrateful but blames the scientist for every misfortune that ever occurred. Naturally the scientist would tend to prefer not to bother with the additional work load created by analyzing papers sent to him. The following is a specific example:

It has been shown that you cannot trisect (divide into three equal parts) an angle by using only a compass and a straight edge. Some people like to play with this puzzle, and proof that something cannot be done has not always stopped people in the past. In 1973, I received a monograph (I call it a monograph because it had "Monograph" written on the front) which contained a discussion of two subjects: 1) why mathematicians were too stupid to listen to the author of the monograph; and 2) how to trisect an angle exactly.[12] The author wrote me a note explaining that his work was not accepted by the mathematical societies of America, so would I please look over it and offer criticisms. Keeping in mind all the times people had said that Velikovsky was wrong, but they did not have time to state why, I took the time to analyze the method of trisecting an angle. The mathematical part was quite logical, but I thought I detected an error where he made the work an approximation instead of remaining exact. I then wrote a computer program to calculate the magnitude of the three angles that would be drawn by his method and had the computer print the size of the trisected angles as the size of the original angle was increased from zero to one hundred eighty degrees. At small angles the method was very close, although it did not exactly trisect the angle. However, the error increased and was nearly two degrees off at 144°. The magnitude of the error then began to decrease. Zero and 180° were the only two angles where the method exactly trisected the angle.

I sent these results to the author and pointed out that his trisection was only approximate, but it was very close. If he checked the journals and found that no approximations were better than his, he could write it up as an approximation to trisecting an angle, of which other methods exist. Later I received a letter suggesting what I could do with my roll of computer tape, and wishing me a speedy, exact trisectomy. Such an experience can make a scientist think its not worth the effort to work on odd subjects.

Scientists also have to waste time refuting stories that are fabricated by someone and foisted upon the public as science. One example is the *missing day* story. This story has recently appeared in a number of newspapers and has had other widespread circulation. It has been reprinted in tracts and columns by various personalities. In Dallas, Texas, a Channel 8 newsman circulated copies of the story with his picture at the top of the page. To the man in the street, the story appeared plausible and from a reliable source.

The story concerns a NASA computer group and some calculations being performed on the past and future movements of the planets. The computer supposedly stopped and the repair man was called to investigate, but he could not find anything wrong. The computer supposedly stopped when it found a missing day. Subsequent investigation supposedly showed that this was the day the sun stood still at the time of Joshua. Part of the time was also allotted to the change of the sundial by ten degrees at the time of Hezekiah.

During the question periods of my lectures I have often been asked about this story and how it affects Velikovsky's work. Since the story is not true, it does not affect Velikovsky's work (see Appendix III). Claiming that this type of calculation is possible would be similar to claiming that a computer program proved that there is a mile missing between anywhere and Chicago. Fighting this type of story adds to the tendency of some scientists to assume that anything odd is wrong.

ASSOCIATION WITH IRRATIONAL WORKS

Some people who have never investigated Velikovsky's work have heard sensationalized reports of some of his conclusions and, without consideration of the evidence, placed his work in the same category as that of fiction writers who invent spacemen to account for all statistical oddities. When enough odd data from the ancient world is not available, they create data. Since publications such as *Science News* and *Scientific American* often associate Velikovsky's work with these people, these publications leave the impression that all the works need not be investigated. It is easy to refute von Daniken, especially since he admits to embelishing available data, so instead of investigating Velikovsky's work, some investigators merely associate him with thrillseekers.

Scientists, refusing to enter properly into this field, have created exactly the problem they claim they wish to avoid. The field has been left open to speculators who exploit the sensational aspects of the ancient world. By not investigating and clarifying some of the data, it is left to opportunists who prefer hypothesizing to critical analysis.

RELIGION

The previous causes were general and create strange reactions to many new ideas. There are two other causes of the affair that are related to what Velikovsky said. One of these is real and the other is speculative.

It has been substantiated that religion played a part in some of the actions against Velikovsky. Oddly, his theory joined the religious and scientific forces in efforts to suppress his work.

The conflict between science and theories about catastrophes originated in the last century. Some religionists claimed that the Earth was exactly six thousand years old and all features of the Earth must be explained by catastrophes. Some scientists claimed that the Earth was millions of years old and all of its features *must* be explained by uniformitarian concepts. Neither side was willing to have an Earth, of any age, with features explained partially by uniformity and partially by catastrophism. When Velikovsky offered this solution, both sides attacked him.

COLLECTIVE AMNESIA

Velikovsky speculates that part of the violent reaction to his book was a result of what he called "collective amnesia". He discusses this in *Worlds in Collision* in connection with the ancients' desire to disguise in mythology the frightening events they experienced. He claims that the events were so terrifying that people do not want to believe that events of this nature ever happened.

Velikovsky notes the similarity to a case of amnesia induced in an individual by a horrible event. Often, when an event of this type occurs, the individual suppresses the memory of the event and does not want to believe that it happened. Velikovsky suggests that the same type of problem exists in mankind as a group. He believes that the events of the past were so frightening that people tried to suppress the memory of these events, and that a hidden fear of catastrophes exists today because this fear has been transmitted from generation to generation.

Recent investigations reveal that this suggestion is scientifically supportable. There is experimental evidence which tends to indicate that emotional characteristics are not entirely a result of environment and that some knowledge can be acquired by processes other than what are considered the normal learning procedures. It has been known for years that knowledge is transferred from one generation to the next in certain species, but we classify it as "instinct" and delude ourselves into thinking that no knowledge is transferred. (Sometimes we mistake naming something for explaining it.) Now, however, evidence is growing that memory and emotions can be transferred, either genetically or chemically, from one animal to another.[13]

So we see that a number of factors may have contributed to the irrational reaction to *Worlds in Collision.* The percentage of each factor varies in each individual, so no one thing can be blamed for this unprecedented blot in the history of science.

CHANGING ATTITUDES

Although a number of my own personal encounters have been with people who react adversely to the mention of Velikovsky's work, I have encountered myriad open minds and often in places where this would not be expected. This was not the "let's be polite until he leaves and maybe he will not become violent" attitude that often is apparent when new ideas are expressed, although that, too, has happened. However, there have been numerous people willing to discuss the theory and its implications even though they may not agree with every detail. Many allowed discussion of the work when it was less fashionable to do so.

In 1971, Texas Christian University allowed, in their Division of Special Courses, a course about Velikovsky's ideas. Soon after that the Director of the Fort Worth Museum of Science and History, Helmuth Naumer, now with the Pacific Science Center in Seattle, approved a suggestion to produce a planetarium program based on Velikovsky's work. Although such people may not necessarily agree with any or all of the points raised by Velikovsky, they recognize that many of the other ideas they present are not completely supported by all authorities either. If the museum had to wait for all authorities to agree, it would have very little to discuss.

More universities are now sponsoring Velikovsky - related symposia and courses. Lewis and Clark College in Portland, Oregon, and McMaster University in Hamilton, Ontario, sponsored general conferences about Velikovsky's work, and specific topics have been discussed at conferences at Duquesne, Notre Dame, and other universities. The number of courses at colleges is growing every semester. At Glassboro State College in New Jersey, the journal KRONOS has been printing quarterly issues of articles about Velikovsky's work. This material is prepared by highly qualified people in all fields. A new journal has recently been started in England. [14]   A poll of scientists and engineers conducted by *Industrial Research* indicated that of those replying, over 80% thought that Velikovsky's work deserved more attention.

CONCLUSION

Because of the theoretical and observational support for a theory of the type presented by Velikovsky, a growing number of authorities in various fields are taking a new look at the evidence. This is putting an ever-increasing strain on the "mediocrities" of science and history. Propaganda is abundant in resulting attempts to convince other scientists and the public that no authority would ever consider investigating anything mentioned by Velikovsky. Unfortunately, the fact that there are experts on both sides of the question makes the problem more difficult for the interested person, who must take the time to evaluate the evidence and form an opinion based on facts which must be sifted from assumptions and traditions. Any person who is not interested in doing this can best serve science by not expressing opinions based on out-dated concepts.

Many have considered the evidence and found substantial support for Velikovsky's idea. A small fraction of this support has been presented here. It has been demonstrated that complaints about method or procedure used by Velikovsky are either not true or apply equally to many accepted scientists and their theories. This places those complaints in the category of rationalizations for not considering the evidence. Other theories and scientists cannot pass the test they require of Velikovsky.

It has also been demonstrated that the main theory in opposition to Velikovsky's has been wrong about many major points.

If that theory is correct, why is it wrong so often? Even if Velikovsky had not proposed a reasonable alternative, people should have by now (and many have) become suspicious of the theory of uniformity.

We have seen that a number of irrational acts have occurred in the Velikovsky affair, and that there are divergent reasons for these actions. Although we like to think that we would act differently in similar circumstances, we can understand why some of these acts occurred. However, it is time to look ahead. We could argue forever over what Velikovsky did or did not mean, what he did or did not predict, and miss the total concept he presented. Enough information now exists to show that his ideas are worthy of continued study. Whether he as an individual is right or wrong about some point is irrelevant. Velikovsky's work now belongs to the world, and the world will lose by continuing to ignore it.

HISTORICAL SUPPLEMENT

OEDIPUS OR AKHNATON?

In 1960 Velikovsky published *Oedipus and Akhnaton* which was based on research that was done when he first came to the United States in 1939. This work had been set aside when the clues that eventually led to the publication of *Ages in Chaos* and *Worlds in Collision* were discovered. In *Oedipus and Akhnaton,* Velikovsky identified the legendary character, Oedipus, as the Egyptian Pharaoh Akhnaton and suggested that the so-called Oedipus legend was not a legend, but possibly the life-story of Akhnaton as told by the Greeks.

This work is almost totally independent of Velikovsky's other books. There is one major connection to *Ages in Chaos* and perhaps a minor connection to *Worlds in Collision* the latter being, that, if the equation is valid, it is one more indication that many of the ancient legends have some basis in fact. If the reconstruction of Egyptian history, as presented in *Ages in Chaos* (and earlier in the *Theses for the Reconstruction of Ancient History*), is basically sound, then the Oedipus legend could have sprung up in Greece soon after the events occurred in Egypt. Otherwise there is over a five hundred year delay between the events and the creation of the story.[1] Since the Oedipus legend is mentioned in the *Odyssey,* the story can be placed before the seventh century B.C. (Akhnaton is conventionally treated as the first monotheist. We shall see later, however, that Akhnaton was probably not a monotheist at all, and that in any case he lived a number of centuries *after* the earliest known monotheism.)

With only these tangential connections to his other works, the book was largely ignored by scholars, although a leading classicist, Professor Gertrude E. Smith, of the University of Chicago, wrote a favorable review of *Oedipus and Akhnaton.* [2] This was remarkable since the atmosphere at the time was such that it was not easy to give favorable opinions about anything Velikovsky wrote. Part of this atmosphere was created by scientific intimidation, and part by W. F. Albright, a previous opponent of *Ages in Chaos.* [3] He opposed the conclusions presented in *Oedipus and Akhnaton* on the improbability of a cultural exchange between Egypt and Greece at such an early time. This, despite the fact that "Mycenaean ware was found in abundance in the capital city of Akhnaton, and a seal bearing the name of Akhnaton's mother turned up in a Mycenaean grave in Greece." [4]

THE LEGEND

A number of treatments of the Oedipus theme exist. [5] Sophocles presented three plays: *Oedipus Rex, Oedipus at Colonus* and *Antigone.* Aeschylus also wrote three plays, of which only *The Seven Against Thebes* remains. The names and details change, but the major plot is recognizable in each. It generally proceeds along the following lines: A royal couple have a baby son and, wishing to know what great things are in store for the child, consult a local blind soothsayer. Unfortunately, instead of the usual niceties provided by fortune tellers, the royal couple are told that the son will grow up and kill his father, marry his mother and corruption will ruin the kingdom. Disturbed by this prophecy, the couple decide to allow the child to die by abandoning him in the wilderness. He is rescued, however, and taken to live with a royal family of another country. Very little is known about his childhood.

When Oedipus, which means "swollen-footed", became a young man, there was gossip around the royal residence which made him wonder about his past and future. As was the custom, he went to a soothsayer to ascertain his destiny and was told that he would kill his father, marry his mother, and bring disaster to the kingdom. Since he loved whom he thought were his parents, he decided to leave the country. While traveling, he encountered a man whom he argued with and killed. As it happened, this was his real father. Oedipus then ventured to the city of Thebes outside of which stood a Sphinx who desired human sacrifice. The Sphinx asked Oedipus a riddle, and when Oedipus correctly answered it, the Sphinx killed herself. The people of the city were so happy about the demise of the Sphinx that they offered to let Oedipus marry their recently widowed queen. He accepted, although she was a bit older than he.

The country started to decay and the people began to suspect some cause related to the morality of the monarch. An investigation revealed that the king was living in not-so-holy matrimony with the queen, who was none other than his mother. When she discovered this, she committed suicide. Oedipus blinded himself, lived in seclusion for awhile, and then went into exile.

There is also a side plot where an ambitious uncle helps to increase the unpopularity of Oedipus so his sons will become the rulers. The uncle then causes the sons to fight After they kill each other, he marries the wife of one son. (She was also the dead husband's half-sister.) The uncle then becomes the ruler. It sounds like day-time television, yet it was written over twenty-five hundred years ago.

CORRELATIONS TO EGYPTIAN HISTORY

While reviewing the life of Akhnaton, Velikovsky noticed a number of striking parallels between the life of Akhnaton and that of the Greek figure called Oedipus. In addition, several items of the Greek legend *were of Egyptian origin and, theoretically, should not have been included in a story created in Greece by Greeks.*

(Pages 248 and 249 contain family trees of Oedipus and Akhnaton respectively.)

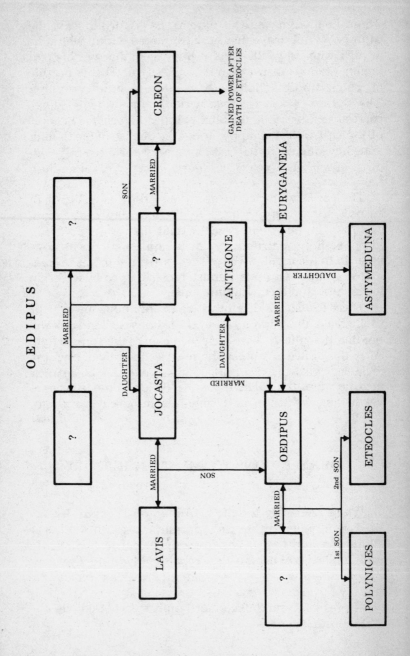

AKHNATION

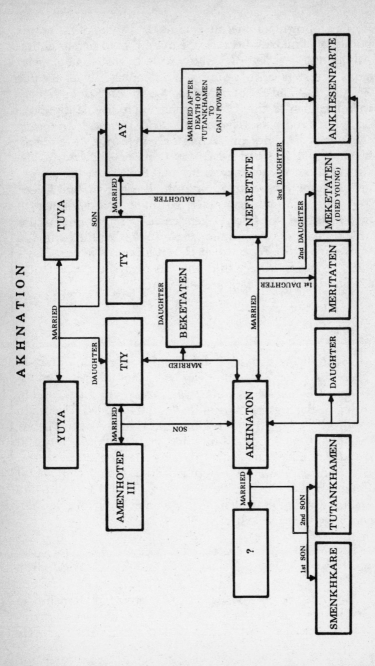

The following material summarizes some of the major points of similarity between the lives of both personalities. Additionally, a few of Velikovsky's intermediate conclusions are stated. This outline is intended only as a guide to the book and is not intended as a proof. For extremely well-documented material presented in a fascinating manner, the reader is referred to *Oedipus and Akhnaton.*

Two of the lines on Akhnaton's genealogy are not always found in standard descriptions of Akhnaton's life. One of these is the line connecting Beketaten, the daughter of Queen Tiy, with Akhnaton. It is known that Queen Tiy was Akhnaton's mother, so under today's mores it is difficult to consider Beketaten as a by-product of the union of these two. Some people prefer to think she was the daughter of Amenhotep III, Akhnaton's father. However, records indicate that she was born after Amenhotep III had been dead for about six years.

Thebes

Most of the action in the Oedipus story took place in Thebes. A Greek, Boeotian city was called the "seven-gated" Thebes because of its outer wall with seven gates, and in order to distinguish it from the "hundred-gated" Thebes in Egypt. The legendary creature that watched over Thebes in Boeotia was not a familiar Greek mythical figure. It was the Sphinx and called that by the Greek tragedians. The Sphinx, however, originated in Egypt. From actual images preserved in relief, it is known that there was an historical Egyptian Theban Sphinx to whom human sacrifices were made in the 18th Dynasty.

Soothsayer

Amenhotep, son of Hapu-no known relationship to Amenhotep III or Amenhotep IV (Akhnaton)-was considered extremely brilliant and able to see the future. He was renowned as a soothsayer and frequently consulted by royalty. Tiresias, of the Oedipus legend, possessed the same characteristics as Amenhotep, son of Hapu. Both were blind as well.

The Son

Queen Tiy, comparable to Jocasta of the legend, had a son of whom nothing is known until he claimed the throne after his father's death. The son, Akhnaton, appears to have had swollen thighs, since the court artists depicted him in such a way as to emphasize this particular characteristic. Interestingly enough, Oedipus in Greek means a swelling of the foot or a swelling of the leg.

When Akhnaton was a young ruler, he used the epithet "Who lived long" or "Who survived to live long". This is possibly a result of his having survived some crucial event in childhood which might have caused him to consider any additional life as "living long". This event may have been similar to the attempted killing of Oedipus. Akhnaton also called himself son of the sun. Some ancient sources have Oedipus change his parentage from Laius to Helios.

Killing The Father

Akhnaton (Amenhotep IV) erased the name of Amenhotep III from the various momuments on which it was inscribed. Erasing the name or memory of a person meant eliminating that person forever in the spiritual world; hence, Akhnaton "killed" his father.

After this act, Akhnaton instigated new religious practices. These actions earned Akhnaton the title of the "first monotheist". He probably was not a monotheist at all, let alone the first mon otheist! If the revised chronology is basically correct, Akhnaton lived several hundred years after other known monotheists.

Part of the reasoning which lead to the conclusion that he was monotheistic was that he changed his name from Amenhotep IV which contained the name of a god he wanted to phase out of the religion. More significantly, he erased his father's name which also contained the name of the god, Amen. It is thought that, if he went to all the trouble to chisel out the name, he was serious about stopping the worship of this god. However, Velikovsky suggested that, since Akhnaton did not remove the name of Amenhotep II, Akhnaton's interest was not only in religion, but also in "killing" his father for eternity.

Marriage

Mitanni, where Akhnaton probably lived as a child, had Iranian customs which considered mother-son marriages holy. Akhnaton used the epithet "Living in Truth" possibly because he openly portrayed this relationship and tried unsuccessfully to have it accepted by the Egyptians in general. This added to the dissatisfaction that later helped in the removal of Akhnaton. There were other indications that Akhnaton was knowingly married to his mother. Akhnaton insisted that he was "husband of his mother" (a big clue!), and his mother Queen Tiy was called "King's Mother and Great Royal Wife". Under today's customs, translators find this phrase incomprehensible.

Akhnaton apparently was polygamous. In addition to the implied marriage to his mother, Queen Tiy, he had some younger wives. One of these was the well-known

Nefretete. Akhnaton, Nefretete and their offspring are often pictured facing Queen Tiy and Beketaten. Tiy and Nefretete did not appreciate each other and the conflict seems to have eventually caused a reduction of Nefretete's power. Oedipus had the same problem. His mother-wife Jocasta was not overly fond of Euryganeia, who was referred to as his "younger wife". Jocasta also had the younger wife's influence decreased or eliminated.

Ruin

Problems with other kings and famine made the Egyptians think they were being punished because of the acts of Akhnaton. Details of some of the trouble can be found in the el-Amarna letters (Chapter III). The displeasure of the people was also significant in the Oedipus legend.

Length of Rule

Ay (see chart) advertised the problems and encouraged revolt against Akhnaton, as did Creon against Oedipus. Akhnaton possibly lived for awhile in seclusion at a minor palace located near the main one. Depending on the source, both Akhnaton and Oedipus were credited with reigns of both seventeen years *and* twenty years. The time in seclusion may have been three years which was probably not counted as actual regnal time.

Blindness

Akhnaton and Oedipus became blind in their old age. Oedipus blinded himself, but Akhnaton possibly was blinded by the same disease which caused his enlarged thighs.

Suicide

In the legend, Jocasta comitted suicide. The mummy of Queen Tiy was identified as such only in October of 1976. The news report from the University of Michigan discussed only the identification procedure and did not mention a possible cause of death.

The Brothers

After Ay helped to depose Akhnaton, he may have encouraged Smenkhkare and Tutankhamen, two of Akhnaton's sons, to alternate their rule. In the legend, Creon created a similar situation with Polynices and Eteocles. Ay and Creon then each encourage Tutankhamen and Eteocles, respectively, to retain the throne; this incited Smenkhkare and Polynices, who each acquired armies and attempted to regain power. In the ensuing battles, real and supposedly legendary, all four characters were killed. Ay then married the widow of Tutankhamen since the power in Egypt was acquired through the female blood line. In the Greek version, Creon married the widow of Eteocles. Both Ay and Creon had also had previous wives who died young. Eventually Ay and Creon were both dishonored after their own deaths.

The Burials

In the legend, Creon decreed that Polynices should not be buried, but that the great hero and defender of the land, Eteocles, should have the most lavish burial possible. In

real life, Ay made the burial of Tutankhamen an unfor-
gettable event. In fact, about the only thing King Tut is
noted for is having the honor of an extravagant funeral.

The sister of Polynices, Antigone, buried the body of
Polynices, and for her efforts Creon had her entombed
without benefit of death. When Creon finally decided to
free her, she had already hanged herself with her scarf.
Some evidence indicates the hastily buried body in Tiy's
tomb may have been the body of Smenkhkare. Not far
from this tomb was a pit with evidence that perhaps someone had been entombed alive. Also found was a scarf with
the name that Smenkhkare's wife called him. No remains
of a body were found.

Miscellaneous

The rock tombs used in the legend were not common to
Greece, and the Greeks did not place as much importance
on burial methods as did the Egyptians.

In the legend, Antigone performed some mutually ex-
clusive acts, such as going into exile with her father and
then being buried alive near the tomb of her brother. In
the life of Akhnaton, Beketaten may have gone into exile
with her father, while Meritaten was probably emtombed
near Smenkhkare.

Recent Evidence

When Velikovsky published *Oedipus and Akhnaton*,
there was some question about a few of the relationships
discussed. For example, it was not clear that Tutankhamen and Smenkhkare were brothers. However, recent

investigations support this identification. Harrison, Abdalla, and Connelly have performed analysis of the remains of Tutankhamen and Smenkhkare.[6] X-rays of the skulls show that they are the same basic shape. Special blood tests were made, and one conclusion was that Tutankhamen and Smenkhkare had the same parentage. Also King Tut probably lived to be only nineteen years old and did not die from tuberculosis, as previously thought. Apparently his death was caused by a blow to the head with a standard blunt instrument which would be more in accord with death in battle. An ancient painting does show Tut in battle.

Harrison *et al.* also felt that these two brothers and Akhnaton (Amenhotep IV) may have been sons of Amenhotep III. However, Dr. I. E. S. Edwards, Keeper of Egyptian Antiquities at the British Museum, took a more non-committal approach by saying that Amenhotep III "was either Tutankhamen's grandfather or his father."[7] That Amenhotep III must have been Tut's grandfather is more in line with the chronological analysis given by Velikovsky.[8]

Prof. Lewis M. Greenberg has also presented a new dimension regarding the religious innovations of Akhnaton.[9] He suggested the possibility that the worship of the god Aten may have been the result of a synthesis of Egypt's solar theology with a new cosmological phenomenon (Venus) of considerable importance. Greenberg refers to the conflicts between the religious leaders and Akhnaton, partly due to the Pharaoh's novel marriage arrangements, and also points out the probable needs of the new religion. He then poses some questions about the new religion if it were merely a revised form of sun worship. For example: "Why was Aten represented with rays emanating in arcuated fashion from one side only, as a comet's tail, (which Venus may then have possessed), as opposed to the standard portrayal of the sun's rays in a 360 degree sweep", and why does the Hymn to Aten say it "rises like the living Sun" when one would not normally say that the sun rises like the sun?

Conclusion

Until potent evidence to the contrary comes along, it seems that Velikovsky's provocative and well supported concept should be considered along with other analyses of the Oedipus legend. Ph.D.'s in literature have probably been granted for far less substantial investigations.

Dr. Cyrus Gordon, Chairman of the Department of Mediterranean Studies at Brandeis University, recently wrote a short article reviewing Velikovsky's *Oedipus and Akhnaton.* [10] In the article, Gordon said: "However much one may cavil on this detail or that, Velikovsky has succeeded in identifying Oedipus as the Greek reflex of the historical Akhnaton." Not long before this, another noted scholar mentioned Velikovsky's identification of Oedipus as Akhnaton. Dr. Cyril D. Darlington, Sherardian Professor of Botany, University of Oxford, a renowned geneticist, has written about many subjects. In his book, *The Evolution of Man and Society*, Darlington listed the comparisons detailed by Velikovsky and stated that the similarities indicate the Oedipus legend was truly an Egyptian story which was transplanted to Greece. [11] As previously mentioned, under conventional chronology, the Oedipus "legend" arose some five hundred years after the lifetime of Akhnaton. If these noted scholars are correct, then this adds another item to the vast list of five hundred year discrepancies associated with the conventional chronology.

APPENDIX

APPENDIX IA

There are historical indications that the Sun once rose in the west. Some of them are not vague and do not need interpretations for this result. In fact just the opposite is true. They need to be interpreted if you do not want them to say the Sun rose in the west. Egyptian sources make it clear that the Sun "rose where he now sets", and "set where he now rises". About the complete quote Velikovsky said: "This passage has been the subject of exhaustive commentaries, the authors of which tried to invent every possible explanation of the phenomenon, but failed to consider the meaning which was plainly stated by the priests of Egypt, and their efforts through the centuries have remained fruitless".[1] The Egyptians also had a name Harakhte, for the western Sun. Again this must be "interpreted: if one is to assume it is just the normal Sun since they said "Harakhte, he riseth in the west".

Numerous Greek authors (e.g. Plato, Euripides) discussed a time when the Sun rose in the west. The Chinese say that the stars moving from east to west is a new arrangement. The Chinese Zodiac moves retrograde.[2] Some Indians of Mexico called the Sun that moved to the east Teotl Lixco.[3] There are also Hebrew sources (e.g. Teaclate Sanhedrin of the Talmud) discussing the reversal of east and west.

The Aztecs relate a story about a time of gloom when the sky was too dense to see the Sun. People placed bets on which direction they thought the Sun would rise. No one guessed east.[4] There is a similar Mayan legend except in this one people did guess the east.[5] Arabia lies to the east of the countries with which it is associated; however, it had the name Erev, the evening land.

A first thought about the reversals might be that it is relatively easy to flip the poles by 180°, and this would create the effect. Reflecting on this point, however, one would soon realize that turning the earth over would not make the Sun rise in the west. This requires having the surface of the Earth spinning in the opposite direction.

APPENDIX IB

Concerning the nearest Venus-Earth encounter, Velikovsky wrote: "This approach, if one is to believe the sources, was followed by a disturbance in the rotation of the Earth". This area of Velikovsky's reconstruction of natural historical events requires the most additional theoretical work. It is probably safe to say that if the Earth should drastically change its rotation rate tomorrow, within two weeks *Nature* would publish several theoretical explanations. Since this has not happened recently, theoreticians have not worked on an explanation. However, there are some interesting data and speculations about this subject.

In 1960, A. Dajon, Director of the Paris Observatory, reported that after a strong solar flare, the rotation rate of the Earth changed about .85 milliseconds.[6] The next year a Soviet astronomer, Vaisberg, discussed mechanisms which could lead to the retardation of rotation of the Earth during solar flares such as the one mentioned by Dajon.[7]

Some papers were written in opposition to Dajon[8], and at the AAAS meeting, when Velikovsky mentioned the work of Dajon, it was claimed that his work had been refuted. However, it was not mentioned that interest in Dajon's result had been revived since Gribbin and Plagemann had claimed a similar result after a great solar flare in August of 1972.[9]

Whether or not the electromagnetic interaction of the Earth with a solar flare can produce changes of rotation rate, it is possible to change spin rates and create heating in cosmic bodies through electromagnitic interactions. This has recently been discussed relative to bodies in the solar system by Sonnett *et al.*[10] This is the mechanism for heating that Velikovsky discussed in *Earth in Upheaval.*[11] It has also long been known that electromagnetic fields affect the spin rates and orbits of artifical satellites.[12]

However, the influences on satellites are no where near the order of magnitude about which the ancients implied. They indicated a rotation rate on the order of days, if not actually zero. This would not only take a large (approximately 2×10^{36} ergs assuming the total mass stopped) amount of energy, but the energy would have to be expended in stopping the Earth's spin. A complete theoretical explanation of this has not been presented yet. (This situation is certainly not unprecedented in scientific hypothesis. Laplace offered, without any mathematical development, his nebular model of the origin of the solar system.)[13]

An ingenious observation has been made by Dr. Irving Michelson of the Illinois Institute of Technology in Chicago. He calculated that if one assumes a net charge on the Earth which is consistent with some published calculations, then the Earth's electrical energy is almost identical to its rotational (spin) kinetic energy. He noted that the charge represents just sufficient energy that stopping the rotation of the Earth could remove the charge. He stated: "While it is by no means clear that such processes did occur, it is of singular interest to observe that the energies tabulated (of various solar system interactions) and ranging from a million times smaller to a million times greater than the Earth's rotational kinetic energy, the electrical energy corresponding to the present consistent hypothesis so nearly coincides with the rotational value."[14]

As early as 1963, Juergens was following a line of thinking similar to that presented by Michelson. Juergens noted that angular momentum is a function of angular velocity and moment of inertia, and that if an electric charge is added to a spinning body, its moment of inertia increases. Therefore, if charge is added and angular momentum is conserved, the body must reduce its angular velocity. He suggested that if, during the interplanetary encounters, the Earth acquired an excess charge then the Earth's rotation rate would temporarily decrease until leakage of the excess charge restored the moment of inertia to its equilibrium value. Although this would require an infinite charge to completely stop the Earth, small changes of rotation rate could be caused by more reasonable amounts of charge. Juergens did not offer this as a total solution, but he points out that it does have some interesting qualitative features. [15]

There is another possibility, for reversing the apparent movement of the Sun, which may not have the same energy problem, but which may have other more imposing problems. Suppose that the Earth's mantle could slip around the core if a sufficient external force were applied properly. The mantle could then acquire a position wherein it rotated in the opposite direction of the core. Friction between the core and mantle could eventually stop the core and start it rotating in the opposite direction. It is now thought that the axis of rotation of the mantle is a few degrees off the axis of rotation of the core. [16] Could it be that the tilt is 87° instead of 3°?

Eric Crew has recently re-emphasized the work of Dr. C. E. R. Bruce. [17] Bruce has, since the early 1940's, advocated cosmological theories involving electromagnetic fields. Because of this approach, he was able to explain a number of astronomical effects and predict a number of others that have since been discovered such as quasars. Crew noted that one of the practical problems that could be explained by this approach is the charge of rate of spin of a body. The line of reasoning is similar to that discussed by Sonett and involves currents induced in the solid surface of one body approached by another body.

APPENDIX II

A few examples of these correlations will be given; however, this is only to present the basic picture. For an in-depth analysis, the reader should refer to *Ages in Chaos*. It should be kept in mind that in many cases the vowels are chosen arbitrarily, so that some names which have been translated differently may actually be the same, such as the city Sumur may also be read Semer. Differences can also be caused by translating to one language and from that language to a third language. Names in Russian can be translated into French and then the original Russian and the French could be translated into English. This might provide two similar, but not identical spellings in English. This is why the sequence of events and activities of the people involved are important in determining that the names refer to the same individuals.

Second Chronicles lists some of the captains of Judah under Jehoshaphat. (II Chron. 17:14-19) Among these are Adnah, Jehohanan, Amasiah the son of Zichri, Eliada, and Jehozabad (Iehozabad). These positions were inherited from the father or from the older brother. The next generation had captains such as Ishmael, the son of Jehohanan, and Elishaphat, the son of Zichri, and Adaiacadaja, who ruled Edom when it was without a king. (II Chron. 23:1) Among the recovered letters of Tell-el-Amarna were found the names Addudani (Addadani), and "son of Zuchru", Izhzibada, and Addaia. These were important officers in Judah and they could report directly to the Pharaoh, and Adaia who was the Pharaoh's chief deputy.

In addition to the similarities in these names, Velikovsky also pointed out that Zuchru or Zichri was the only attached name of a father. He also noted that in II Chronicles it states that because of an act of Zichri, his descendents were honored by having his name attached. (*Ages in Chaos*, pg. 240) These could be one and the same person under the revised chronology. Under conventional chronology, about five hundred years before the event in Chronicles a Zuchru lived in the same area and performed an act which caused his descendents to be honored by being called "sons of Zuchru". These sons were associated with people of the same name and position as the later ones described in Chronicles.

In all the letters known to be from Tell-el-Amarna, only one was from a woman. She was called Baalat-Nese and apparently lived in either Shunama or Burkuna in Palestine. Baalat-Nese can more properly be translated as "a woman to whom occurred a wonder" instead of the sometimes used "Mistress of Lions" (*Ages in Chaos*, p. 290). If the revised chronology holds, and there was a noteworthy woman in the area at this time, it seems reasonable that Hebrew history would mention her. In II Kings a "great woman" is mentioned who lived in Shunem. It also says that Elisha, who may have been an early practitioner of artificial respiration, breathed life into the lady's dead son. This would easily classify her as a person to whom a wonder occurred. Since she was known to the king of Israel, it is not unreasonable to think that she was also known to the Pharaoh.

Velikovsky pointed out that there is a word *elippe* that is frequently encountered in the el-Amarna letters and is translated as "ship". There are apparently two meanings for the word since sometimes these ships travel overland and enter into conspiracies with people. With only one translation, some places that never dreamed of being a port are said to have ships going there. Velikovsky suggested that *Elippe* came from the Hebrew word *ilpha*, which was derived from a Syrian word meaning ship, and the Hebrew word *aluph* meaning clan leader, family leader, or prince. The *elippe* that float and carry cargo and people were ships and the *elippe* that dabbled in the affairs of men are possibly chieftains. If so, it would also explain some apparent exaggerations in the Hebrew record. For example, since "eleph" is "thousand", a wall falling and killing twenty seven thousand people would more likely have been a wall falling on twenty seven "chieftains". The words ilpha, aluph and eleph *all* have the forms *aleph, lamed, phe.*

Gold and silver are always popular, but the popularity of some items is a function of time. During the time of Amenhotep III and IV (Akhnaton) ivory was very stylish. These Pharaohs often filled requests for various items which were either solid ivory or olive wood inlaid with ivory. The el-Amarna letters tell of a number of shipments of this nature to the kings of the Asian provences (*Ages in Chaos*, p. 27). Ivory furniture was an especially popular item. Since Velikovsky's revised chronology synchronizes the time of King Ahab with the time of Amenhotep III and Amenhotep IV, it would not be surprising to find that ivory was exceptionally favored during the time of Ahab.

The Scriptures contain references to elaborate ivory accumulations of Ahab. The "houses of ivory" (Amos 3:15) in which were the "beds of ivory" (Amos 6:4-5) were thought to be figments of the imaginations of the writers of the Scriptures. However, evidence from the excavations of ancient Samaria indicates that the vast collection of ivory objects did exist, and they unquestionably belonged to the time of Ahab.

Because of the conventional chronology, the archaeologists were surprised by the artwork on the Hebrew ivory pieces. During this time period, the area is supposed to have been under Assyrian domination, yet the styling is all Egyptian with no indication whatever that the area was influenced by Assyria (*Ages in Chaos*, p. 329). This problem does not exist with the revised chronology, since Velikovsky's analysis indicates that Amenhotep III and Amenhotep IV (Akhnaton) were the dominant rulers of Samaria around the time of Ahab.

The Pharaoh Tutankhamen was related to Akhnaton in a number of possible ways (see Supplement) and ruled soon after Akhnaton. Ivory objects found in his tomb were similar to some found in Samaria. Two Winged sphinxes with human forms are guardians at the corners of a shrine of King Tut, and similar ones existed at the time of Ahab. No artificially devised scheme of chronology can ignore the fact that the ivory objects of Egypt and Samaria are exceptionally similar. Conventional chronology requires strained suggestions, such as Egypt being great and powerful and dominating Samaria but not influencing its art, whereas five or six hundred years later when Assyria rules the Samarians, they are finally inspired to copy buried Egyptian art. This problem does not exist with the revised chronology.

Here are listed only a few examples of the similarities between the el-Amarna letters of supposedly ca. -1400 and portions of the Scriptures of ca. -900; in *Ages in Chaos*, Velikovsky described over fifty in detail.

The conventional chronology, on the other hand, requires that two groups of people with the same or similar names perform the same acts in the same places centuries apart. The result is that the same people go to war with each other with the same winner collecting materially and artistically similar booty and gifts. The events are then described using the same idioms. The second group accomplishes all this five to six hundred years after the first group. Under the revised chronology, the letters and scriptures were written about the same events and the similarities are no longer astonishing.

APPENDIX III

So many people asked me about the "missing day" supposedly calculated by a NASA computer that I sought the origin of the story. Thanks to the research efforts of Dr. David Huebner, the inventor of the story was discovered.

Harold Hill admitted to being the originator of the missing day story, but he claimed it was true. He had only "misplaced details regarding names and places". [18] However, for those interested in actual calculations, he referred the reader to a book published in 1890 by C. A. Totten. Totten claimed to have made some calculations showing that there actually was a missing day at the time of Joshua. However, Totten said: "The mere figures are of no interest save to the verifier," so they were not included. [19] First we went from a computer program and programmers who cannot be found, to hand calculations which were never shown to anyone.

It is apparent from reading Totten's book that the missing day story is an updated version of Totten's prevarication. The modern touch of NASA, computer and scientists replaced the less believable situation in the Totten book.   To perform a calculation of the type Totten claims to have performed, accurate calendar points before and after the event would be required. If you had an accurate calendar, you would not need to perform the calculations. If you used astronomical data before and after the event, you would need very exact data, but none exists. To do his calculations, Totten assumed he knew exactly how long ago the Earth started and worked from then to the present. He noted that scientists complained that he needed to start at the present and work backward and have his theory fit known eclipses and other data, assuming it existed. Totten admitted that this was a reasonable request and said that "this is exactly what I can do, and in fact what I have already done in order to verify my calculations to my own satisfaction, and with this result"; the result being that he could fit all eclipses past and future. Again no support for this statement was given.

NOTES

Chapter I

1. *KRONOS* is a journal created as a forum for the discussion of Velikovsky's work. It is published by KRONOS Press,Glassboro State College, Glassboro,N.J. 08028. From 1972 to 1974, *Pensee* Magazine printed a 10 issue special series about Velikovsky's work. Information about these issues is available from *KRONOS*.
2. *The Velikovsky Affair*, ed. Alfred de Grazia, University Books, Inc., p. 8, 1966. (To be updated and reprinted by KRONOS Press).
3. Ibid, p. 26.
4. Ibid, 20.
5. Ibid., 21.
6. Ibid, p. 29.
7. Ibid, p. 25.
8. F. G. Bratton. *Myths and Legends of the Ancient Near East*, Thomas Crowell Co., New York, 1970, p. 13

Chapter II

1. *Worlds in Collision*, 49.
2. Exodus 7:20,21.
3. *Worlds in Collision*, 50.
4. Exodus 7:24.
5. Exodus 7:24.
6. *Worlds in Collision*, 49.
7. Ibid, 59.
8. Exodus 10:22.
9. *Worlds in Collision*, 58.
10. Ibid, 61.
11. Exodus 12:29.
12. *Ages in Chaos*, 32.
13. *Analog*, 1975.
14. Dr. James A. Durham, Letter to Analog.
15. *Worlds in Collision*, 65.
16. Ibid, 74.
17. Psalms 68:22.
18. *Ages in Chaos*, 45.
19. Exodus 14:9.
20. *Ages in Chaos*, 45.
21. *Worlds in Collision*, 69.
22. Ibid, 182.
23. Ibid, 181.
24. Ibid, 166.
25. Galileo was the first in modern history to see the phases of Venus, and he used a telescope. Of course a lot of people claimed they could "see" them with the unaided eye after they were discovered; however, this would not adequately explain the ancients fascination with the "Horns of Venus".
26. There is a difference between a drawing and a photograph of the same comet. An ultraviolet wavelength of light that the eye cannot see washes out the fine structure in the photographs and this often produces the common image of a comet. However, the drawings are more likely to give the type of impressions the ancients received, since we can probably assume that they observed first hand instead of forming opinions from newspaper photographs.
27. *Worlds in Collision*, 181.
28. Ibid, 128.
29. Ibid, 132.
30. Ibid, 139.
31. Ibid, 140.
32. Ibid, 39.
33. Ibid, 244.
34. Ibid, 364.

35. *Worlds in Collision*, 216.
36. Ibid, 237.
37. Ibid, 256.
38. Ibid, 218.
39. Ibid, 245.
40. Ibid, 252.

Chapter III

1. I. Velikovsky, "Astronomy and Chronology", Supplement to *Peoples of the Sea* (Doubleday, 1976), and *Pensee IV*, Spring-Summer, 1973, p. 38. This article was first set in type in the early 1950's to be part of the vol. of *Ages in Chaos*.
2. I. Velikovsky, *Pensee IV*, 38, 1972.
3. Ibid, 39.
4. Ibid.
5. Ibid, p. 40.
6. A. Gardiner, *Egypt of the Pharaohs*, p. 53., 1961.
7. I. Velikovsky, "Astronomy and Chronology", ref. 5, M Knapp, Pentagramma Veneris (Basel, 1934)p22.
8. I. Velikovsky, *Pensee IV*, 43, 1972.
9. I. Velikovsky, "Astronomy and Chronology"
10. KRONOS I, #2, 1975,p72,ref. #33.
11. Eva Danelius, *Kronos, I* #3, p. 3, 1975.
12. L. M Greenberg, *Pensee*, p. 36, Winter 1973.
13. J. Van Seters, J. F. *Egyptian Arch. 50*, 24, 1964 and
14. I. Velikovsky, *Ages in Chaos*, p. 55.
15. Ibid, p. 55, ref. 2
16. Psalms 78:49.
17. I. Velikovsky, *Ages in Chaos*, p. 69.
18. Numbers 24:7.
19. I. Velikovsky, *Ages in Chaos*, p. 72.
20. I. Velikovsky, *Worlds in Colision*, p. 151.
21. I. Velikovsky, *Ages in Chaos*, p. 76.
22. II Chronicles 9 and I Kings 10.
23. I. Velikovsky, *Ages in Chaos*, p. 107.
24. Eva Danelius, KRONOS I, #3, 1975, p3 contains additional support for the identification of Hatshepsut as the Queen of Sheba.
25. *Ages in Chaos*, p. 155.
26. Ibid, 169.
27. Ibid, 158.
28. Ibid, 168.
29. Ibid, 183.
30. Ibid, 222.
31. Robert H. Hewsen, *Kronos I,* #3, p. 22, 1975
    This sounds similar to interpretations given in a short note in the July, 1967 issue of *Art and Archaeology Newsletter* entitled "A Forward Look Backward" by Otto F. Reiss. He describes the way archaeologists of the future might view our mythological World War II. This contest of primitive technologies involved the *Hewer of Iron* or "Eisen Hower" and a *forger of daggers*, "Messer Schmitt", and the *Honest Man* (good guy or "True Man"). France was part of the conflict because of the mention of the hero of *France*, "de Gaulle". Reiss said some names would be difficult since the spelling varies, such as "Hitler" and "Himmler" who were obviously the same person. This future archaeologist's final conclusion? "It adds up to the struggle between true man and death, or between good and evil. A great allegory, to be sure. But historical fact? Certainly not!"

33. I. Velikovsky, *Ages in Chaos*, p. 338.
34. I. Velikovsky, *Ages in Chaos*, p. 232.
35. Ibid, 237.
36. See KRONOS, vol. I, #'s 2, 3, and 4, vol. II #1 and future issues. Also examples available in *Pensee III, IV, V, VI, IX, and X* and in *The Exodus Problem* by Courville, and the S.I.S.R. newsletter (see ref. 13 of Chapter 8.)
37. Eva Danelius, KRONOS I, #4, 1976, p. 9

Notes Chapter IV

1. J. G. Porter, *The Moon, Meteorites and Comets*, ed. Middlehurst and Kuiper, p. 559, 1963, University of Chicago Press.
2. JPL33-297.
3. E. Roemer, *Astro. J. 66*, 368, 1961.
4. Proceedings of the Tenth Lunar and Planetary Exploration Collopuium,   p. 75, May, 1961.
5. NASA-CR-83113 JPL TECH. MEM. 33-297, 1967.
6. NASA-SP-198, p. 126
7. N. T. Bobromikoff "Comets", in *Astrophysics*, ed. Hynch, McGraw-Hill,   1951. Bobrovnikoff calculated that fine particular comets were the debris of one comet which split into five comets. The mass of the original comet he calculated to be on the order of the mass of the moon.
8. Max Wallis N71-25726 rept. 70-35, Avil NT15, Dec., 1970. This was later published in *Cosmic Electrodynamic 3*, 45, 1972.
9. H. S. Bridge, et. al. *Science 183*, 1293, 1974.
10. W. C. Straka, *Pensee II*, p. 15, 1972.
11. H. Alfven and A. Mendis, *Nature, 246*, 410, 1973.
12. G. Kuiper, *Astrophysics*, ed. Hynek, p. 400, 1951, F. Whipple, *Moon, Meteorites and Comets*, ed. Middlehurst and Kuiper, p. 639, 1963, Oort, J., *Moon, Meteorites and Comets*, p. 665, 1963.
13. S. K. Vsekhsvyatskii, *Comet International Colloquim*, Liege, ed. P. Swings, p. 500, 1966.
14. See e.g.
    S. K. Vsekhsvyatskii, *Soviet Astron. AJ 11*, 473, 1967; Pub. *Astro. Soc. Pac. 74*, 106, 1962; and NASA TT-F-80.
15. P. V. Smith, *Science 111*, 437, 1952.
16. J. Oro, *Nature 190*, 389, 1961.
17. Oro and Han, *Science 153*, 1393, 1966.
18. *Time*, 37, March 1, 1971.
19. D. F. Saunders, G. L. Thomas and F. E. Kinsman, NASA-CR-131150, March, 1973.
20. I. Rich, "Goddard Space Flight Center Symp. on Significant Results from *ERTS-1*," Vol. 1 list A and B, p. 395, 1973.
21. *Worlds in Collision*, p. 369.
22. B. Zeitman, S. Chang, and J. G. Lawless, *Nature 251*, 42, 1974.
23. Alan C. Nixon, *Science News, 106*, 99, 1974.
24. *Nature 229*, 79, 1971.
25. Wong Kee Kuong, *Pensee. III*, p. 45.
26. This was republished *Velikovsky Reconsidered*, Doubleday, 1976.
27. R. J. C. Atkinson, *Nature 210*, 1302, 1966; *New York Review of Books*, 1966;
28. *Antiquity*, Sept., 1966.
    Science News 104, 28, July 14, 1973.
    It is interesting to observe Velikovsky's description of Hawkins. In 1967 when Velikovsky's article about Stonehenge was written, he had undergone 17 years of libelous abusive name calling. Four years earlier Hawkins had presented a theory which was used repeatedly, although incorrectly, as a "proof" that Velikovsky was wrong. With all the unwarranted and unethical personal attacks on Velikovsky, what did he call the author of an opposing idea? He said " a young and talented astronomer, Professor Herald S. Hawkins", published this theory.
29. A. Fleming, *Nature*, p. 575, June 19, 1975.
30. A. Thom, *Megalithic Sites in Britian*, 1966.
31. For measurements made by the ancients, see KULIKOV, 24,25, NASA TT 143. Oddly enough, the person who first brought these data to my attention left out some data and misplotted other points in order to make the data fit the theory.
32. Allen, *Astrophysical Quantities*, University of London, Atholone Press, 2nd ed., 1963.
33. E. Schatzman, *The Physics of the Solar System*, ed. Rasool, NASA SP 300, p. 409, 1972.
34. Roberta S. Sklower, in *Mexico Mystique* by Frank Waters, p. 302, 1975. She wrote Appendix VIII for that book.
35. *Velikovsky Affair*, 117.

36. R. W. Bass, *Pensee VIII*, 11, 1974.
37. M. M. Nieto, *The Titius-Bode Law of Planetary Distances: Its History and Theory*
38. Velikovsky's reply to Stewart. See *Velikovsky Affair*, p. 17.
39. R. W. Bass, "A Variational Principle, Determining all Periodic, Auto-Symmetric Almost-Periodic, and Fixed-Boundary-Configuration Solutions of the N-Body Problem", *XIth International Astronauticl Congress*, Stockholm, 1960. Also, *Aeronca-Aerospace Technical Report 60-5*.
40. This states "The 'least unstable' almost periodic orbits of any homogeneous, definite, conservative dynamical system, for each compatible value of the energy constant, are precisely those closed curves in configuration space along which the average of the systems potential energy has a minimum value (relative to all nearly admissible closed curves)". (The minimization should be done as follows: a) fix angular momentum b) fix mean value of kinetic energy c) vary hypothetical path in 6 m-dimensional phase space until mean value of potential energy has a stationary (critical) value. Then the correspond has a stationary (critical) value. Then the corresponding motion actually satisfies Newton's equations for gravitational n-body problem). This principle is generalization of what is called the Lagrange-Pirichlet *Principle of Least Potential Energy*.
41. It states "A planetary or satellite system of N point masses moving solely under their mutual gravitational attractions spends most of its time close to a configuration for which the time mean of the action associated with the mutual interactions of the planets or satellites is a minimum".
    See M. W. Ovenden, *Vistas in Astronomy 18*, 473, 1975.
42. J. G. Hills, *Nature*, 225, 840, 1970.
    Hills said "Because the initial conditions in these satellite systems which were studied are not likely to have been the same as in the planetary system, this suggests to me that Bode's Law may have resulted from a process of dynamical relaxation".
43. G. J. F. MacDonald, *Reviews of Geophysics*, 2, 467, 1964.
44. S. F. Singer, *Science*, 170, 438, 1970.
45. A. G. W. Cameron, *Nature 240*, 299, 1972.
46. L. Rose and R. Vaughan, *Velikovsky Reconsidered*, 102, Doubleday, 1976.
47. L. Rose, *Velikovsky Reconsidered*, 100, Doubleday, 1976.
48. Harrington and T. Van Flandern, *Bull. of the Am. Astro. Soc.*, 6, 433, 1974.
49. A. V. Fokin, *Soviet Astro. AJ 2*, 628, 1958.
50. Middlehurst and Kuiper, *Moon, Meteorites and Comets*, University of Chicago Press, 559, 1963.
51. R. W. Bass, *Pense VIII*, 8, 1974.
52. M. W. Ovenden, *Recent Advances in Dynamical Astronomy*, ed. Tapley and Szebehely, D. Reidel Pub. Co., 319, 1972; *Nature 239*, 508, 1972.
53. R. W. Bass, *Pensee VIII*, 8, 21, 1974.
    Kronos I, #3, 1975.
54. I. Velikovsky, *Worlds in Collision*, 384, 1950.
55. D. R. Long, *Nature 260*, 417, 1976.

Chapter V

1. W. H. McCrea, *Proc. Roy. Ast. Soc., Series A*, 256, 1960.
2. J. G. Hills, Ph.D. Thesis, Michigan University, Ann Arbor, 1969.
3. H. Alfven, *Astro. Physical J.*, 137, 981, 1963.
4. R. A. Lyttleton, *The Comets and Their Origin*, p. 13, 1953. Although the orbit change was of a comet, Bass pointed out (Chap.*IV*) that the mass of the third body does not matter if it is small compared to the other two masses. (In this case the sun and Jupiter).
5. N. D. Suvorov, *Natur Wissenschaften 43*, 214, 1971.
6. I. P. Williams, *Astrophysics and Space Science 12*, 165, 1971.
7. R. A. Lyttleton, "Man's View of the Universe" (Boston, Little and Brown),   p. 36, Monthly Notices, *Roy. Astro. Soc., 121*,6.
8. For example see Straka in *Pensee II*, 1972, and other references listed in the replies to Straka.
9. T. R. McDonough, *Nature 251*, 17, 1974.
10. R. Smoluchowsky, NASA SP-300, p. 283, 1972.

11. Hess and Mead, *Introduction to Space Science*, 2nd ed., Gordon and Breach, Inc., p. 823, 1965.
12. J. D. Anderson, *E⊕S 55, #5*, 515, 1974.
13. A. H. Cook, *Proc. Roy. Soc. Lond. A 328*, 301, 1972.
14. Edison Pettit, "Planetary Temperature Measurement", p. 400, *Planets and Satellites*, ed. Kuiper and Middlehurst, University of Chicago Press, 1961.
15. I. Asimov, *Adding A Dimension*, 193, Avon Books, N. Y., 1964.
16. F. G. Smith, *Radio Astronomy*, Penguin Books, Ltd., 1960.
17. *Velikovsky Affair*, p. 39. (Comments attributed to Einstein in Sullivan's *Continents in Motion* were made before Einstein's renewed interest).
18. *Velikovsky Affair*, p. 39.
19. James Warwick, talk presented at a conference held at McMaster University in June, 1974.
20. R. Hide, *Nature 190*, 895, 1961.
21. R. Hide and A. Ibbetson, *Icarus 5*, 279, 1966.
22. *World in Collision*, p. 184.
23. Ibid, p. 186.
24. Ibid, p. 187.
25. E. Koch, NASA TT F13905, (from 1961 *Sterne Und Weltraum* article).
26. The one item that was considered as a possible exception will be discussed later.
27. Shklovskii and Sagan, *Intelligent Life in the Universe*, p. 324, Holden-Day Inc., 1966.
28. P. Moore, F.R.A.S., *The Planets*, p. 45, W. W. Norton and Co., 1962.
29. Shklovskii and Sagan, Ibid, p. 325.
30. S. F. Singer, *Science 170*, 1196, 1970.
31. J. S. Lewis, *American Scientist, 59*, 557, 1971.
32. F. Kopal, *The Solar System*, p. 53, 119, Oxford University Press, 1973.
33. R. M. Goldstein, *Moon and Planets*, p. 131, North Holland Pub., A. Dollfus ed., 1967.
34. R. W. Bass, *Pensee VII*.
35. Lynn Rose, Personnal communication.
36. Lynn E. Rose, KRONOS II, #1, 16, 1976.
37. H. Urey, *The Planets*, Yale Press, 1952.
38. D. H. Menzel and F. Whipple, *Pub. Astro. Soc., Pac. 67*, 161, 1955.
39. C. H. Mayer, *Planets and Satellites*, ed. Kuiper and Middlehurst, University of Chicago Press, p. 459, 1961.
40. G. P. Kuiper, *The Atmospheres of the Earth and Planets*, ed. G. Kuiper, p. 372, The University of Chicago Press, 1952.
41. J. Shaw, and N. T. Bobrovnikoff, Wright Patterson AFB, contract #AF 33 (616) -5914, Project #1111, task #115, Feb. 1959.
42. See e.g. S. I. Rasool and C. DeBergh *Nature 226*, 1037, 1970.
43. C. Sagan, *Astron. Journal 65*, 352, 1960.
44. V. I. Moroz, *Soviet Ast. AJ 7*, #1, 109, 1963.
45. See e.g. S. I. Rasool and C. DeBergh, *Nature 226*, 1037, 1970.
46. *Worlds in Collision*, p. 369.
47. Ibid.
48. Glasstone, *Sourcebook on the Space Sciences*, Van Nostraud, 1965.
49. Shklovskii and Sagan, *Intelligent Life in the Universe*, p. 324, 1966, Holden-Day.
50. J. E. Hensen and A. Arking, *Science 171*, 669, 1971.
51. Immanuel Velikovsky, *Pensee, VI*, p. 21.
52. B. Hapke, *Science 175*, 748, 1972.
53. D. G. Rea, *Rev. Geophys. Space Phys. 10*, p. 369, 1972.
54. R. Beer, R. H. Norton, and J. V. Martonchick, *Astrophys. J. 168*, p. L121, 1971.
55. W. T. Plummer, *Science 163*, 1191, 1967.
56. *Science News 109*, 234, 1976.
57. I. Velikovsky, *Pensee, VI*, p. 21.
58. Andrew T. Young, NASA-CR- 142056, Jan. 31, 1975.
59. J. Gribbin, *Nature 254*, 657, 1975 report about the conference.
60. C. Sagan talk at AAAS meeting.
61. A. L. Bradfoot, et. al., *Science 183*, 1315, 1974.
62. *Aviation Week and Space Technology*, Nov. 3, 1975.
63. C. Sagan, *Nature 261*, 31, 1976.

64. R. Jastrow and S. I. Rasool, *Introduction to Space Science*, 2nd ed., 1968, Ed. Hess and Mead, Gordon and Breach Publishing, p. 792.
65. W. F. Libby, *Science 161*, 916, 1968.
66. *Pensee VII*, p. 36.
67. G. Colombo, *ESRO Planetary Space Missions,* Vol. 1: Basic Data on Planets and Satellites, p. 29, Nov., 1970.
68. A. B. Binder, *Science 152*, 1053, 1966.
69. F. F. Fish, *Icarus*, 7, 25, 1967.
70. A. Binder and D. W. McCarthy, Jr., *Science, 176*, 279, 1972.
71. *Science 186*, 721, 1974.
72. *Worlds in Collision*, p. 364.
73. E. J. Opik, *Science 153*, 255, 1966.
74. H. C. Urey, *The Planets, Their Origin and Development*, p. 104, Yale Press, 1952.
75. E. C. Slipher, Sc. D., LL.D., *The Photographic Story of Mars,* p. 67, Sky Pub. Co., and Northland Press, 1962.
76. Goldstein et al, *Science 174,* 1324, 1974.
77. *Sky and Telescope*, Dec., 1969, p. 381. Reference given to article by Pettengill et al in the April, 1969 *Astronomical Journal*.
78. *Nature 235*, 251, 1972.
79. *Science News 101*, 228, 1972.
80. 46°C for Black Body, See Allen, *Astrophysical Quantities*, p. 151.
81. NASA TT-F-16339, BERTO, et al.
82. A. B. Binder, *Science 152*, 1053, 1966.
83. S. Glasstone, *Sourcebook on the Space Science*, D. Van Nostrand Co., Inc., p. 704, 1965.
84. V. V. Sharonov, *Soviet Astronomy AJ 5*, 199, 1961.
85. V. I. Moroz, *Soviet Ast. 8*, 273, 1964.
86. A. B. Binder, and D. P. Cruikshank, *Icarus 5*, 521, 1966.
87. F. F. Fish, Jr., *J. of Geophy. Res., 71*, 3063, 1966.
88. A. B. Binder, *Science, 152*, 1053, 1966.
89. *Sky and Telescrope*, p. 291, May, 1975.
90. V. I. Moroz, NASA-TT-F-16823, from *Zh. Pisma v Astron.* (Moscow) 1, #6, 36, 1975.
91. *The Atmospheres of the Earth and Planets*, ed. G. P. Kuiper, University of Chicago Press, 1949, p. 266. In the 2nd edition in 1951, Brown has a note explaining that Professor H. Seuss independently arrived at the same conclusion in 1949.
92. H. Urey, *The Planets, Their Origin and Development*, p. 104, Yale Press, 1952.
93. S. Siegel, L. Halpern, C. Giumarro, G. Renwick, and G. Davis, *Nature 197*, 329, 1963.
94. P. H. Abelson, *Proc. of the Nat. Academy of Sciences, 54*, 1490, 1965.
95. I. S. Shklovskii and C. Sagan, *Intelligent life in the Universe*, Holden-Day, 1966, p. 373
96. *Science News, 110*, 212, 1976.
97. Work by Greenberg, Sizemore and Cordona, and book by David Talbott to be published by Doubleday, and H. Tresman, England, Private communication.

98. B. A. Smith, E. J. Reese *Science 162*, 1275, 1968.
99. W. E. McGovern, S. H. Gross, and S. I. Rasool, *Nature 108,* 375, 1965.
100. I. P. Williams, *Nature 249*, 234, 1974.
101. H. C. Urey, *The Planets*, p. 113.
102. *Velikovsky Affair*, p. 52.
103. Ibid, p. 36.
104. R. Burman, *J. and Proc., Royal Soc. of New South Wales, 102*, 157, 1969.
105. These claims are found in *Worlds in Collision* (1950) and in the following documents: memos submitted to Prof. H. H. Hess, Chairman, Space Science Board, National Academy of Sciences, dated March 14, 1967 and May 19, 1969; a letter to Hess, dated July 2, 1969; and article written at the invitation of the editors of the *New York Times* and published in the early City Edition ("Man Walks on Moon") of July 21, 1969 (but omitted in the Later City Edition); a letter to Prof. A. W. Burgstahler, Chemistry Department, University of Kansas, postmarked July 23, 1969; and a transcript of a passage from a lecture at Guyot Hall, Princeton University, October 21, 1969, given in memory of Hess (deceased August 25, 1969). Correspondence with Hess are re-printed in *Pensee*.

106. *Nature 221*, 415, 1969.
107. Strangway et al, *Science 167*, 690, 1970.
108. Letter from Urey to *Cosmos and Chronos*, 1971.
109. S. K. Runcorn and H. Urey, *Science 180*, 636, 1973.
110. *Nature 249*, 209, 1974.
111. E. H. Levy, *Science 178*, 52, 1972.
112. *Science 181*, 615, 1973.
113. T. Gold and S. Soter, *Planetary and Space Science, 24,* 45, 1976.
114. V. D. Krotikov and V. S. Troitskii, *Sov. Ast. AJ 7,* #6, 822, 1964. Krotikov and Troitskii detected a heat flow from the interior of the moon. This was not based on any theory, but was a result of measurement. This result does not seem to have been widely accepted, possibly because it was not explainable by the then popular theories.
115. Urey letter to *Cosmos and Chronos*
116. Lunar sample preliminary examination team, (IS-PET), *Science 165,* 1211, 1969.
117. R. K. Wanless, et al, *Science 167*, 479, 1970.
118. D. Heymann, et al, *Science*, Jan. 30, 1970.
119. J. G. Funkhouser, et al, *Science 167*, 561, 1970.
120. *Science, 181*, 615, 1973, 4th Lunar Conference.
121. *Am. Jour. Phys., 44*, 5, p. 495, May, 1976.
122. J. G. Funkhouser and J. J. Naughton, *J. of Geophy. Res. 73*, 4601, 1968.
123. D. York, *Pensee I*, p. 18, May, 1972.
124. Leon T. Silver, *Transactions, Am-Geophy. Union 52*, 534, 1971.
125. R. C. Wright, *Pensee I*, 20, 1972.
126. Work by R. Walker, et al, Washington University, St. Louis.
127. *Aviation Week* and *Space Technology,* p. 15, May 15, 1972. The explanation as basalt flow. No theory was given for what created structures that would cause domes when flowed upon by lava.
128. NASA SP 246, p. 16.
129. L. A. Sukhanov, NASA TT-T689, p. 266, 1973.
130. L. B. Ronca, *Icarus, 5*, 515, 1966.
131. A. A. Mills, *Nature 224*, 863, 1969.
132. Ralph Jergens, *Pensee IX,X.*
133. This statement was from an article prepared by the Lunar Sample Analysis Planning Team. *Science 181,* 615, 1973.
134. Ibid
135. Y. Nakamura, private communication.
136. David W. Hughes, *Nature 262*, 175, 1976.
137. LSPET, *Science, 165,* 1224, 1969; C. Ponnamparuma, et al *Science, 167,* 760 1970; B. Nagy, et al, *Science 167*, 170, 1970; G. Eglington, et al, *Nature,* Vol. 226, pp. 251-2, April 18, 1970.
138. P. Gorenstein, and P. Bjorkholm, *Science, 179*, 792, 1973.
139. R. E. Juergens, *Pensee VIII,* 45, 1974.

Chapter VI

1. W. F. Libby, *Pensee IV*, 7, 1973.
2. H. C. Sorensen, *Pensee IV*, 15, 1973.
3. Letter from Dr. Klaus Baer to Rev. Benjamin N. Adams,   Trinity Presbyterian Church, San Francisco.
4. R. Stuckenrath, Jr., *Archaeology, 18*, 281, 1965.
5. H. E. Wright, Jr., *Minnesota Messenia Expedition*, 189.
6. *Velikovsky Affair*, p. 167.
7. K. V. Flannery, et al, *Science 158*, 445, 1967.
8. Frank Waters, *Mexico Mystique: The Coming Sixth World of Conciousness*, p. 149, The Swallow Press, Inc., Chicago, 1974.
9. J. Anderson and G. W. Spangler, *Pensee IX*, 31, 1974.
10. R. V. Gentry, *Am. J. Phy. 33*, 878, 1965.

Chapter VII

1. R. K. Chadwick, *Nature 256*, 570, 1975
2. P. K. Chadwick, *Nature 260*, 397, 1976

3. H. E. Wright, *Science, 161*, 334, 1968.
4. *Catastrophic Geology, I*, 1976, address Caixa Postal 41003, Rio de Janeiro - RJ, Brasil.
5. *Earth in Upheaval*, p. 215.
6. J. Tallis, *Nature*, Aug. 7, 1975.
7. D. V. Ager, *The Nature of the Stratigraphical Record*, 1973.
8. *Earth in Upheaval*, p. 218.
9. W. Francis, *Coal, Its Formation and Composition*, Edward Arnold Publishers Ltd., London, 2nd ed., 1961.
10. Ibid, p. 46.
11. Ibid, p. 625.
12. Ibid, p. v.
13. L. W. Sullivan, personal communication about his book, *Continents in Motion*, 1975.
14. Dwardu Cardona, KRONOS I, # 4, 77, 1976.
15. *Nature, 237*, 10, 1972.
16. Paul S. Wesson, *J. of Geology 80*, 185, 1972.
17. A. J. Mantura, *The American Association of Petroleum Geologists Bulletin,* 56, 1552, 1972, and 56, 2451, 1972.
18. D. V. Ager, *The Nature of the Stratigraphical Record*, p. 7, 1973.
19. Ibid, p. 26.
20. Ibid, p. 43.
21. Ibid, p. 44.
22. Ibid, p. 75.
23. *Earth in Upheaval*, p. 259.
24. L. M. Greenberg, KRONOS I, #4, 98, 1976.
25. *Earth in Upheaval*, p. 146.
26. C. J. Ransom, *Nature 242*, 518, 1973.
27. *Nature 234*, 441, 1971, and Morner, et al *Nature Physical Science*, Dec. 27, 1971.
28. M. Barbetti and M. McElhinny, *Nature 239*, 327, 1972.
29. Ager, p. 83.
30. N. O. Opdyke, B. Glass, J. D. Hays, J. Foster, *Science 154*, 349, 1966.
31. N. D. Watkins & H. G. Goddell, *Science 156*, 1083, 1967.
32. C. J. Waddington, *Science 158*, 913, 1967.
33. J. D. Hays, N. D. Opdyke, *Science 158*, 1001, 1967.
34. G. G. Simpson, *Science 162*, 140, 1968.
35. H. C. Urey, *Nature 179*, 556, 1957.
36. W. Urbanowski, R. W. Ure, Jr., and H. C. Urey, *Nature 197*, 228, 1963.
37. R. A. Lyttleton, *Roy. Soc. London Proc. Series A, 272*, 457, 1963.
38. S. C. Lin, *J. Geophy. Res., 71*, 2427, 1966.
39. R. R. Lyttleton, *Geophy. J. of the Roy. Astro. Soc. 15*, 191, 1968.
40. S. A. Durrani and H. A. Khan, *Nature, 232*, 320, 1971.
41. J. P. Kennet and N. D. Watkins, *Nature, 227*, 930, 1970.
42. D. H. Tarling, *Nature, 253*, 307, 1975.
43. B. Glass and B. C. Heezen, *Nature, 214*, 272, 1967.
44. *Earth in Upheaval*.
45. H. C. Urey, *Nature, 242*, 32, 1973.
46. H. Urey, *Science 147*, 1262, 1965.
47. N. Herz, *Science, 164*, 944, 1969. Discussion, *Nature 222*, 923, 1969. If the moon were captured 1,300 million years ago and caused a cataclysm on the earth, it could be expected that there would be a noticeable effect on the moon. It is revealing to note that Herz did not consider it unscientific to postulate that a major event on the moon happened at a time less than the accepted "age" of the moon.
48. *Earth in Upheaval*, p. 43.
49. Ager, p. 37.
50. D. A. Ross. E. T. Degens, and J. MacIlvaine, *Science 170*, 163, 1970.

Chapter VIII

1. Lynn Rose, *Pensee III*, 27.

2.   Lynn E. Rose and Raymond Vaughan, *Pensee VIII, p. 27*

3.   R. F. Stephenson, *Nature,* 1970.

4.   J. D. Mulholland, *Science 172,* 963, 1971.

5.   *Mercury,* Nov.-Dec., 1975, p. 35.

6.   E. Everhart, *Astro. J. 74,* 735, 1969.

7.   S. J. Weidenschilling, *Astro. J. 80,* 145, 1975.

8.   In defense of Sagan, it can be noted that there is a sentence in *Worlds in Collision* which, if taken by itself and the rest of the book totally ignored, could be con-strued as suggesting what Sagan claimed; however, it is probably not in his defense that the context of the statement was so grossly neglected.

9.   See *Kronos* for additional information about the greenhouse effect.

10.   I. Michelson, *Science,* 1974.

11.   A. Koestler, *The Sleepwalkers.* p. 427

12.   Paul Morgan "Beyond the Magic Circle or How to Trisect Any Angle" EPO-TAI Press, 1973 (with World Rights Reserved?)

13.   See review in *Science News 100,* 308, 1971.

14.   *Society For Interdisciplinary Studies Review,* Ed. R. M. Lowery, 11 Adcott Road, Acklam, Middlesborough, Cleveland, England.

Historical Supplement

1.   *Velikovsky Affair,* p. 44.

2.   For twenty years, Albright was the undisputed authority for dating Palestinian pottery. Danelius, in *Kronos 1, #3,* p. 3, 1975, described how Albright, near the end of his career, was greatly embarassed because he dated certain pottery to the 10th to 6th century B.C. and it was later related to the 14th to 12th century of conventional Egyptian chronology. Albright would have had no problem under the revised chronology. Danelius surmised that this may have been why Albright, just before his death, suddenly and unexpectedly began attending Velikovsky's lectures.

3.   *Velikovsky Affair,* p. 45.

4.   *New Scientist, 18,* p. 369, May 1972; *Nature 244,* p. 325, 1969.

5.   I. E. S. Edwards, *Nature 236,* p. 324, 1972.

6.   *Oedipus and Akhnaton,* p. 179.

7.   L. M. Greenberg, *Pensee I,* p. 41, May, 1972.

8.   Cyrus Gordon, *Pensee I,* 1972.

9.   C. D. Darlington, *The Evolution of Man and Society,* Simon and Shuster, N. Y., p. 118-120, 1969.

Appendix

1.   *Worlds in Collision,* p. 105.

2.   Ibid, p. 112.

3.   Ibid, p. 113.

4.   Ibid, p. 118.

5.   Ibid

6.   A. Dajon, *Comptes rendues des seances de l'Academie des Sciences,* 250, 1960.

7.   O. L. Vaisberg, *Soviet Astronomy AJ 5,* 406, 1961.

8.   N. N. Paviov and G. V. Staritsyn, *Sov. Ast. AJ 6, #1,* 90, 1962.

9.   Gribbin and Plagemann, *Nature, 243,* 26, 1973. (see N. O'Hora and C. Penny, *Nature, 244,* 426, 1973 for reply to Gribbin and Plageman.)

10.   C. P. Sonett, D. S. Colburn, K. Schwartz, and K. Kiel, *Astrophysics and Space Science 7,* 446, 1970.

11.   *Earth in Upheaval,* p. 133.

12.   Yu. V. Zonov, NASA TT-F-37, 1960, W. Hollister, Lockheed Special Bibliography SB-61-66, Jan. 1962, R. H. Greene, The Mitre Corporation, TM- 3641, ESD TDR 63-477.

13.   E. Schatzmann, NASA SP-300, 409, 1972.

14.   Irving Michelson, *Pensee VII,* p. 15, 1974.

15.   Ralph Juergens, *Pensee VII,* p. 39, 1974.

16.   S. C. R. Malin, and I. Saunders, *Nature 245,* 25, 1973.

17.   E. W. Crew, *Nature, 252,* 539, 1974; *The Observatory 95,* 204, 1975; *Society for Interdisciplinary Studies,* Vol. I, 8, 1976.

18.   H. Hill, *How to Live Like a King's Kid,* Logos Int., Plainfield, N. J., 1974, p. 73.

19.   C. A. L. Totten, *Joshua's Long Day and the Dial of Ahaz,* reprinted 1968, Destiny Pub., Merrimac, Mass, p. 17.